MONOGRAPHS OF THE
SOCIETY FOR RESEARCH IN
CHILD DEVELOPMENT

Serial No. 248, Vol. 61, Nos. 4–5, 1996

INTERVIEWING YOUNG CHILDREN ABOUT BODY TOUCH AND HANDLING

Margaret S. Steward
David S. Steward

IN COLLABORATION WITH
Lisa Farquhar
John E. B. Myers
Michael Reinhart
Jane Welker
Nancy Joye
Joseph Driskill
Julia Morgan

WITH COMMENTARY BY
Lucy S. McGough
Maggie Bruck and Stephen J. Ceci
Peter A. Ornstein

AND A REPLY BY THE AUTHORS

MONOGRAPHS OF THE SOCIETY FOR RESEARCH IN CHILD DEVELOPMENT
Serial No. 248, Vol. 61, Nos. 4–5, 1996

CONTENTS

ABSTRACT

STEWARD, MARGARET S., and STEWARD, DAVID S., in collaboration with FAR-
QUHAR, LISA; MYERS, JOHN E. B.; REINHART, MICHAEL; WELKER, JANE; JOYE,
NANCY; DRISKILL, JOE; and MORGAN, JULIA. Interviewing Young Children
about Body Touch and Handling. With Commentary by LUCY S.
MCGOUGH, by MAGGIE BRUCK and STEPHEN J. CECI, and by P. A. ORNSTEIN;
and a Reply by MARGARET S. STEWARD. *Monographs of the Society for Research
in Child Development*, 1996, **61** (4, Serial No, 248).

Children aged 3–6 years were interviewed following a scheduled pediatric clinic visit to assess the efficacy of two independent variables—interview
strategy and number of interviews—on the accuracy, completeness, and consistency of children's reports. Four experimental interviews were created—a
verbal interview and three interviews enhanced with anatomically detailed
cues (dolls, line drawings, and computer graphics), photographs, and props.
Initially, 130 children were interviewed after the clinic event. One month
later, 124 were interviewed again, and 74 were interviewed a third time after
6 months. Children's reports were compared to videotapes and medical records of their pediatric visit in order to create three dependent reporting variables—accuracy, completeness, and consistency.

In addition, the predictive power of four sets of covariates on reporting
was assessed: (1) age and gender; (2) ethnicity, medical history, family stress,
and mother's education; (3) number of invasive medical procedures, number of body touches, health status, and child's pain judgments; and (4) number of outpatient and inpatient visits between the initial and the follow-up
interviews at 1 and 6 months.

Initially, children's spontaneous reports of body touch were highly accurate, but sparse. After a 1-month delay, accuracy and completeness dropped
significantly: accuracy was stable from 1 to 6 months; completeness re-
bounded at 6 months. Three-year-olds' reports of body touch were less complete and less consistent, but rarely less accurate, than those of older age
groups. After 1- and 6-month delays, consistently reported information was

more accurate than new information. Children's pain ratings contributed positively to predictions of completeness at the initial and 1-month interviews and to completeness and accuracy at 6 months. Complex events were reported more accurately but less consistently. Anatomically detailed cues in the three enhanced interviews increased completeness of reporting of total body and genital touch. Photos elicited more useful information for identification of persons and places than did questions, while medical props initially offered no advantage and subsequently led to errors. Children's feelings also influenced reporting: higher ratings of anger, sadness, and fright were positively related to reporting of extremely painful touch, while some children who failed to report painful, invasive medical procedures displayed shame when interviewed. The relative privacy of the computer-assisted interview holds promise for disclosure of sexual topics.

I. INTRODUCTION

Young children often witness crimes or violence in their homes (Kenning, Merchant, & Tomkins, 1991; Pynoos & Eth, 1986) and schools (Pynoos & Nader, 1989). Tragically, many children are victims of physical and sexual maltreatment (Finkelhor, Williams, Burns, & Kalinowski, 1988; Terr, 1979, 1983, 1990; Zimmerman, Wolbert, Burgess, & Hartman, 1987). Obtaining trustworthy testimony from young children is a central concern of both prosecutors and defenders in a range of criminal, civil, and family court proceedings.

The ability of a young child to remember and report the facts (who, what, where, and when) of an event is particularly important in sexual abuse cases. Child abuse is often very difficult to prove in court. Medical or laboratory evidence exists in only a small percentage of cases (DeJong, Hervada, & Emmett, 1983; Enos, Conrath, & Byer, 1986; Jones & McQuiston, 1988; McCann, 1990; Paradise, 1990; Sauzier, 1989). Unlike the physically abused child, whose injuries provide convincing evidence of maltreatment (Caffey, 1946; Kempe, Silverman, Steele, Droegmueller, & Silver, 1962), sexual abuse usually leaves no physical clues. Even when medical evidence of sexual abuse exists, such evidence may fail to persuade a jury unless it is accompanied by testimony from the child (DeJong & Rose, 1991). The U.S. Supreme Court has observed that "child abuse is one of the most difficult crimes to detect and prosecute, in large part because there often are no witnesses except the victim" (*Pennsylvania v. Ritchie,* 1987, 60). In child sexual abuse litigation, the scarcity of eyewitnesses and physical evidence focuses extraordinary forensic attention on the child.

When a child is asked to remember and describe sexual abuse, what is he or she asked to do? Sexual abuse may take many forms. Abusive conduct ranges from gentle fondling to brutal anal or vaginal penetration with resulting injury. The child's psychological and physical experience may range from pleasure at receiving attention and tender body touch to terror at the physical restraint and pain. The child may be an innocently willing participant, a fighting, feisty protester, or a withdrawn and helpless victim. When

1

abuse is repeated over months or years, the acts and the child's role may evolve. Moreover, what is considered "naughty" by the child may bear little resemblance to the legal definition of sexual abuse. Because sexual abuse is a complex phenomenon, interviewers often find it necessary to sift through a child's recollection to uncover and interpret acts of forensic significance.

Disclosing sexual abuse is not an easy task for children (Sorenson & Snow, 1991). Abuse is often a complex event that children are ill prepared to describe. Words and concepts that define and describe sexual abuse are readily available to adults but may be beyond the ken of the child. Abusive events can be novel and fraught with mixed emotions. It is difficult for a sexual abuse victim of any age to "tattle" on a parent, an older sibling, or a family friend, to speak to strangers about private body parts, or to describe embarrassing, forbidden. "nasty" acts. Helping young children disclose is an enormous challenge.

The most common disclosure of sexual abuse by a young child is the direct, although often unintentional or "accidental," statement of the child victim to a parent, older sibling, or preschool teacher (Conte & Schuerman, 1987; Sauzier, 1989; Sorenson & Snow, 1991). A carefully conducted investigative interview is required to transform a child's initial disclosure of abuse into verbal evidence. The purpose of the investigative interview is to elicit as accurate and as complete a report as possible of the alleged abusive event. The results of the initial investigative interviews with the child are of crucial relevance to clinicians, the police, and the courts (Jones & McQuiston, 1988).

Children's statements describing sexual abuse inform legal proceedings at several levels (Myers, 1992). The child's disclosure statements weigh heavily in the decision to commence legal proceedings, including criminal prosecutions and juvenile court proceedings to protect children. Once legal proceedings are under way, the child's early disclosures play a vital role in the legal system. For example, a child's disclosure may be used effectively to convince a perpetrator to admit guilt, thereby obviating the necessity for a trial (Sas, 1991). If a trial is held, the child's early disclosure statements may be repeated in court by the adults to whom the child disclosed (Goodman et al., 1992). In most trials, the child testifies, and the child is nearly always the most important witness (Gray, 1993; Runyan, Everson, Edelsohn, Hunter, & Coulter, 1988). Thus, the capacity of the legal system to protect children and find the truth depends in large measure on the words of little children.

CURRENT INTERVIEWING PRACTICES

In the United States, Great Britain, Canada, and Australia, the issue of just how to conduct forensic interviews with young children has been brought to professional and public awareness owing in part to the fact that, unlike most European countries, these countries have an adversarial rather than an inquisitorial trial system. In the "clash of conflicting accounts" that is the hallmark of the adversarial trial, the process of obtaining evidence, as well as the content of the evidence, is fair game for challenge (Spencer & Flin, 1990). At present, in the United States, the demand for investigative interviewing of young children is shaped largely by the needs of the legal system, but the process is quite uneven (Gray, 1993; McGough, 1994; White, 1988). Three features of current practice that make investigative interviewing problematic are the source and training of interviewers, uneven and unskilled use of props and anatomical dolls, and the need to conduct multiple interviews.

Interviewers

Investigative interviewers are drawn from several professions, each with a particular perspective on child abuse, a unique assignment by their agency, and different training in how to interview children (Goldstein, 1987). Professionals from health, mental health, education, social services, law enforcement, and the legal profession all find themselves involved in the investigative process. Currently, there is no required training for investigative interviewers who work with children.

Legal and child protection agencies sometimes assign responsibility for investigative interviewing to junior staff members. The use of inexperienced interviewers leads to enormous variability in technique from one interviewer to another and reliance on questioning techniques that are more appropriate with adults. Even staff from legal and child protection agencies, who are experienced in adult interviewing, are frequently unfamiliar with the cognitive, linguistic, and communication skills of young children and use different behavioral indicators to infer that abuse occurred (Kendall-Tackett, 1992; Kendall-Tackett & Watson, 1991). Interviewers are often unaware of the way in which young children approach situations in which they are asked to report events. A poorly conducted interview may so upset a child that he or she simply refuses to repeat information in subsequent interviews, further undermining the credibility of his or her testimony (Jones & McQuiston, 1988).

When the courts assign the task of investigative interviewing of young children to health and mental health clinicians who possess skill and experience with a wide range of techniques to communicate with young children, there are problems of a different sort. Few of these professionals have training in investigative, as opposed to therapeutic, interviewing and risk confounding the purity of the child's verbal evidence with their own empathy or psychodynamic interpretation (Faller, 1990; MacFarlane & Krebs, 1986; Mason, 1991; White & Quinn, 1988).

Protocols have been developed for medical staff who are assigned the task of gathering and preserving physical evidence of abuse, but no interview protocol has been accepted uniformly across the disciplines to elicit verbal evidence from young children when there are suspicions or allegations of sexual abuse. What children say during an investigative interview depends in large part on how well an interviewer enables them to remember the allegedly abusive event and then to report what they remember. Aware of the importance of obtaining verbal evidence from a child victim, some interviewers, regardless of their professional training or agency assignment, have employed techniques borrowed from adult interviewing such as suggestive or aggressive interrogation, threats, and intimidation (Ceci & Bruck, 1995). Others have dipped into the repertoire of therapists, who employ materials such as toys, drawings, and dolls to facilitate both verbal and nonverbal communication with children (Goldstein, 1987).

Use of Props and Anatomically Detailed Dolls

Props, especially anatomically detailed props, are easily acquired and commonly used by investigative interviewers with little or uneven training. Boat and Everson (1988) surveyed approximately 300 frontline interviewers from law enforcement and mental health agencies, child protection workers, and physicians in North Carolina in 1985. The survey revealed that about one-third of the respondents, ranging from 68% of the child protection workers to 13% of the physicians, had used anatomical dolls for at least a year. In each professional category, approximately 20% of those who had not used dolls indicated that they intended to use them in the future, although fewer than half had even minimal training in their proper use. Conte, Sorenson, Fogarty, and Dalla Rosa (1991) surveyed 212 professionals in 40 states and found that respondents indicated use of a variety of techniques, including anatomical dolls (92%), free drawings (88%), anatomical drawings (66%), other dolls (50%), and puppets (47%). More recently, Boat and Everson (in press) reviewed videotaped investigative interviews conducted by child protection professionals of 52 2–5-year-old children and 45 6–12-year-old children and found that anatomical dolls and drawings were used as frequently with the younger as with the older children: anatomical dolls were used with 86% and 80% and anatomical drawings with 10% and 7% of younger and older children, respectively. They also observed interviewers using drawing materials, other dolls, puppets, and miscellaneous toys.

Concern has been building over the past decade that unskilled or inappropriate use of props—particularly sexually explicit props such as anatomically detailed dolls—during initial, pretrial interviews may contaminate the child's memory of what occurred or suggest the possibility of abuse that never happened (Boat & Everson, 1988, in press; Ceci & Bruck, 1995; Everson &

Boat, 1994; Freeman & Estrada-Mullaney, 1988; Kendall-Tackett, 1992; Mason, 1991; Perry & Wrightsman, 1991; White, 1988; White & Santilli, 1989; Yates & Terr, 1988a, 1988b). Everson and Boat (1994) reviewed 20 guidelines developed to aid interviewers with prop use and identified the five most frequently recommended uses of anatomically detailed props: comforter, icebreaker, anatomical model, demonstration aid, and diagnostic screen.

Boat and Everson (in press) conducted the first empirical study of the use by child protection professionals of props, including anatomical dolls and drawings. They coded 97 videotaped investigative interviews for "concerning practices," which they defined as the use of props in potentially inappropriate or misleading ways. The most frequent use of the anatomical dolls was as an anatomical model (to assess sexual knowledge, general knowledge of sexual abuse, and personal sexual exposure or experience) and as a demonstration aid to clarify a verbal disclosure. Interviewers were significantly more likely to use dolls with younger children as an icebreaker to introduce the topic of sexuality and as a diagnostic screen where the child freely interacts with the dolls and the interviewer follows up on graphic behavior or statements. When dolls were used as a demonstration aid, the most common interviewer practice that was potentially worrisome was an overreliance on the dolls. In 35% of the cases, the dolls were either introduced prematurely or offered in lieu of obtaining a verbal description. The authors note the need for continued training for interviewers who use anatomical dolls—so that they understand what particular function the props are serving at any point in the interview, understand the potential errors associated with that use, and can articulate their reasons for using the dolls.

It should be noted that courts routinely permit children who are testifying in court to use anatomical dolls to help them describe their abuse when the children experience difficulty testifying in the normal manner (*Kehinde v. Commonwealth,* 1986; Myers, 1987, 1992; *People v. Rich,* 1987; *State v. Eggert,* 1984). Perry and Wrightsman (1991) report that some states have enacted statutes authorizing the use of anatomical dolls to facilitate the testimony of young children.

Multiple Interviews

Multiple interviews are another feature of current practice. Children as young as 3 years of age are often subject to several interviews during the initial phase of an investigation, and they are often reinterviewed by different legal staff in preparation for testifying in civil or criminal court (California Child Victim Witness Judicial Advisory Committee, 1988; Goldstein, 1987; Jones & Krugman, 1986; Jones & McQuiston, 1988; Myers, 1994; Nurcombe, 1986; Whitcomb, Shapiro, & Stellwagen, 1985; Yates, 1987). Service providers testifying before the U.S. Attorney-General's Task Force on Family Violence (U.S. Attorney-General, 1984) estimated that a child victim averages at least a dozen investigative interviews throughout the course of child protective proceedings, criminal prosecution, and custody proceedings. An empirical study by Tedesco and Schnell (1987) of 48 child victims indicated that children were interviewed on average 7 times, with a range from 1 to 40 times. While research documents that repetition of material attenuates forgetting of neutral stimuli such as word lists (Howe, Kelland, Bryant-Brown, & Clark, 1992), paired comparisons (Fisher & Chandler, 1991), and book passages (Foos & Fisher, 1988), many professionals working with child victims believe that being required to repeat the story again and again is traumatic for the child and may compromise reporting (Whitcomb et al., 1985). In the Tedesco and Schnell study, the greater the number of interviews, the more negative the child's reaction to the experience. Two troubling observations of repeated interviews about personally salient, distressing events are that children may begin to relate their experience in a nonemotional, rote fashion, thus weakening the believability of their testimony (Faller, 1990; Haugaard & Reppucci, 1988), and that over time children may become reluctant to talk repeatedly about material that is emotionally distressing for them and withhold information (Yates, 1987). Thus, multiple interviews may affect event memory of neutral stimuli and the reporting of traumatic events differentially (Warren-Leubecker, 1991).

Multiple interviews are problematic, not only because of the stress on the child, but also because each interview may yield a slightly different set of information from the child (Fivush & Hamond, 1990; Fivush & Shukat, 1995; Sauzier, 1989; Sorenson & Snow, 1991; Summit, 1983), especially if the child is interviewed by different interviewers (Fivush & Hamond, 1990). While repeated interviews may provide an opportunity for a more complete report of an event, Rose and Blank (1974) and White and Quinn (1988) note that repetitive questioning may communicate to children that they have been giving "incorrect" or "inadequate" answers and place demands on them to supply the "correct" information. It has been argued that young children may benefit from repeated interviews because they learn, with repeated experience, how to engage in or cue talk about remembered events (Hudson, 1990; Rogoff & Mistry, 1990). Yet Fivush and her colleagues (Fivush, 1994; Fivush, Hamond, Harsch, Singer, & Wolf, 1991) have conducted longitudinal research that reveals that young children incorporate information introduced by the adult interviewer in describing events subsequently.

Although in their studies the amount of information that a child incorporates into later interviews is small, approximately 9%, Fivush and her colleagues note that in a legal setting this could be critically important. The consistency of a child's report was rated in a recent national survey as one of the top three criteria that professionals use to assess the accuracy of allegations of child abuse—following the presence of physical indicators and a child's precocious sexual knowledge (Conte et al., 1991). The law is also concerned with consistency of report. Legal staff are often frustrated by lack of consistency in child interviews. Mock juries have judged inconsistencies to be more damaging to the credibility of the report of 6-year-old eyewitnesses than to the reports of 10- or 30-year-old witnesses (Leippe, Mannion, & Romancyzk, 1991). But children may consistently err. Terr (1979, 1983) conducted clinical interviews 4 months and 4 years after children had been kidnapped. She found that some children consistently erred in describing their captors, the setting, and events immediately preceding and following the event. However, little research has been conducted on the consistency or accuracy of children's reports over time, especially when the events had been personally experienced and were traumatic (Bulkley, 1989; Conte et al., 1991).

The relative vulnerabilities of very young children subject to multiple interviews were revealed in studies conducted by Ornstein and his colleagues (Baker-Ward, Gordon, Ornstein, Larus, & Clubb, 1993; Merritt, Ornstein, & Spiker, 1994; Ornstein, Gordon, & Larus, 1992). Ornstein et al. (1992) found that, at the initial interview immediately after a mildly stressful physical examination, 3-year-old children remembered significantly fewer features than did 6-year-old children, 81.8% and 91.7%, respectively. At the follow-up interviews, 6-year-old children continued to remember more than did the 3-year-old children, whether they were reinterviewed at 1 or 3 weeks. Both 3- and 6-year-old children forgot: 3-year-old children remembered more than 70% of their original report, while the 6-year-old children remembered more than 90%. Both 3- and 6-year-old children, however, generated new, accurate information. Baker-Ward et al. (1993) interviewed 3-, 5-, and 7-year-old children following a physical examination and found a positive correlation between age and total recall on the initial interview that paralleled the Ornstein study. Again, children forgot some features of their original reports over time. Total recall scores dropped significantly for 3- and 5-year-old children but not for 7-year-old children. By comparison with a control group, they failed to find an "inoculation advantage" for the subsequent memory for children who participated in the initial interview (Brainerd & Ornstein, 1991; Howe, O'Sullivan, & Marche, 1992). However, results of multiple interviews differ when children are asked to recall repeatedly more stressful events. Merritt et al. (1994) found little or no loss of total recall on multiple interviews about a painful medical procedure, even from 3-year-old children.

Although there is a tendency to assume that a child's experiences in the intervals between multiple interviews are "held constant," those of us who work clinically with abused children know that this is rarely true. A child may be reabused between the first and the second interview or between an initial interview and a court appearance 6 months or a year later. It is important to understand and document the role of intervening experience. In the Baker-Ward et al. (1993) study, between the initial and the follow-up interviews, 25% of the children made a return trip to the doctor for treatment of an illness or accident or to accompany a sibling for a checkup. By comparing children who returned to those who did not, the authors determined that intervening visits interfered with the recall of some children and facilitated the performance of others—but there was not sufficient information presented to identify characteristics of children whose responses were affected. Unfortunately, in the period between interviews, children may be subjected to deliberate attempts to introduce misinformation, which Bruck, Ceci, Francoeur, and Barr (1995) have demonstrated can effectively "reconstruct" a child's memory and result in erroneous reports of a previous event. Further research needs to be conducted to determine the features of the child and the intervening event that may affect subsequent recall. Both the clinical and the research data suggest that intervening events may contribute to inconsistent reports when multiple interviews are conducted over long periods of time.

In sum, at present the practice of investigative interviewing of young children involves interviewers from many different agencies, who have neither required training nor common protocols and who frequently use a wide variety of props. Given this state of affairs, it is not surprising that children are subject to multiple and repetitive interviews, which can compromise their testimony. Appellate court judges reviewing child abuse convictions have expressed concern that multiple interviews might lead, bias, or "taint" a child's report (*Idaho v. Wright,* 1990; *New Jersey v. Michaels,* 1993, 1994). Researchers, child development specialists, and child advocates are also expressing concern about whether children are being "reabused" by multiple interviews or "educated" by the repeated use of props and/or questions (Bruck, Ceci, Francoeur, & Barr, 1995; Davies, 1991; Dunning, 1989; King & Yuille, 1987; Melton & Limber, 1989; White, Santilli, & Quinn, 1988).

INVESTIGATIVE INTERVIEWING OF YOUNG CHILDREN IS LIKELY TO EXPAND

While the practice of interrogating young children about alleged abuse is relatively new, and while many of the features of the current scene are troubling, we believe that investigative interviewing of young children is likely to expand dramatically in the future for several reasons. First, estimates of the incidence of sexual maltreatment grew from 0.86 per 10,000 children in 1976 to 20.89 in 1986 (National Research Council, 1993). Current estimates are that one girl in four and one boy in seven will have experienced abuse before reaching adulthood (Finkelhor, 1993). Second, although the number of children reported for child abuse and neglect has topped 2 million per year, the Study of National Incidence and Prevalence of Child Abuse and Neglect found that professionals still failed to report half the maltreated children they saw, including 40% of their sexual abuse cases (Besharov, 1990). As professional training improves and reporting laws are enforced, more children will enter the system. Third, more children will be interviewed as research data documenting children's relative accuracy in reporting sexual abuse are available to law enforcement and social welfare professionals (Jones & McGraw, 1987). It is important that children be interviewed directly about their own experiences because there is mounting evidence that allegations of abuse made by adults on children's behalf are fraught with error ranging from deliberate falsification (e.g., accusations made by a parent in a custody battle; Benedek & Schetky, 1985; Myers, 1989; Thoennes & Tjaden, 1990) to misperception or confused interpretations of nonsexual events (Everson & Boat, 1989; Yates & Musty, 1988). Finally, it will be possible to interview more children in the future because legal reforms in the United States, Canada, Australia, and Great Britain are liberalizing the admissibility of evidence from children (McGough, 1994; Melton, 1981; Myers, 1987; Spencer & Flin, 1990; Warner, 1990; Yuille, 1988) and ensuring that the conditions under which children testify will be more developmentally sensitive and less traumatic (Goodman, Levine, Melton, & Ogden, 1991).

NEED FOR RESEARCH: CHILDREN AS PARTICIPANT EYEWITNESS REPORTERS

The courts have looked to social scientists for empirical research to help them understand many facets of child abuse (*Maryland v. Craig,* 1990) and the appropriateness of relying on children as witnesses (Goodman, 1984; *Idaho v. Wright,* 1990; McGough, 1994; Melton, 1987; Melton, Petrila, Poythress, & Slobogin, 1987; Monahan & Walker, 1991; Saywitz, Goodman, & Myers, 1990). The current research literature on children's eyewitness reports consists of two types of studies: (1) those in which children are bystander eyewitnesses, observing but not participating in the event, and (2) studies in which children are participant eyewitnesses, reporting their experience from the vantage point of involvement in the event.

The bulk of the new bystander research refocuses the questions originally raised at the turn of the century with respect to the accuracy, suggestibility, and reliability of children as bystander eyewitnesses (Ceci, Ross, & Toglia, 1987a, 1987b; Clarke-Stewart, Thompson, & Lepore, 1989; Cole & Loftus, 1987; Doris, 1991; Goodman, 1984; McCloskey & Zaragoza, 1985; Poole & White, 1991; Zaragoza, 1987, 1991). Bystander research with children is an extension of a voluminous experimental literature on the performance of adult bystander eyewitnesses (see Loftus, 1979). In bystander eyewitness studies, the subject is presented, typically, with an event through a series of pictures, stories, slides, or videotape in the laboratory; or the subject observes a staged event in a controlled setting and is then asked to report what occurred (Loftus & Davies, 1984).

The results of the bystander eyewitness research help courts understand the ability of young children to provide eyewitness testimony that might be required, for example, in cases of domestic violence (Goodman & Rosenberg, 1987; Kenning et al., 1991; Pynoos & Eth, 1986). However, we believe that the results of bystander eyewitness research may underestimate the report of the child who has been physically and/or sexually abused. The potential sensory information encoded and later available for recall and reporting by a participant in an event extends beyond the visual and auditory information available to the bystander. A participant eyewitness in a child abuse case— often referred to as a *victim witness*—may experience kinesthetic (movement of the body or body parts), proprioceptive (body orientation—standing, sitting, lying down), and, in some cases, nocioceptive (painful) stimuli. The encoding, retention, and report of crucial events may be influenced by tapping into these physical experiences and by strong emotions such as anxiety, fear, embarrassment, or rage—emotions that reveal personal distress and are often in sharp contrast to the emotionally neutral experience of most bystander eyewitnesses (Dent & Stephenson, 1979; Terr, 1979, 1983, 1990). There has been a call by Goodman (1984), Melton (1981), and many others for more ecologically valid research that approximates the experience of child abuse victims. In order to increase the validity, and therefore the generalizability, of research on children's memory of abusive events, research settings need to be identified in which children experience a range of kinesthetic, proprioceptive, and nocioceptive stimuli in addition to the visual and auditory stimuli that the victim eyewitness shares with bystander eyewitnesses.

In sum, there is currently a debate about how best to interview allegedly abused young children so that accurate information is obtained and the rights of those accused are protected (Davies, 1991; Weissman, 1991; Yuille, 1988). Both the manner in which evidence in child abuse cases is collected and the way in which the truth of the evidence is tested in our court system have highlighted a series of contradictions and questions that invite empirical investigation. To begin to address the problems encountered by young child abuse victims who face interrogation, we drew together an interdisciplinary clinical research team with expertise in child development, pediatrics, early childhood education, child clinical psychology, and the law. All of us had worked in some capacity with sexually abused young children and were aware of the uneven, and often uninformed, handling of children by law enforcement officials and the courts. We were determined to develop and test interview protocols that would enable young abused children to report their experiences as accurately and fully as possible. To that end, our team sought a research setting in which we could test interview protocols with participant eyewitnesses.

THE MEDICAL SETTING—AN ETHICAL ANALOGUE FOR STUDYING CHILDREN'S EXPERIENCES OF BODY TOUCH AND HANDLING

In order to study the interviewing process and to test the design of new interview protocols with young children in a manner that will inform the courts, it is critical to identify a natural research setting that offers children a potentially wide range of experiences of body touch and handling. It is, of course, neither moral nor legal to abuse children in order to study the effect of cues and props on their subsequent recall and report of the event. Nor should parameters of the interview process be studied employing allegedly abused children as participants, for the use of experimental research protocols might jeopardize any subsequent legal proceedings. Furthermore, without access to the original abusive event, the differential effectiveness of the inclusion of cue/prop enhancements in an investigative interview cannot be determined.

The medical setting was selected as an appropriate analogue for studying children's experience of body touch and handling. Children's memories of the facts (who, what, where, and when) of pediatric care can be particularly vivid and are sometimes more accurate than those of their parents or doctors (Bearison, 1990; Beuf, 1979; Massie, 1985; Robertson, 1956). Three factors present in the ecology of a child's visit to a pediatric outpatient clinic offer a compelling parallel for some children's experiences of physical and/or sexual abuse (Faller, 1990; Finkelhor, 1979; Jones & McQuiston, 1988; Mrazek & Mrazek, 1981; Russell, 1984). The first factor is that in both situations any place on the child's body may be inspected, touched, and handled. During a physical examination, a good pediatrician should touch the child "from head to toe." Increasingly in pediatric settings across the country, the routine, well-child physical examination includes inspection and handling of genitalia (McCann, 1990). For some children, a visit to the clinic provides an analogue that may help us understand the reports of young children who have experienced body touch, including genital fondling, which is probably the most common sexually abusive experience for young children. Although almost every type of abuse has been perpetrated on young children (Sauzier, 1989), fondling is often the first step in a pattern of grooming the child for incestuous abuse that begins in the preschool years and progresses to oral copulation or mutual masturbation in the early school years and to full intercourse in the preadolescent and adolescent years (Waterman & Lusk, 1986).

The second factor that offers a parallel between the pediatric visit and an abusive experience is that in both situations body touch may be distressing for the young child (Faller, 1990). Steward (1988) has observed that during medical procedures both the relative painfulness of the touch and whether the child's body boundaries have been broken (e.g., a needle penetrating the skin or an instrument entering body orifices such as the ear or mouth) contribute to children's distress. While the parent may view medical treatment and abuse as polar opposites—one entirely good and in the child's best interest, the other entirely bad—the child may not. The cognitively immature child lacks an appreciation for the reasons for medical care (Steward, 1988; Steward & Steward, 1981) and does not understand adult intentionality well (Fabes, Eisenberg, McCormick, & Wilson, 1988). In a child's mind, there may be little to differentiate necessary but painful touch administered by a doctor or nurse from abusive touch. Young children do know when they are hurt (Ross & Ross, 1988), but their pain is often underestimated by adult observers such as parents and/or the medical staff who administer necessary medical procedures (Manne, Jacobsen, & Redd, 1992), even as perpetrators apparently underestimate the distress they cause child victims. The pediatric literature reveals that children often believe that they have become ill or injured or require painful medical procedures because they have been bad, and the medical staff is seen as meting out the punishment (Brewster, 1982). Similarly, therapists have found that many abused children believe that their distressing maltreatment is their own fault (Berliner & Conte, 1990; Sauzier, 1989).

The third factor that offers a parallel between the pediatric visit and the abusive experience is that in both situations the child is expected to comply with an adult's request, even when the experience is painful or private parts are touched (Berliner & Conte, 1990; Finkelhor & Browne, 1985; Russell, 1984). During a medical procedure, parents usually encourage their child to cooperate with the medical staff and rarely interrupt medical procedures. Even the parent who accompanies a child for necessary medical procedures intending to provide emotional support may "join the opposition" by, for example, helping medical staff physically restrain a child whose defensive body movements may jeopardize a procedure or result in injury to him or her. Sometimes parents become angry at a child's verbal protest or uncooperative behavior (Blount et al., 1989). Some children experience their parents' harsh behavior: coercion, threats, or even temporary abandonment in the clinic (Bush, Melamed, & Cockrell, 1989). Parents in the pediatric setting can develop feelings of shame and embarrassment that distance them from their child, even as some mothers, terrorized by a spouse's threatened abuse or fearful of losing a new partner, may withdraw nurturance and protection at the very time their child experiences physical or sexual victimization (Everson, Hunter, Runyon, Edelsohn, & Coulter, 1989).

In summary, the medical setting provides an ethical abuse analogue for the study of children's memory of experiences of body touch and handling. In our society, this is the only setting in which parents permit other adults to touch their children anywhere on their bodies (including genitalia). The touch may range from a gentle probe to necessary but very painful, invasive procedures. Adults often underestimate children's distress, and some withdraw their emotional support. Finally, children must comply.

Our research team decided to observe children in the medical setting and assess their memory of a visit to an outpatient clinic for specific features that related to body touch and handling. In the next section, with an eye toward the development of experimental interview protocols, we review research studies that examine the role of external cues, the interviewer-child relationship, and the stressfulness of the event being remembered—each of which may enhance, inhibit, or distort children's reports of their memories during an interview.

USE OF CUES IN INTERVIEWS WITH YOUNG CHILDREN

In order to use cues effectively, what do investigative interviewers need to know about the role of cues in young children's memory? There are three general memory processes—encoding, storage, and retrieval—each of which is potentially sensitive to improvement with increasing age and experience (Bjorklund, 1987; Brainerd, 1985; Brainerd & Ornstein, 1991; Kail, 1989). Davies (1991) has noted that it is the retrieval process that is of most interest to investigative interviewers, for retrieval is the only process over which interviewers may exert some influence—through the incorporation of a broad range of verbal and nonverbal cues. Nelson (1989) observed that for young children the encoding process is rarely deliberate and that the content stored in early childhood memories consists primarily of events that were directly experienced by the child. She noted that memory can be manifested in a variety of intentional behaviors, including verbal response—but she warned that retrieval can be difficult because the young child may remember more than he or she can relate.

Mandler (1990) cautions that even after children develop expressive language it may not be safe to assume that verbal protocols are straightforwardly associated with what a child remembers about an event. Pillemer and White (1989) assert that memory of faces, places, and emotions—three components critical to determine in most investigative interviewing—is especially difficult to elicit with verbal cues alone. We also know that young children may be hampered in reporting their experiences because they have difficulty gaining clear and quick access to their memories (Emmerich & Ackerman, 1978; Kobasigawa, 1974; Perlmutter & Ricks, 1979; Ritter, Kaprove, Fitch, & Flavell, 1973). Children as young as 4 years old know that retrieval cues help (Gordon & Flavell, 1977; Wellman, 1977, 1978), and young children can use cues to increase reporting (Price & Goodman, 1990). But young children have difficulty generating retrieval cues for themselves (Ritter, 1978; Schmidt & Schmidt, 1986) and often rely on adults to provide retrieval cues for them (Fivush & Hammond, 1990; Hudson, 1990).

Researchers examining the nature and onset of very early personal memories, often termed *autobiographical recall,* have shifted our attention from the traditional focus on memory of arbitrary bits of information, typically learned in a laboratory setting and tested after brief intervals, to memory for real-world events that individuals have experienced in "everyday" settings and remembered over long periods of time (Banaji & Crowder, 1989; Bronfenbrenner, 1979; Fivush, 1993; Howe & Courage, 1993; Hudson, 1986, 1990; Loftus, 1991; Neisser, 1978, 1988, 1991; Nelson, 1988, 1989, 1993; Sheingold & Tenney, 1982; Wagenaar & Groeneweg, 1990). This is especially important to investigative interviewers for it has been documented that children's performance and memory are often underestimated in a laboratory setting (Ceci & Bronfenbrenner, 1991) and that the range of children's emotional expression—especially of negative emotions—is more limited in the laboratory setting than in a natural setting (Fabes et al., 1988; Fabes, Eisenberg, Nyman, & Michealieu, 1991; Peterson, Moreno, & Harbeck-Weber, 1993). Howe and his colleagues (Howe, 1995; Howe & Courage, 1993; Howe, Courage, & Peterson, 1994) assert that the development of autobiographical memory coincides with the emergence of the cognitive sense of self, thus emphasizing the active, constructive role of the child in the recall process.

Autobiographical memory offers a compelling and useful framework for investigative interviewers, for, as the child develops language (Brown, 1973; Miller, Potts, Fung, Hoogstra, & Mintz, 1990), the capacity of self-evaluative reflection and emotional response (Lewis, 1991), and a sense of agency (Howe, 1995; Pillemer & White, 1989), personal experiences can be shared effectively with others. Fivush (1993) asserts that the single most important finding to emerge from research on children's autobiographical memory is that children's recall can be very accurate. Fivush and her colleagues (Fivush, 1995; Fivush & Hammond, 1990; Fivush et al., 1991; Hudson & Fivush, 1987) have demonstrated that children's recall remains accurate over multiple interviews and across time. Autobiographical researchers have made the critical methodological point that the accuracy of memory, the exhaustiveness or completeness of memory, and the consistency of memory across time are three distinct features. The rich complexity of real-world events heightens the relevance of clearly differentiating accuracy from consistency. As Terr (1979, 1983) reminds us, inconsistent data can be new and accurate, and, conversely, consistently reported data may be erroneous.

Researchers contrasting children's and adults' autobiographical memory have noted that development influences each of these three features of memory differently. For example, while the contents of both adults' and children's autobiographical memory appear to be highly accurate, Fivush (1993) notes that the completeness and consistency of children's autobiographical recall are quite dependent on the availability of cues. The younger the child, and/or the more distant the event to be recalled, the more the individual must rely on external and often very specific cues (Baker-Ward et al., 1993; Ornstein et al., 1992). More and/or better cues increase the completeness of recall, but different sets of cues and/or different interviewers may evoke recall of different subsets of an experience, leading to inconsistent reporting (Hudson, 1990).

Eisenberg (1985), Engel (1986), and Fivush and Fromhoff (1988) observed that parents initially provide the entire conversational framework, including verbal retrieval cues, during discussions with their young children about past events. In child abuse cases, interviewers may also have to be ready to provide retrieval cues to young children. Direct questions and even leading questions can serve as verbal retrieval cues for young children, but such questions are included at a price, for the number of errors of both omission and commission usually increases when these strategies are employed (Dent, 1982). Mandler (1990) identified some further problems that children face when adults attempt to cue children's recall. She noted that adults often give children the wrong retrieval cues and that adults typically do not wait long enough for children to report. Furthermore, the adult may remind and fill in for the child. The work of Nelson, Mandler, and Fivush and their colleagues strongly suggests that a broad range of verbal and nonverbal cues should be included in interview protocols in order for the investigator to obtain as full a report as possible of a young child's previous experience.

Cole and Loftus (1987) note that, because all children can report at least something accurate about their past experiences, the challenge for the researcher is to learn how to elicit information that is maximally accurate. They specifically note the need to understand children's use of prop and location cues and to experiment with methods of interviewing children that decrease the characteristics of the inquiry that push a child to respond in a particular way. Mandler (1990) asserts that all recall is cued. Children's earliest verbal memories appear to be prompted by external cues rather than by questions (Nelson & Ross, 1980). Cues may spark recognition memory or through manipulation may allow a child to reconstruct a memory of the event (Daehler & Greco, 1985). Cues may also enable a child to express the details of a remembered event. Cues are especially helpful for children who simply do not have the vocabulary necessary to express some or all of the components of an event, particularly if the event is novel or complex, if the child was very young when the event occurred (Terr, 1990), or if the event was a highly emotionally charged memory (Pillemer & White, 1989).

In the next section, we present a review of the results of the experimental

15

use of toys, objects, images, and sexually explicit props to enhance children's recall.

Toys, Objects, and Photo Arrays

Parents of 21–27-month-old children, keeping diaries of their toddlers' memories for Nelson and Ross (1980), reported that in 48% of the cases the sight of an event stimulated a verbal memory, in 32% the memories were stimulated by the sight of a person, while in only 5% were they prompted by a parent's question. Similarly, Todd and Perlmutter (1980) found that approximately half the memories of a group of 3- and 4-year-old children were prompted by toys or friends. During a recall test about a visit to the "wizard's room" in their laboratory, Price and Goodman (1990) found that 4-year-old girls were able to reenact with props a greater number of actions than 5½-year-old girls were able to describe. In addition, both 2½-year-old and 4-year-old girls ordered sequentially the activities they remembered in the prop condition with as much success as girls in the verbal recall condition who were a year and a half older.

Research by Saywitz, Goodman, Nicholas, and Moan (1991) supports the use of props in eliciting a more complete report of body touch. In an interview following a special pediatric examination, children increased reports of touch to body locations when they could demonstrate that touch with toy medical equipment. For example, when using a toy otoscope, reports that their ears had been touched increased from 18% to 47%; when using a toy stethoscope, reports that their hearts had been touched increased from 21% to 72%; and, when using a toy hammer, reports that their knees had been touched increased from 24% to 76%.

Jones and McQuiston (1988) and Leventhal, Hamilton, Rekedal, Tebano-Micci, and Eyster (1989) suggest that toys and dolls can be used in investigative interviews, not only to elicit nonverbal demonstration, but also to encourage children's recall and speech. Smith, Ratner, and Hobart (1987) demonstrated that the presence of objects cued kindergarten children's memory of making clay but that children who were given the opportunity to reenact the experience reported significantly more information and more of the action. Jones, Swift, and Johnson (1988) found improvement in the accuracy with which young children recalled objects they had previously manipulated in a visit to a farmhouse museum when either the objects or photographs of the objects were available. The objects and photographs were equally effective for both the 3- and the 4½-year-old children on same-day and 1-week interviews, but the photographs were more helpful than the objects in eliciting recognition from the younger group of children at 8 weeks.

One reason toy props may lose their cuing property for young children over time has been offered by DeLoache and her colleagues (DeLoache, 1987, 1989, 1990; DeLoache, Kolstad, & Anderson, 1991). They have found that it is difficult for young children to generalize from toy props to the real object. Miniature, scale-model equipment is apparently understood and used by young children "as is" rather than being seen as symbolic of another, larger object. This supports our clinical observations that, when young children prepare for a new medical procedure by manipulating small, toy replicas of medical equipment, they are surprised, confused, and sometimes angry when confronted with the real medical equipment during a procedure. Furthermore, child patients in our pediatric playroom consistently select the real medical equipment over toy equipment when replaying a medical procedure they have experienced.

We believe it is important that, when props are used by an investigative interviewer, both the purpose and the selection of props must be distinguished from therapeutic play (Faller, 1990; MacFarlane & Krebs, 1986; Mason, 1991; White & Quinn, 1988). In therapeutic play, the adult has no expectation or demand that the child's playful use of props reveal or approximate reality. Instead, the props are selected and manipulated by the child to enhance his or her ability to express thoughts, feelings, and fantasies. The way in which props have been used in pediatric settings differs from therapeutic use in three important ways. First, in clinical pediatrics, props are used for the purpose of preparing children, not for fantasy, but for the very specific realities of the body touch and handling they will experience during medical procedures and to debrief children or correct their misconceptions after a procedure has been completed (Golden, 1983; McCann, 1990; Petrillo & Sanger, 1980; Plank, 1971). Second, props are selected and controlled by the adult to enhance the child's anticipation of or memory of the particulars (the who, what, where, when) of an experience (Peterson & Mori, 1988). Third, many props are lifelike (e.g., such as anatomical body outlines) or life-size (e.g., the dolls in our medical center are the size of a 2-year-old child and are anatomically correct both inside and out) and include real medical equipment such as syringes, bandages, induction masks, and blood pressure cuffs (Melzack, 1975; Savedra & Tesler, 1989). The use of props by investigative interviewers can be informed by the pediatric use of props, but research attention is also required to discover how props might facilitate children's reporting beyond the hospital in settings where abuse is investigated.

Photo arrays have been used experimentally with young children to test both face recognition (Bruck, Ceci, Francoeur, & Barr, 1995; Davies, Stevenson-Robb, & Flin, 1988; Davies, Tarrant, & Flin, 1989; Goodman, Hirschman, Hepps, & Rudy, 1991; King & Yuille, 1987; Marin, Holmes, Guth, & Kovacs, 1979; Oates & Shrimpton, 1991; Peters, 1987) and place recognition (Goodman, Aman, & Hirschman, 1987; Goodman & Reed, 1986; Peters, 1987). Photo arrays, or "rogues' galleries," have long been used by police to cue adult bystander eyewitnesses' recognition of criminal suspects (Davies, 1981). There is a vast experimental literature on the use of photographs in laboratory eyewitness research in which the number of correct identifications increases with the child's age and the number of false positives decreases with age up to early adolescence (Chance & Goldstein, 1984; Yarmey, 1984).

Recently, researchers have found both adults and elementary school children equally accurate as mock eyewitnesses when using photo lineups for initial suspect identification; children, however, were less stable in their choices on retest (Parker, Haverfield, & Baker-Thomas, 1986), and they appear to have a greater tendency to produce false positive errors when the photograph of the target person is absent (Davies et al., 1988; King & Yuille, 1987; Peters, 1987). After witnessing a live incident, however, there were no differences in accuracy between children and adults on a photograph identification task (Marin et al., 1979). Goodman, Hirschman, et al. (1991) found no significant differences between parents and children in the average correct identification of nurses who administered injections to the children or in the proportion of false identifications made by the two groups. Overall, parents' identification skills were comparable to those of the 5–6-year-old children in the study. Jones and Krugman (1986) reported the use of an actual police photo lineup with a 3-year-old child, who was able to identify the person who physically and sexually abused her and left her in a remote area to die.

Photographs and line drawings of faces have been used, not only for person identification, but also as a primary signal system of emotional expression (Craig, McMahon, Morrison, & Zaskow, 1984; Ekman & Friesen, 1975; Izard, 1977; Izard, Hembree, & Huebner, 1987; Mehrabian & Wiener, 1967). Preschool children can match photographs showing the same expression posed by different persons, identify the facial expressions that correspond to emotion terms or emotion-eliciting situations, and imitate facial expressions (Borke, 1971; Fridlund, Ekman, & Oster, 1987; Greenspan, Barenboim, & Chandler, 1976; Izard, 1977; Odum & Lemond, 1972; Paliwal & Goss, 1981). Photographs and line drawings of the face have been used effectively by children as young as 3 years to communicate the intensity of their physical pain (Beyer, 1984; Kuttner, Bowman, & Teasdale, 1989; McGrath, deVeber, & Hearn, 1985; Wong & Baker, 1988).

The results of current research suggest that props such as photographs, toys, or dolls may elicit a more complex reenactment of an event in which children actively participated than can be elicited solely by verbal interview (Goodman & Aman, 1990; Jones et al., 1988; Peters, 1987; Price & Goodman, 1990; Saywitz, 1989; Smith et al., 1987; Todd & Perlmutter, 1980). There is both research and clinical observational support for the selection and testing of real, as opposed to scale-model, equipment for cuing young children.

Moreover, the limited research to date does not suggest that these props increase the incidence of false reports.

Sexually Explicit Dolls and Drawings

Everson and Boat (1994) reviewed 20 guidelines for the use of anatomical dolls. Two of their recommendations for the use of these dolls were as anatomical models and demonstration aids in investigative interviews with children. The dolls are helpful as anatomical models when it is necessary to verify a child's comprehension of the meaning of sexual terms and behavior (Melton, 1981) or the meaning of *touch* (Hashima, Barton, & Steward, 1988). Some children have learned an esoteric set of labels for actions, persons, or objects that is not commonly understood outside the family. For these children, the limitation on their ability to communicate lies less in their expressive vocabulary than in the communication value of that vocabulary for an interviewer who is unfamiliar with it (Goodman & Aman, 1990). It may be especially difficult for the interviewer to understand the names for primary and secondary sexual characteristics because children use idiosyncratic nicknames (Goldman & Goldman, 1982, 1988; Gordon, Schroeder, & Abrams, 1990) that may differ not only from anatomical terms but also from the names that their parents report as being used in the family (Schor & Sivan, 1989; Sivan, 1987). Furthermore, Schor and Sivan (1989) found that more than half the parents of the 144 young children they studied did not have separate names for the sexually related body parts, with words such as *bottom* being used for anus, buttocks, and vagina. Preschool and kindergarten sex education and sexual abuse prevention curricula represent another source of new words and phrases, such as *private parts,* that may be repeated but are often poorly understood and should be checked when used by young children (Berrick & Gilbert, 1991).

There is an important role for dolls as anatomical models to assist children whose sparse or esoteric responses might otherwise lead an investigative interviewer to underestimate their memory or, more critically, to disbelieve their accurate, but otherwise unverifiable, report. There are six published reports that investigate the efficacy of including anatomical dolls as a demonstration aid in interviews with children about experiences of body touch. In each of these studies, body touch was introduced experimentally in a laboratory setting or observed and documented in the medical setting so that the accuracy of children's reports could be independently verified.

Goodman and Aman (1990) have conducted the only laboratory study to date directly comparing the role of anatomical and regular dolls as stimulus cues to the reports of 3- and 5-year-old children about a tea party, a puppet play, and a Simon Says touching game that children played with a male confederate in a laboratory setting. In the touching game, each child was asked to touch his or her own body (e.g., ear, toes) and to touch the confederate's knee; the child's knee was touched in turn by the confederate. It is not possible to ascertain from the data presented if access to either type of doll enhanced reporting of the knee touch, but neither type of doll significantly increased the amount of information that the children gave about their whole experience in the laboratory over the information offered by children in a parallel verbal interview. In fact, the dolls were interpreted by the authors as perhaps distracting young 3-year-old children's ability to answer objective questions about their previous experience, although there was no increase in suggestibility or frequency of false alarm errors, that is, unfounded allegations of sexual abuse, when 3-year-old children used the dolls.

In another laboratory study, DeLoache and Marzolf (1995) tested the usefulness of anatomical dolls with very young children. Building on their previous work documenting children's difficulty using toys, props, and scale models as symbols, they argue that, for an anatomical doll to be useful in revealing body touch, children must be able first to use the doll as a representative of themselves. Then children must take the second step, which is to be able to map from themselves to the doll. DeLoache and Marzolf interviewed 2½-, 3-, and 4-year-old children about a play session with a male experimenter who placed stickers on four body locations (the child's arm, knee, foot, and cheek) and then touched them twice (hand and foot) during a Simon Says game. Before interviewing the children with the dolls, the authors sought to help children establish correspondence between themselves and the doll with parallel capes, necklaces, and floor pillows. On the sticker task assessing the children's ability to map from their body to the doll, performance improved significantly with age. Only 20% of the 2½-year-old children were able to meet the criterion of placing three of four stickers correctly, while 84% of the 4-year-old children did so. On the memory task, there were no age differences in accuracy of location of body touch in response to direct questions. However, when the dolls were used as demonstration aids, the 2½- and 3-year-old children showed on the doll only half the touches they had previously reported to the interviewer, while the 4-year-old children demonstrated 79% of the previously reported touches on the doll. No child spontaneously used the dolls to communicate with the interviewer. Some children accurately located touch on their own bodies but erred as they moved to demonstrate it on the dolls.

In a study conducted in a medical setting, Ornstein, Follmer, and Gordon (1995) examined the memory of 3- and 5-year-old children for a recall of the features of a routine visit to the doctor. Children were asked to recall features of their experiences without dolls, to recall features of their experiences with dolls as a representational figure, or to demonstrate using dolls for role-play. Ornstein et al. report that the dolls did not facilitate the reporting accuracy of children from either age group. The 5-year-old children made fewer errors than the 3-year-old children did when dolls were used.

In another study conducted in a medical setting, Saywitz et al. (1991) used anatomical dolls and direct questions as stimulus cues in a study of 5- and 7-year-old girls' memories of a specially designed pediatric examination. Half the girls in each age group received a vaginal and an anal examination, and half received a checkup for scoliosis (which involved a special tapping sequence along the spinal column) incorporated into the physical examination. All the girls were questioned three times during the interview about the event. Although the girls reported more body touches during the second round of questioning, after the dolls were introduced, than they did in the initial free recall condition (29% vs. 10%), when specific disclosure of touch to the vagina and anus was examined, the dolls did not enhance the number or consistency of reports. In fact, 22% of the girls reported genital touch in the free recall condition, but only 17% did so in the subsequent inquiry with the dolls, while the same number of girls, 11%, reported anal touch in both free recall and demonstration conditions.

Saywitz et al. noted that four of the eight children who reported vaginal touch in free recall failed to demonstrate it and that only one of the four children who reported anal touch during free recall continued to demonstrate it with the dolls. In fact, when they had access to the dolls, only two children first reported vaginal touch and one anal touch. Only one of the girls reported spinal touch in free recall, and none reported it in demonstration with the doll. In response to doll-assisted direct questioning, 92% of the girls reported genital touch, 82% anal touch, but only 60% spinal touch (a reporting rate that did not differ from chance). No girl from the back-touch group falsely reported genital/anal touch spontaneously or in the demonstration condition with the anatomically detailed dolls. The authors believe that the difference in reporting rates for touch to different body parts may be a function of the fact that genital touch may be more stressful from a socioemotional perspective and therefore more memorable than back touch to little girls. In response to direct inquiry, errors increased, but errors of omission were more frequent than errors of commission, and no child in the back-touch condition falsely reported genital touch.

Bruck, Ceci, Francoeur, and Renick (1995) repeated the Saywitz study with younger children (3-year-olds), half of whom received a genital examination during a routine physical examination, half of whom did not. However, the interviewers did not solicit children's free recall initially; rather, immediately after the examination, an experimenter pointed to the genitalia or buttocks of the doll and asked whether the child had been touched there. In response to the doll-assisted direct question, only 47% of the children accurately confirmed the genital touch, while 50% of the children who had not received the genital examination erred by saying yes. When children were then asked to use the anatomical dolls as a demonstration aid, only 25% of the children were coded as accurate. The authors coded children's insertion of a finger into the doll's anal or genital cavity as an error. When children who had not received a genital examination were told to show on the doll how the doctor touched their genitals and buttocks, 50% of the children complied with the request and erred by showing either genital or buttocks touch. Children's reporting accuracy was similar when demonstrating with the doll or their own body.

Katz, Schonfeld, Carter, Leventhal, and Cicchetti (1995) interviewed 21 3–7-year-old children 1–2 weeks after they had received a forensic medical examination for suspected sexual abuse. The interview included open-ended questions, open-ended questions with the dolls, and doll-assisted direct questions. Access to dolls did not improve the amount of information children reported; however, doll-assisted direct questions yielded significantly more accurate information than the other two conditions. Access to anatomically detailed dolls did not elicit false reports of sexual contact.

Goodman, Quas, and Dunn (1995) interviewed 46 3–10-year-old children approximately 2 weeks after the children experienced a voiding cystourethrogram (VCUG), an invasive medical procedure that is stressful, embarrassing, and painful. It involves forced genital contact as the urethra is catheterized and the bladder infused with liquid, and it requires that the child void on the X-ray table. Parents are usually not allowed to remain with the child for the whole procedure. Initially, children were asked to freely recall their examination experience; then, anatomically detailed dolls and relevant prop cues were introduced. As anticipated, significant age differences among children (grouped into 3–4-year-olds, 5–6-year-olds, and 7–10-year-olds) were found when total correct and incorrect units of information were analyzed. Children in each age group recalled more accurate than inaccurate information. With props and dolls, the youngest group produced significantly more incorrect additional information than did children in the older groups. Props benefited both the 5–6-year-old children and the 7–10-year-old children. However, all three groups of children were significantly more likely to report genital touch when they had access to dolls than in the free recall conditions (M's = 70% and 20%, respectively). In this study, doll-assisted direct questions were not asked.

Four points can be made to summarize the research data collected to date in laboratory and medical settings on the use of dolls as demonstration aids. First, in the experimental studies, when 2½- and 3-year-old children were interviewed about benign or mildly distressing touch, they did not benefit from access to the anatomical dolls. Their verbal recall was more informative and more likely to be accurate. DeLoache and Marzolf (1995) note that these findings are counterintuitive for most adults, who easily understand the symbolic function of the dolls. Second, access to dolls may have helped some 3–7-year-old children report benign genital touch during a physical or forensic medical examination, but specific enhancement over free recall cannot be discerned from the Saywitz et al. (1991) study, and, in studies by Bruck, Ceci, Francoeur, and Renick (1995), Katz et al. (1995), and Saywitz et al. (1991), the efficacy of the doll demonstration is confounded with the order of presentation. It is possible that some children in these studies may have been confused by repeated questioning, perceived that their initial report of genital touch must have been wrong or unacceptable, and therefore changed it. Others, possibly believing that their first answer was sufficient, failed to demonstrate the touch when asked a second time.

Third, when reporting genital touch that was painful, access to the dolls as demonstration aids strikingly increased the reporting of children across the age range from 3 to 10 years. Seventy percent of the children in the Goodman et al. (1995) study used the dolls to demonstrate painful genital touch, compared to 25% in the study by Bruck, Ceci, Francoeur, and Renick and 17% in the study by Saywitz et al.—a magnitude of difference that both was statistically significant and could be clinically important if the abuse analogue is considered. We believe that both the differential contribution of interview strategies and the relative painfulness of the touch may be important factors in the assessment of the efficacy of the use of dolls as demonstration aids with young children. Fourth, doll-assisted direct questioning elicited high rates of accurate response from 5- and 7-year-old children in the Saywitz et al. (1991) study and from 3–7-year-old children in the Katz et al. (1995) study. In striking contrast, high error rates, not differing from chance, characterized the 3-year-old children in the study by Bruck, Ceci, Francoeur, and Renick (1995).

Next Steps in Research

The weight of the research data reviewed above suggests that young children need and can use external cues to aid in both the recall and the reporting of what they have previously experienced. The research by DeLoache and her colleagues (DeLoache, 1989, 1990; DeLoache et al., 1991; DeLoache & Marzolf, 1995) and our own clinical observations in the pediatric playroom suggest that the effectiveness of real medical equipment, as opposed to toy props, might further enhance young children's reporting. We believe that the efficacy of sexually explicit props merits further testing. One issue is to determine whether there is a link between the use of dolls as models and as demonstration aids since many investigative interviewers use the dolls for multiple purposes in a single interview. Another issue is to test the usefulness of a broader variety of sexually explicit cues. No studies have been identified that employed anatomically detailed drawings to cue children's memory of body touch or to support disclosure. Anatomically detailed drawings have been used effectively in pediatric settings to communicate with children about body touch (Plank, 1971). As two-dimensional cues, they do not offer the same "pull" to the curious young child to explore body openings, explorations that might be misinterpreted as a replay/report of sexual experience (Boat & Everson, 1994; Ceci & Bruck, 1995). The courts have not objected to the anatomical drawings (White, 1988), and professionals are reportedly using them to investigate abuse (Conte et al., 1991; Everson & Boat, 1994). It would be helpful to compare the differential enhancement of anatomically detailed dolls and drawings in children's reporting of body touch. Given the finding by White, Strom, Santilli, and Halpin (1986) that the 4- and 5-year-old children in their study typically did not use the dolls, and given the reticence of the 7-year-old children in the study by Saywitz et al. (1991) to use the dolls to demonstrate anal touch, it may be that older children would find anatomical drawings less "babyish," more symbolic and remote, and thus safer and more useful than anatomically detailed dolls.

INTERVIEWER-CHILD INTERACTIONS

Mandler (1990) described recall as a reconstruction of information about the past *to ourselves*. The task of the investigative interviewer is to enable a child to report recalled information to others. What factors might support or inhibit disclosure? Fivush et al. (1991) found that young children (30–35 months old) reported more accurate autobiographical information when conversing with a stranger than with their mothers. Their study does not test whether distressing social, personal, and interpersonal experiences may inhibit some young children from reporting what they recall to an interviewer who is an unfamiliar adult. Shy children simply will not talk to people they do not know, and even naturally effusive children have often been taught to inhibit their inclination to talk to strangers. Moreover, even when children can be persuaded to speak to an unfamiliar interviewer, they may avoid the central topic because they have learned that some things "we just don't talk about to strangers."

The quality of the relationship established between the interviewer and the child before and during the interview may play a significant role in lowering these inhibitions (Melton & Thompson, 1987). Unfortunately, investigative interviewers are often rushed, particularly during the initial interview. They are "under the gun" and need to obtain sufficient information to determine whether legal, health, or mental health protection is needed in as short a time as possible (Goldstein, 1987; Jones & McQuiston, 1988). Interviewing can be harsh and frustrating work, and, when children feel intimidated by any stress they might perceive in an interviewer's manner or tone of voice, they may "shut down" and respond less often to questions (Dent, 1977; Hill & Hill, 1987; Peters, 1987). Worse still, children's suggestibility may also be increased by the interviewer's stress (Goodman et al., 1992).

The content of events recalled may inhibit disclosure. Children regularly withhold information that is laden with affect. Cole (1986) found a general masking of negative feelings by boys, and Saarni (1984) demonstrated that girls are even less likely than boys to display disappointment. Saywitz et al. (1991) suggested that the differential reporting of 7-year-old but not 5-year-old girls following a physical examination that included either genital or back touch was a function of the older girls' feelings of shame or embarrassment, which reduced their motivation and ability to report the experience. Young children may choose to withhold information about bad experiences because they do not want to elicit a negative response from their listeners. For example, children who have a life-threatening illness have confided to our medical staff that they know they are going to die but that they don't want their parents to know because their parents would be "too sad." Clinicians and researchers alike report that maltreated children learn to remain silent when they sense that a parent might become angry or excessively alarmed were the truth told (Sauzier, 1989; Summit, 1983). During an investigative interview, when a child begins to disclose a particularly frightening or brutal event, a horrified response from the adult interviewer, particularly one who has not been trained adequately, may stop the child mid-sentence (Jones & McQuiston, 1988). This response can be seen in children as young as 28 months, who are beginning to read their own and adults' emotions (Bretherton & Beeghly, 1982).

Perceived lack of control over an event may be another inhibitor of disclosure (Seligman, 1975). Band and Weisz (1988) interviewed preschool and elementary school children and found that children report that they cope more actively with physical accidents and injuries that are self-inflicted or caused by other children than with medical procedures in which they are a passive and sometimes even resistant partner. The perception of helplessness often promotes the adoption of a resigned stoicism, a quiet forbearance. The relative helplessness of the hospitalized child (Bowlby, Robertson, & Rosenbluth, 1952) or the abused child can thus limit disclosure of detail. This may be why parents so often underestimate children's pain (Lollar, Smits, & Patterson, 1982) and why medical staff inaccurately believe that children adapt to repeated painful procedures over time (Katz, Kellerman, & Siegel, 1980). Adults sometimes actually promote this passive style of coping. While parents and medical staff understand that sometimes one must hurt a child in the process of necessary medical care, it is difficult for adults to tolerate a feisty, crying, or noncompliant child, and adult stoicism is portrayed as the ideal.

We believe that a child's willingness to talk subsequently about an event in which he or she has been rendered helpless can be dampened further if the interviewer assumes a powerful asymmetrical role with respect to the child. Mischler (1986) has long been a critic of authoritarian interviewing practices that can compound and reinforce the helpless role of the person being interviewed. He believes that this results in impoverished data. He has called for a redistribution of power between the interviewer and the interviewee. By empowering the interviewee, a strategy often found in ethnographic work, Mischler asserts that the quality, interpretation, and personal meaning of the event being reported will become clearer and the data more accurate.

The weight of the research and clinical observations reported above supports attention to the psychosocial interaction of the child and the interviewer. The data suggest that, rather than increasing the interaction between interviewer and child, disclosure of difficult, negative events might be enhanced if the possibilities for interaction were limited. Interviewer-induced error might be less of a problem, and, given more freedom and control, the child might be willing to reveal negative, embarrassing information. Both the interviewer and the child would benefit.

In searching for interview techniques that seemed particularly applicable to young children and that also met our concern to limit interviewer-child interaction, we rejected strategies from the therapeutic literature that commonly encourage rapport building, engagement, etc. We considered our observation of young children in preschool, hospital, and home settings. We have found that, for children, the opportunity to work actively with computers is even more compelling than passively watching television. In our experience, even very young children are hard to interrupt or "call for dinner" when they are absorbed in a computer game. Our research team decided initially to explore the presentation of stimulus cues via computer and ultimately to create a computer-assisted interview protocol in order to limit the personal interactions between interviewer and child. The evolution of this is described below in some detail in the section on research design.

THE EFFECT OF STRESS ON CHILDREN'S MEMORY

Mandler (1990) asserts that, if we are to understand what young children recall, we must determine the relationship between what they remember and what they say. In child abuse cases, the potential discrepancy between remembering and reporting is important to the legal system since it is the child's report rather than the memory per se that is critical when it comes to testimony. Child abuse is not a single phenomenon, and abused children's experiences vary widely. Still, distress and negative emotions are common responses of the abused child to experiences of coercion, physical restraint, or painful injury. We believe that distress may be a critical mediator that filters children's reporting of remembered events. Much of the developmental theory and research on memory has focused on children's memory of emotionally neutral information or events and has been conducted in laboratory settings (Schneider & Pressley, 1989; Steward, 1993). Although there have been some studies with children in laboratory settings of the effect of experimentally induced moods on memory (Forgas, Burnham, & Trimboli, 1988; Masters, Barden, & Ford, 1979; Nasby & Yondo, 1982), rarely have researchers explored children's memory of events as emotionally complex or as experientially vivid as sexual abuse. Schneider and Pressley (1989) call for work on intraindividual variations in children's memory across situations.

Children's Experiences of Pain and Intrusion

A child's experience of body touch is personal and unique, and touch that is physically painful is clearly distressing (Elliott, Jay, & Woody, 1987; Jay & Elliott, 1986). There are clinical vignettes and case studies in the pediatric literature extending back more than 50 years that document children's distress as a result of illness, medical and surgical procedures, and hospitalization (Bergmann & Freud, 1965; Jackson, 1942; Jessner, Blom, & Waldfogel, 1952; Levy, 1945; Pearson, 1941; Plank, 1971). And there is a growing clinical and experimental research literature focused more sharply on childhood pain (Bush & Harkins, 1991; Gaffney & Dunne, 1986; Harbeck & Peterson, 1992; Ross & Ross, 1988).

Pain has been defined by the International Association for the Study of Pain as "an unpleasant sensory and emotional experience associated with actual or potential tissue damage, or described in terms of such damage" (Merskey, 1979, 249). McGrath (1987) asserts that there is no simple physiological, neurological, or biochemical marker of pain that is valid independent of the judgment of the individual. Ross and Ross (1982) conducted interviews with nearly 1,000 5–12-year-old children about pain experienced at home, in school, in pediatric clinics, in hospitals, and in dentists' offices. Most children described pain caused by external events such as accidents, heat, surgery, or aggressive acts by other children and emphasized the general discomfort of their own painful experiences using descriptors such as *stabbing, burning, squeezing, jabbing,* and *dull.* Investigators who have studied childhood pain understand that the "unpleasant sensory and emotional experience" (Merskey, 1979) may include feelings of fear, anxiety, loneliness, anger, and sadness. The fact that the experience of pain is associated with "actual or potential tissue damage" highlights the dynamic role of memory in the assessment of previous experience with medical procedures and of cognitive appraisal informed by that memory in anticipation of subsequent procedures (Merskey,

1979). Jay, Elliott, Ozolins, Olson, and Pruitt (1985) believe that the complex set of sensory, emotional, and cognitive variables that are included in the childhood experience of pain can be more parsimoniously conceptualized as *distress.*

In order to explore the link between pain and memory, three critical issues need to be addressed: (1) What aspects of body touch might children experience as stressful? (2) What instruments are available to assess children's pain? (3) Will children's pain judgment parallel or differ from adults' judgment?

Steward (1988) identified three potential sources of distress from her clinical work with ill children: painfulness, invasiveness, and the incongruence of a medical procedure with the child's understanding of his or her needs. Painful touches are more stressful than benign touches, and touches that break body boundaries or enter body orifices are more stressful than those that touch only the body surface. Broome and Hellier (1987) administered the Children's Medical Fears Scale to 84 5–11-year-old children. Across the whole age range, two of the most feared of the 29 items were "getting a shot" and "having my finger stuck." However, even non-needle-mediated procedures were frightening to the younger children. The kindergarten children rated fear of the "doctor or nurse looking in my ear" significantly higher than did older children, and kindergarten and first-grade children both rated fear of the "doctor or nurse looking down my throat" higher than did the older children. Eland and Anderson (1977) found that, for the young child, even the anticipation of receiving an injection or a venipuncture evokes an extremely negative response. Peterson, Harbeck, Farmer, and Zink (1991) note that the pain of most medical procedures is of high intensity but of short duration. They suggest that, if a young child is not cognitively able to decenter to evaluate both aspects of the stimulus at the same time, then the short duration would not substantially detract from the evaluation of anticipated intense pain. Ross and Ross (1988) note that, whether pain is spontaneous or treatment induced, it is almost always an attention-directing event. Howe et al. (1994) suggest that the increased arousal and alertness that accompany the anticipation and the distress of an invasive medical procedure may contribute to the uniqueness of the event and that the event would therefore more likely be remembered.

The initial work on the clinical assessment of children's pain was conducted by pediatric nurses because of their concern about the undermedication of postsurgical and burn patients (Eland, 1974; Eland & Anderson, 1977). In the past 20 years, a wide variety of tools has been developed to assess the quality (Savedra, Holzemer, Tesler, & Wilke, 1993) and quantity (Beyer & Wells, 1990; Kuttner & Lepage, 1989; Lollar et al., 1982; McGrath, 1987) of young children's self-report of pain and to code the behavioral (Jay, Ozolins, Elliott, & Caldwell, 1983) and biochemical (Gunnar, Hertsgaard,

Larson, & Rigatuso, 1991) distress that pain evokes. Face scales have been used to elicit self-report of pediatric pain from children as young as 3 years of age (Beyer, 1984; Kuttner et al., 1989; LeBaron & Zeltzer, 1984; McGrath et al., 1985) and were preferred by children from 3 to 18 years of age over five other scales that utilized numbers, words, color, volume, or quantity of objects for self-rating pain (Wong & Baker, 1988). Face scales used by Wong and Baker (1988), as well as those developed by Kuttner et al. (1989) and McGrath et al. (1985), range from smiling through neutral to a painful grimace. They also demonstrate tears on the most extreme face, a cue that Kuttner and Lepage (1989) noted may be age related. We believe that tears may also introduce gender bias and result in underreporting by boys. The newest face scale, a well-designed instrument with strong psychometric properties, is based on drawings by Australian schoolchildren (Bieri, Reeve, Champion, Addicoat, & Ziegler, 1990). The Faces Scale registers the continuum from no pain to extremely intense pain with changes in the mouth, eyes, and brow—the same critical facial components identified by Ekman and Friesen (1975) in their analysis of the facial expression of human emotions. None of the faces in this new Australian scale has tears.

While the documentation of children's pain during and immediately following medical and surgical procedures is common, and while there has been attention to the role of a child's cognitive and linguistic ability to understand and describe pain (Gaffney & Dunne, 1986; Harbeck & Peterson, 1992), investigation of the role of pain in children's memory of procedures is rare (Peterson et al., 1991; Steward, 1993). Three research teams have studied the relation between children's pain ratings of a medical procedure and their later memory of the event. Oates and Shrimpton (1991) found that, while children who had blood samples taken rated their experience as more painful (on a five-point scale from "very stressful" to "enjoyable") than did control children, pain neither enhanced nor depressed children's memory of the total event when interviewed 1 week or 3–6 weeks later. Bruck, Ceci, Francoeur, and Barr (1995) also had children rate an inoculation, using a chip scale and a cartoon faces scale. They found no relation between children's self-rated pain and photograph identification of the pediatrician or his actions 4–18 months later. Merritt et al. (1994) asked children to rate the pain of a VCUG using the Oucher Scale. Although the VCUG is acknowledged to be more painful and of longer duration than a blood draw or an inoculation, children's pain ratings did not correlate with either immediate recall of features of the event or subsequent recall 6 weeks later.

On the other hand, Merritt et al. (1994) did find two aspects of children's memory of the painful VCUG procedures different from the memory of children experiencing a benign physical examination documented in earlier studies (Baker-Ward et al., 1993; Ornstein et al., 1992). First, 3–7-year-old children ($M = 5$ years) who had experienced the painful procedure did not demonstrate the anticipated age-related forgetting between initial and delayed interviews. In fact, children recalled 88% of the features of the medical procedure initially and 83% 6 weeks later, while they rejected misleading questions at both the immediate and the delayed interviews. Second, younger children reporting the more painful experience gave more information in response to open-ended questions and were therefore less dependent on verbal cuing by direct questions to recall features of the experience than were younger children in the less painful experience. Open-ended questions accounted for 65% of the recall of the children in the study by Merritt et al. but only 42% of the recall of 5-year-olds in the Baker-Ward et al. study.

The findings with respect to the relation of adults' judgment of children's distress to children's memory are somewhat contradictory, as the clinical literature would suggest (Manne et al., 1992; Watt-Watson, Evernden, & Lawson, 1991). Research teams have introduced a variety of visual analogue scales anchored by words such as *anxiety, fear, distress,* and *pain* to elicit adults' judgment of children's pain. Ornstein et al. (1992) found no significant relations between ratings of 3- and 6-year-old children's anxiety by nurses or physicians following a physical examination and children's immediate or delayed memory of a physical examination. Parents' ratings of their 6-year-old children demonstrated an inverse relation such that children rated with higher anxiety demonstrated depressed recall. Baker-Ward et al. (1993) found no relation between children's total recall performance of a physical examination at the immediate or delayed interviews and anxiety ratings by parents, doctors, or nurses. Goodman, Hirschman, et al. (1991) asked experimenters to judge children's anxiety during an injection. They found no main effect for distress, but children judged to be most distressed during the procedure reported the most information and were least suggestible in follow-up interviews. Children judged to be most distressed before the procedure were most accurate in identifying the medical staff. On the other hand, Peters (1987) found accuracy of person recognition to be impaired when children identified the photograph of a person (a dentist) with whom they interacted when they were more stressed, while the same children were more accurate when they identified the photograph of a person (a research assistant) with whom they interacted when they were less stressed.

In addition to the child's self-rating noted above, Merritt et al. (1994) collected multiple assessments of children's distress by others. Parents' ratings of their children's fear and predictions of their children's anxiety and cooperation did not relate to the children's recall, nor did ratings of children's pain by the medical technician. The technician's rating of children's fear was significantly related to depressed total recall in initial and delayed interviews. Assays of children's distress employing salivary cortisol did not predict children's recall, but high scores on the Observation Scale of Behavioral Distress were negatively correlated with children's recall of features of the painful medical procedure only at the 6-week follow-up.

In sum, both painful body touch and intrusive body touch are distressing to children, and instruments to assess the magnitude of distress can be used reliably by children. To date, there are few empirical studies that have tested the effect of pain on children's memory, and there is little agreement on the relation between adults' and children's estimates of pain. There are mixed results from five research teams about the accuracy of children's recall when the experiences are judged by adult observers as mildly to moderately stressful. The pediatric literature would anticipate finding a positive relation between children's own pain ratings and the accuracy of their subsequent memory of the event (Bearison, 1990; Beyer, Berde, & Bournaki, 1991; Freud, 1952; Manne et al., 1992), whereas none was found by three research teams. When adults judge a medical procedure to be highly stressful, children required less verbal cuing and demonstrated relatively little forgetting compared to children who experienced a mildly distressing procedure. In the studies reviewed above, the selection of instruments to rate pain, differences in children's health status, and the limited invasiveness of the procedures may have constrained the findings. The findings reported above suggest that researchers interested in the link between children's pain and memory could fruitfully broaden the range of memory variables beyond accuracy. It is clear that, in order to test the models of the link between memory and emotion in the context of medical procedures, the assessment of a child's distress must be made by the child. It may also be useful, both theoretically and clinically, to collect judgments from adult observers (e.g., parents, medical staff, research assistants) about the child's distress, for discrepancies between adults' and children's judgment can provide another independent variable that may contribute to the predictive power of any of the models. However, adults' judgments of children's distress should never be substituted for the children's judgment, for it is the children's experience of pain and distress that is immediately available to be woven into their memory of the event.

Family Stress

Many abused children live in chaotic, dysfunctional families (Finkelhor, 1993; Finkelhor & Baron, 1986; Long & Jackson, 1991). Our clinical experience with abused children suggests that a background of chronic stress may drain children's cognitive and emotional energy so that their memory for a specific event may be depressed. We have been unable to identify experimental research that attempts to determine the truth of this clinical observation, but we feel that it is an important variable to assess in our study, for family stress may function in conjunction with or independently from the relative distress of a specific event to inhibit memory.

II. THE CHILD INTERVIEW STUDY

RESEARCH OBJECTIVES

The primary objective of our study was to design and compare the effectiveness of four parallel interview procedures to elicit children's reports of critical features of the clinic visit that are directly relevant to the legal testimony of children who are participant eyewitnesses: body touch and handling, persons present, and place. Four interview strategies were developed for our study: (1) a verbal interview unsupported by props; (2) a drawing interview that was enhanced with anatomical drawings to support the reporting of body touch, pain faces to aid the report of the relative painfulness of body touch, and feeling thermometers to aid in the report of positive and negative feelings; (3) a computer-assisted interview enhanced with the anatomical drawings, pain faces, and feeling thermometers used in the drawing interview but presented on the computer screen; and (4) a doll interview enhanced with anatomically detailed dolls and medical equipment to support reports of body touch, pain faces, feeling thermometers, and photo arrays to support the reports of person and place. Since the drawing and computer-assisted interviews shared the same cues, by comparing the results from them we were able to assess the effect of the computer on the interviewer-child interaction.

The efficacy of the four interviews was assessed employing independent groups of children rather than using a within-subjects design, in which the effects of type and repetition of question format are confounded. The research was designed as an analogue study that might inform our understanding of the reliability of reports from children who have been physically and/or sexually abused. Participants included boys and girls from pediatric outpatient clinics at a large university medical center. During their visits, all children experienced body touch and handling by our medical staff, and some children also experienced necessary, but painful, medical procedures. Judgments about the intensity of painful touch were made by the participants—the medical staff who administered each procedure and the children who experienced the procedures—rather than by observers such as parents or experimenters. A videotape record was made of the children's visits to the pediatric clinics, instead of employing an observer to check procedures during or asking staff to check off procedures after the clinic visits. Information obtained both from the videotapes and from the children's medical records enabled the coding and analysis of three memory variables: the accuracy, completeness, and consistency of children's reports.

We identified the following research questions. First, how accurately and completely do children report body touch, and what are they able to report about the presence of other persons and the setting? Second, what is the effect on the accuracy and completeness of children's reports when interview protocols are enhanced with prop cues, and do anatomically detailed props support reporting accuracy or error? Third, across multiple interviews, how consistent are children's reports, and is repeated information more likely to be true or false? Fourth, can innovative computer technology be tapped to present stimulus cues that result in effective interviews with young children? Fifth, how do children's reports change if the event the child is asked to report has been distressing, for example, emotionally laden or physically painful?

In addition, during the process of reviewing our empirical findings from the first interview, two issues emerged that raised the clinical curiosity of our research team and merited further investigation. First, we wanted to know in much more textured detail how the presence of the computer affected the child-interviewer relationship. Specifically, we were interested in studying whether the computer limited the intrusion of the interviewer into the child's world.

Second, for most children, the more distressing the experience, the more they told us about what had happened to them. Yet, in comparing the videotapes of the clinic events and the subsequent interviews with the children, we were struck by the fact that some children failed to report very painful medical procedures they had experienced. Our research team wanted to know who the children were who went "underground" rather than report distressing touch and handling, how one might explain their silence, and whether we could uncover a dynamic that might help us understand the parallel problem of the failure of abused children to disclose. Two "spin-off" studies were designed—essentially studies within the larger study—to examine the issues of child-interviewer interaction and to explore the dynamics of the hurt but silent children. A graduate student joined interested members of our research team in the investigations of each of these projects.

The research methodology for the Child Interview Study, including the design of the interviews, the selection of the research population, the dependent and independent variables, and the plan for data analysis, is described below. The results and discussion of the findings of the three interview sessions are presented in Chapters III–VI. The results and discussion of the "spin-off" study comparing the interaction between the child and the interviewer in two of the enhanced interviews are presented in Chapter VII, while the investigation of children who failed to report painful, invasive medical procedures is presented in Chapter VIII. In Chapter IX, we present a set of recommendations for conducting investigative interviews with young children, discuss the limitations of the study, and identify possible next steps for research.

DESIGN OF THE INTERVIEW PROTOCOLS

A prototype was constructed, from which four parallel interviews were developed. Each interview contained the same questions, in the same sequence and grammatical form. The selection of questions was based in part on what our research team had learned in a previous study in which parents and their children were interviewed about touch and handling within the context of normal, everyday caretaking and in part on dialogues with research teams studying different facets of child abuse interviewing (Boat & Everson, 1986; Goodman, 1984; Jones & McQuiston, 1988; Sivan, 1987; White, Strom, & Santilli, 1986; White, Strom, Santilli, & Quinn, 1987). Our intention was to design a straightforward interview that would elicit cooperative responses from young children but not lead them into saying things about their experiences with their doctors that were not true.

The prototype consisted of questions designed to elicit the child's report of the experiences that happened during his or her visit to the doctor. Three major content areas were targeted: (1) body touch, including the location on the child's body where he or she was touched by medical staff during the clinic visit, judgments about how distressing that touch was, and what the child was touched with; (2) the number and description of people present in the room; and (3) the location and description of the clinic room where the procedures took place. For each of the content areas, the query began with an open-ended question to solicit a free-ranging, descriptive, narrative response from the child, for example, "Was anybody in the doctor's office with you? Who?" Verbal prompts were given when appropriate to probe a child's experience fully, for example, "Were there any big people? Were there any other children?" When a medical staff member was identified, a set of seven specific questions was asked, but none was a leading question. For example, if, when describing the medical staff, a child did not mention hair color, he or she was asked, "What color was his/her hair?" But the child was never asked/told, "The doctor's hair was brown, wasn't it?" Children's responses were accepted without challenge or harassment. If a child's spontaneous narrative included all the descriptive information, no further prompts were administered.

The prototype also included a set of nine direct yes/no questions of the sort recommended by Enos et al. (1986) for use in pediatric forensic investigations of alleged child sexual abuse. These nine questions, referred to as the "action" questions, describe common pediatric procedures in which patients are touched. Although we did not control the number of "absent event questions" included in the interview (Ornstein et al., 1992), our pediatric team members anticipated that the typical 3–6-year-old child would experience approximately half the nine actions during a clinic visit. Our research team decided, as an ethical point, to refrain from including knowingly false allegations about the medical staff in the set of direct yes/no questions since, even if the "misleading questions" were accurately denied, they might remain in children's minds and later undermine the ongoing relationship between the children and their doctors.

Finally, the prototype included questions in which children were asked about their feelings during the clinic visit, about coping strategies they had used, and about any preparation they had received prior to the clinic visit. Information on coping strategies and preparation is not reported in this *Monograph*.

Drafts of the interview questions were reviewed and critiqued by the research team consultants from early childhood education, pediatrics, and law. Pretesting of the interview protocols and several of the measurements was completed with children from the Early Childhood Laboratory on the University of California, Davis, campus under the supervision of one of our research team members, Jane Welker.

The Four Interview Formats

Of the four alternative interview formats, one was a traditional verbal interview unsupported by props of any sort. The remaining three interviews were enhanced through either line drawings, dolls, and other play equipment or a computer and computer graphics. The enhanced interviews also included additional questions and occasional requests for demonstrations. (For the questions included in the verbal interview, see the Appendix. For a summary of the topics and a list of the stimulus materials presented in the enhanced interviews, see Table 1.) The differences in interview format provided an opportunity to determine what effect the availability of different materials and equipment had on the accuracy, completeness, and consistency of children's reports as well as on the interaction between the interviewer and the child.

The four interviews differed in ease of administration and in the amount, portability, and flexibility of equipment required. The interview questions for the verbal, drawing, and doll interviews were contained in a notebook; the

TABLE 1

S<small>TIMULUS</small> M<small>ATERIALS</small> P<small>RESENTED DURING THE</small> V<small>ERBAL AND</small> E<small>NHANCED</small> I<small>NTERVIEWS</small>

Event	Verbal	Drawing	Computer	Doll
Body touch	Verbal	Verbal and body outline	Verbal and body outline	Verbal and doll
"Touch with"	Verbal	Verbal	Verbal	Verbal, medical equipment and props
Person	Verbal	Verbal and rogues' gallery[a]	Verbal	Verbal and rogues' gallery[b]
Place	Verbal	Verbal and rogues' gallery[a]	Verbal	Verbal and rogues' gallery[b]
Pain	Verbal	Faces	Faces	Faces
Feelings	Verbal	Thermometer	Thermometer	Thermometer

[a] Presented only in second and third interviews.
[b] Presented in first, second, and third interviews.

questions for the computer-assisted interview appeared one at a time at the top of the screen in somewhat abbreviated form.

The verbal interview used a simple, unenhanced question-and-answer format. The interview was designed to provide an opportunity to determine the efficacy of the strictly verbal interviews commonly used by the staff of law enforcement and social welfare agencies. It also provided a baseline against which to evaluate the three enhanced interview formats. The verbal interview utilized only the core interview questions.

The drawing interview was enhanced with two-dimensional graphics, including anatomical body outlines, a set of four distress faces, and eight emotion-rating-scale thermometers. These materials were included to determine whether they would increase the child's ability to understand the investigative interviewer's request for information, assist the child in retrieving that information from memory, and permit the child to respond in nonverbal (e.g., by pointing or demonstrating) as well as verbal ways. These stimulus cues were designed to be easy and practical for investigative interviewers to use since they could include the drawings with the notepad or clipboard regularly carried to investigative settings outside the office.

The computer-assisted interview included the same set of graphic materials used in the drawing interview except that the graphics were portrayed on a computer screen and presented in an interactive program. This interview required a personal computer, which, with the advent of laptops, was portable. We were interested in testing two facets of the computer-assisted interview. First, would the same stimulus materials be more effective presented on paper in the drawings interview or on screen in the computer-assisted interview? Second, would the presence of the computer hardware change the quality or quantity of interaction between the child and the interviewer? We were particularly interested in determining whether the screen played a role in diverting the child's attention away from the presence of the adult interviewer or whether the mouse gave a covert way to identify body parts and emotions, thereby lessening inhibitions about reporting body touch.

The doll interview was enhanced with two- and three-dimensional materials. These included anatomically detailed dolls, a box of medical equipment and other common items, the distress faces, and the emotion thermometers. The doll interview offered the child a rich collection of potential memory and reporting aides. The anatomical doll and medical equipment were included to determine how the opportunity to demonstrate body touch and handling with three-dimensional models and real medical equipment might influence children's responses. We were particularly interested in how the anatomical dolls influenced the accuracy with which genital touch was reported. Each child in the doll interview was also presented with a set of photo arrays for each staff person the child reported to be present and a photo array of places so that the child's verbal description of the medical staff and clinic room could be contrasted with his or her ability to identify them in a pictorial lineup. Since the materials and equipment required for this interview were cumbersome, the doll interview would be most easily conducted in an office setting.

Stimulus Materials for the Enhanced Interviews

A summary of the stimulus materials presented in the enhanced interviews is presented in Table 1. To enhance the reporting of body touch and handling, outline drawings of the naked bodies of male and female children from the book *Anatomical Drawings* by A. N. Groth (1984) were used in the drawing and computer-assisted interviews. Front and back outlines of a body of a same-sex child were presented, side by side either on a standard 8½ × 11-inch sheet of paper or on the computer screen. Groth's drawing of the girl was modified slightly in order to include ears. In the original, the girl's ears were covered by her hair, but, since inspection of the ears is included in most pediatric examinations, it was necessary that they be visible so that children could point to them if they had been touched. Line drawings of both Caucasian and African-American children were available on paper, but only the male and female Caucasian drawings were available in the computer program.

In the doll-supported interviews, anatomically detailed male and female Caucasian and African-American dolls were used. These dolls, designed by Phyllis Eymann, are sturdy and attractive and have genitalia that are appropriately proportioned (Bays, 1990). They stand 22 inches high, somewhat larger than many dolls used in investigative interviewing. We selected these dolls on

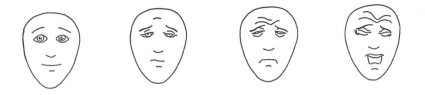

FIG. 1.—Selected faces from the Faces Pain Scale

the basis of our experience in medical play, as the larger size seems to enhance the reality use rather than the fantasy use of the doll. Each doll has an open mouth with a tongue that can protrude, separate fingers rather than mitt hands, and openings for the vagina and anus that are large enough to permit the demonstration of penetration, features identified by Boat and Everson (1986) as enhancing children's reporting of sexually abusive touch.

The doll interviews utilized a large box of items that children could use to identify or demonstrate what they were touched with. Half the items in the box were pieces of familiar medical equipment, such as a stethoscope, bandages, a blood pressure cuff, and a syringe. Half were items originally used for a family caretaking study and included such things as a washcloth, a curling iron, and a feather. In this interview, children were also presented with "Brown Bear," a large, brown stuffed bear. The bear was used to elicit from a child a demonstration of nine touches, including *pat, poke, pinch, rub, bite, wash, tickle, kiss,* and *touch.* Following the child's demonstration of the last word, *touch,* he or she was asked, "Can you show me another kind of touch?"

A set of faces developed by researchers at Macquarie University in Sydney, Australia, was used to elicit a report by the children about the relative distress caused by the touch and handling they themselves had reported (Bieri et al., 1990). Although the original scale has seven faces, for this study only four faces were presented: the first, third, fifth, and seventh (see Fig. 1). These faces, which graduate from a neutral face to one displaying an excruciating grimace, have been used clinically with young children in outpatient settings by Margaret Steward. They have also been used in pediatric hospitals to help children, parents, and medical staff report both the acute distress caused by medical procedures (Juniper, Addicoat, Champion, Cairns, & Ziegler, 1991) and postoperative pain (Malbourne, Ungerer, & Champion, 1991). Children and parents have used them at home between medical visits to monitor fluctuating pain in such chronic diseases as juvenile rheumatoid arthritis and sickle cell anemia (D. Bieri, personal communication, May 1985).

Eight emotion-rating-scale "thermometers" were used to facilitate children's report of the emotions and feelings they experienced during the pediatric visit. For the drawing and doll interview, the eight thermometers were drawn positioned vertically in two rows across a standard 8½ × 11-inch sheet of paper turned broadside. For the computer interview, the thermometers were shown one at a time rather than all simultaneously. Each thermometer included four horizontal crossbars positioned at intervals designating four equal spaces. Children indicated the height of the mercury in each thermometer according to their recall of the strength of the emotion felt during the pediatric visit.

Thermometer rating scales have been used in psychosocial pediatric research most often to measure pain (Beyer & Wells, 1990), and one of our research team members, Lisa Farquhar, has used them in her clinical practice to help children express complex, often quite disparate emotions. After pretesting, we elected to use the thermometers only for the latter purpose. The eight emotions selected were *happy, sad, scared, angry, surprised, sleepy, safe,* and *relaxed*. Research by Bretherton and Beeghly (1982) demonstrated that children as young as 28 months could use those words reliably to describe both their own feeling states and those of others.

Finally, photo arrays were developed to provide stimulus cues for the children's identification of medical staff and clinic location. Our research team took more than 100 photographs of women, men, and places. Color photographs (4 × 6 inches) of the medical staff were assembled in sets of six, modeled on the format of the rogues' gallery used in police investigations. Separate sets were developed for men and women, with careful attention to details such as ethnicity, hair color, general body type, beards, and glasses. We also created a six-picture rogues' gallery of places. The set included color photographs of a child's bedroom, a playroom full of toys, and rooms in four different pediatric clinics. In both the people and the places rogues' galleries, one of the six slots was reserved for the picture of the medical staff (who had been initially identified and described by the child) or the clinic room in which the procedure took place. Sets of pictures and standard instructions were reviewed by John Myers, our legal colleague. The photo arrays were presented to children in the doll interview during the original and two follow-up interviews and to children in the drawing interview only on the two follow-up interviews.

The computer used in the computer-assisted interview was a Mac Plus with a trackball cursor control device.[1] Panasonic camcorders, used in video-

---

[1] We experimented with three different types of cursor control hardware: a standard issue mouse, a "joystick," and a "trackball" (a ball set in a stationary box placed on the table at the side of the computer). It was determined that young children with small hands and limited physical strength could most easily use the trackball. They placed the cursor more accurately, and they had less difficulty clicking the button and selecting the precise screen objects intended. We explored the "touch screen" but rejected its use because the requirement that the child touch a body outline on the screen to identify a body location

taping both the clinic visits and all interviews, were mounted in the upper corners of the rooms. They were visible but unobtrusive.

Special Aspects of the Computer-assisted Interview

When this interview format is used, the interviewer is in charge of the keyboard, and the child is in charge of the trackball, but, as with the other three formats, the interview itself is still conducted verbally, and the child's response can be given verbally, nonverbally, or both ways. Brief versions of the interview questions are displayed across the top of the screen. For some question sequences, for example, the naming of body parts, the interviewer can "check off" the child's response from the list with a single keystroke or type in a child's unique name/nickname for a particular body location. A scroll bar is also available so that the child's additional verbal responses can be typed in by the interviewer. At the end of each set of questions, there is a "tickler," an automatic visual and auditory reminder of any not-yet-asked questions. The interviewer can ask the remaining questions at that time or choose to override and proceed to the next section.

The task of body identification served to pretest each child and, if necessary, to teach each child how the computer trackball worked. In the body-naming task, the program highlights body parts sequentially, from head to toe, in the same order in which the children were questioned in the drawing and doll interviews. The child is asked to name the body part as it is highlighted and then move the trackball to that body part and "click" it. When the child does so successfully, the next body part in sequence is automatically highlighted. The pacing of this task is in the hands of the child, a very nice feature of interactive computer programs in general and of this one specifically.

When prompting children to recall the touches they experienced during the clinic visit, the drawing of the body appears on the screen, and the children can use the trackball to move the cursor around the screen and point to all the places on their own body where they had been touched by medical staff. The set of distress faces then automatically appears on the screen immediately after the children select a body part that had been touched. The body outline and faces are accessible until they indicate that there were no more body touches. The emotion-rating-scale thermometers appear on the screen one at a time, as the visual display of all eight at once appeared too "busy" and possibly confusing on the small computer screen. When the child moves the trackball, the mercury in the thermometer rises or falls, allowing the child to indicate just how "safe" or "angry" or "tired" etc. he or she felt. All

---

is as overt as the requirement that the child touch an outline on paper. We were interested in the "privacy" that the trackball could offer a child.

the child's judgments about body locations touched, pain, and feelings are automatically recorded and saved.

The Role of the Elephant

The "logo" for the research project became the elephant since "an elephant never forgets." The elephant was selected as a stimulus cue that might help children remember previous interviews and their experiences during the pediatric visit. Such a reminder was required since we anticipated that some children would experience additional medical visits between the initial and the follow-up interviews. The elephant would serve to remind them which clinic visit we were questioning them about. The elephant was not anticipated to modify or distort the content reported by the child.

Two rubber stamps showing different, charming elephants were purchased for the project, and the children could choose whichever they preferred to have stamped on their hand at the end of the first interview. Each child received a thank-you note for participating in the study, and it too was stamped with the preferred elephant. Reminders for follow-up appointments were also decorated with appropriate elephant stamps. Follow-up interviews began with use of the elephant cues.

METHOD

Subjects

A total of 130 3–6-year-old children participated in the study, 65 boys and 65 girls. There were 29 3-year-old children (13 boys and 16 girls, $M = 41$ months), 39 4-year-old children (20 boys and 19 girls, $M = 53$ months), 33 5-year-old children (14 boys and 19 girls, $M = 66$ months), and 29 6-year-old children (18 boys and 11 girls, $M = 78$ months). The children were all visiting a pediatric outpatient clinic at our university medical center. An additional 13 children and their families agreed to participate in this study and completed the first interview. However, owing to equipment failure (in which the quality of the video signal, the audio signal, or both was damaged), their videotaped interviews were judged uncodable, and these children were dropped from the study.

The children came from diverse ethnic backgrounds: 59% were white, 20% Hispanic, 9% black, 7% Native American, 2% Asian, and 2% not identified ethnically. The sample included children whose families represented a broad range of social classes: the income of 38% of the families was less than $10,000; 30% of families fell in the $10,000–$25,000 range; 23% were in the

$25,000–$40,000 range; 7% had incomes greater than $40,000; and there was no information about income from 2% of the families. Parents' education ranged from grade school to postgraduate/professional school; the modal education of both parents was high school graduation. The demographics of the study population closely match the demographics of the families who are served by the university medical center in terms of social class and ethnicity. The only bias that we could identify that might differentiate the sample who participated from the total pool of children attending the pediatric outpatient clinics during the period of data collection is the absence of children from the study population who were brought to the outpatient clinics by an adult (such as a transportation worker) who did not have the legal authority to give consent for a child's participation in a research study.

Children were recruited from the following pediatric clinics: Continuity, Child Protection, Cardiology, Endocrinology, Pulmonary, Rheumatology, and Hematology/Oncology. The majority of children participating in the study experienced a routine pediatric physical examination as described by Ornstein et al. (1992), the only difference being that, whereas physician and nurse roles were sharply defined in the Ornstein et al. study, at our medical center pediatric care is delivered by health care teams in which physicians and nurses share flexible role assignments. This is especially true in the Continuity Clinic, our general pediatric acute-care clinic, where doctors and nurses are often accompanied by medical students or residents. In addition, some children in the Cardiology, Endocrinology, Pulmonary, and Rheumatology Clinics also experienced additional diagnostic procedures such as a blood draw. Children in the Child Protection Center received both a physical examination and a careful inspection of the anogenital area and a throat swab as deemed appropriate, as described by Katz et al. (1995) and Steward, Schmitz, Steward, Joye, and Reinhart (1995). Most children in the Hematology/Oncology Clinic were receiving treatment for cancer as described by Bearison and Pacifici (1989). While the clinics were scheduled on different days, they occupied one of two locations at the medical center, and children therefore experienced the same registration procedure, waiting areas, and interview room.

Children were randomly assigned to four interview conditions. (For the distribution of children from pediatric clinics by interview strategy, see Table 2.) The focus of this study was on the children's ability to report on their own experience of body touch and handling. Review of the videotapes of the pediatrics visits confirmed that children in all the clinics were touched by medical staff. Post hoc analyses were conducted to determine whether several experiential features of the pediatric visit and demographic characteristics of the children were evenly distributed across the four interview strategies. There were no differences in total body touch or in frequency of touch to the following body locations: head/hair, eyes, ears, nose, mouth, tongue, chin, neck, nipples, chest, abdomen, umbilicus, genitals, buttocks, anus, back,

TABLE 2

Distribution of Children from Pediatric Clinics by Interview Strategy

Clinic	Verbal	Drawing	Doll	Computer
Continuity	9	6	10	13
Child Protection	5	9	10	8
Cardiology	1	0	5	0
Endocrinology	0	0	0	2
Pulmonary	1	0	0	0
Rheumatology	0	0	0	3
Hematology/Oncology	17	17	8	6
Total	33	32	33	32

arms, wrist, fingers, legs, toes. Children in the verbal interview did receive fewer touches to the side and knee than did children in the enhanced interviews (p's $< .05$). Invasive medical procedures, defined as procedures administered by medical staff that break body boundaries or enter body orifices (Steward, 1988), were analyzed into two major categories: those that involved needles (e.g., shots, tuberculosis tests, venipuncture, spinal tap) and those that did not (e.g., otoscope). Both types of invasive procedures were equally frequently experienced across interview strategies. No differences were found among the interview groups on age, gender, or ethnicity of the child, family income, or mother's education.

The families of all children who kept their appointments between February 1988 and July 1989 and whose children were between 3 years and 6 years, 11 months, of age were invited to participate in our study when they arrived at the clinic. The acceptance rate for families whose children met the eligibility criteria was high; the majority of families we approached agreed to allow their children to participate.[2] There was no financial reimbursement for the first interview, but families whose children participated in the second and/or third interviews received $10.00 for each. In addition, free hospital parking passes were given.

All 130 initial participants were solicited for a second interview 1 month later. The rate of return at the second interview was 98.5%; two children (one boy and one girl) did not return. In addition, the interviews of four children (one boy and three girls) could not be used owing to interruption or equipment failure. Only the first 80 children interviewed initially were contacted for a third interview 6 months later. The rate of return was 92.5%. Table 3

[2] At the request of the clinic directors, the families were not contacted about the study prior to arriving with their child for an appointment in one of the participating clinics. However, the clinic staffs allowed our research team to review the appointment rolls each Friday for the next week to identify which of the clinics might have potential subjects.

TABLE 3

Distribution of Children at the Initial and Follow-Up Interviews

Interview Schedule	Type of Interview				
	Verbal	Drawing	Doll	Computer	Total
Initial interview	33	32	33	32	130
1-month follow-up	31	31	33	29	124
6-month follow-up	19	19	19	17	74

Note.—Children who returned for follow-up interviews participated in the same type of interview each time.

summarizes the distribution of children in each of the four interview types at the initial and follow-up interviews.

The Interviewers

Three persons, one male and two females, served as interviewers. The male interviewed all the boys in the study. One female conducted the initial and follow-up interviews with all but ten of the girls. Owing to illness, she was not able to serve through the end of the study. A second female interviewer was recruited to complete the initial and follow-up interviews with the last ten girls. All three interviewers had completed graduate work in clinical psychology and were highly skilled clinicians, experienced in diagnostic and psychotherapeutic work with young children and their families. All had extensive work experience in outpatient medical settings, and all had participated in prior research.

The interviewers were blind to the events that occurred during each child's pediatric clinic visit, but they were not completely naive. It was necessary for them to know which pediatric clinic a potential subject was scheduled to visit in order to meet families to recruit and screen children for the study. Thus, our interviewers knew which pediatric clinic a child was attending. They also knew the medical staff who were assigned to see each child and were familiar with the range of medical procedures that could be administered in that setting. However, for any specific child on any specific visit, the interviewer was blind to the child's experience of body touch and handling, the medical procedures administered, and the persons from the family or medical staff who were actually present in the clinic room with the child.

Procedures

Pretesting

On arriving at the clinic waiting room, each eligible child was given a language assessment by his or her same-sex interviewer. This was administered in the waiting room and took from 5 to 10 min to complete. It gave the child a brief but intimate time to begin getting acquainted with the interviewer while both were engaged in a language task that was low key and pleasant. Children who did not perform above a normative 24-month level of language proficiency and children whose primary language was not English did not participate further in the study. After the language screen, the interviewer completed an information sheet (which was then clipped to the medical chart) summarizing the results and making recommendations when appropriate for more complete language and/or hearing assessment. Thus, the information from the language screening was available to medical staff to incorporate into their feedback to the parents at the end of the clinic visit.

Parents who agreed to participate and whose child met the age and language criteria were then asked to complete a demographic sheet asking about family constellation, their education and occupation, the child's health history, a measure of family stress, and how the child was prepared for the current pediatric visit. They filled the sheet out in the waiting room prior to their child's clinic visit.

Clinic Procedures

All children had outpatient clinic appointments; however, when a child was actually seen by medical staff depended on factors such as the timing of the family's arrival at the clinic, the number of other children to be seen during clinic that day, and staff availability. Children were called from the waiting room as clinic rooms and medical staff were available. Families made their own decisions about just who would accompany the child. The clinic visit typically lasted about 25 min but could range from 15 min to 1 hour. While each child received individual pediatric attention according to his or her medical needs, all experienced body touch and handling.

Initial Interview

After the pediatric visit, the participating child joined the interviewer in another clinic room, set up as an office. Parents returned to the waiting room. Each child was greeted with the same introduction: "Hi, remember we talked before? I showed you some pictures and told you we were doing a children's memory study. When we are all done, I'll give you a snack and something to take home with you. Now, I am going to ask you a few more questions to see how much you can tell me about what you remember. What happened to you today? What did you do today?" If the child's response did not include any mention of the clinic visit, the child was asked, "What else happened to you today?'' If there was still no mention of the clinic visit, the child was asked, ''Did you visit the doctor's office today?''

Children in the *verbal interview* were then asked a series of open-ended and verbally prompted questions to elicit their report about and description of who was present, what had just happened to them, including location and painfulness of body touch and what they were touched with, and where this event took place. The action yes/no questions were followed by questions about the eight feeling states. Finally, the children were asked to describe coping strategies used and to explain any preparation that they had received prior to the clinic visit. Following the interview, the children were given juice and a snack and allowed to pick an elephant stamp.

The sequence of topics and questions for children in the enhanced interviews paralleled the verbal interview. In addition, children in the enhanced interviews were pretested with the props just prior to the topic where props were used. Children who required help received additional instructions to ensure that they were able to use all the props. Before inquiry about location and relative distress of body touch, children in the *drawings interview* were first shown the anatomical body outlines, told, ''This is a drawing of a boy/ girl just like you,'' and, as the interviewer pointed to fourteen body locations, asked, ''What is this called?'' Then the children were shown the set of pain faces and, in order to anchor each end, asked, ''Has anything ever hurt you this much? What was it?'' If they failed to respond, the children were prompted with the question, ''Which face shows how much it hurts when you skin your knee?''

After eliciting the child's body vocabulary and determining that he or she understood the pain faces, the interviewer proceeded to ask the questions about body touch by medical staff and then to ask the set of ''action'' questions about other interactions that the child might have had with medical personnel. On all three enhanced interviews, a direct question about touch to four body locations (ear, belly button, penis/vagina, and buttocks/anus) was initiated by the interviewer to ''double-check'' if a child had not already spontaneously reported any or all of those body touches. The interviewer pointed on the body outline or the doll to each body location for which there was missing information, and the child was asked, ''Were you touched there?'' The feeling thermometers were introduced by saying, ''I would like you to help me know about the kinds of feelings you had in the doctor's office. Here are some thermometers that measure feelings. How do you feel right now?'' After the child identified a feeling state, he or she was asked to rate the relative amount of that feeling after the interviewer pointed to the top, the midpoint, and the bottom of the thermometers and asked, ''Do you feel ———— a lot, somewhere in the middle, or a little?'' The bulb at the bottom of the thermometer was anchored as ''not at all.'' After establishing the child's ability to use the emotion-rating-scale thermometers, the child was asked to rate eight feelings.

Props were introduced and pretested with children in the *computer-assisted interview* in the same manner as in the drawings interview. However, as noted above, in this interview format, the props were all presented in the form of two-dimensional drawings that appeared on the screen. The interviewer controlled the keyboard to record the child's verbal responses, while the child used the trackball to record his or her nonverbal responses. Both attended to the screen.

Children in the *dolls interview* were first shown the anatomically detailed dolls and told, "This is a boy/girl doll just like you," and, as the interviewer pointed to 16 body locations, the child was asked, "What is this called?" (Note that the child could be asked to label the tongue or the anus on the dolls, but neither is visible on the anatomical line drawings used in the drawing and computer interviews.) The child was introduced to the faces and thermometers in the same manner as the children in the drawings and computer interview. Following the child's spontaneous report of body touch, the action questions, and the "double-check," Brown Bear was introduced, and children were asked to demonstrate different kinds of body touch, beginning with the question, "Can you pat the bear?"

Children in the *dolls interview* were also administered the rogues' gallery of people and places at the end of the session. The photo array for each of the medical staff described by the child earlier in the interview was introduced at the end of the interview in the following manner: "I am going to show you some pictures. You *might* see someone you have seen before, or you *might not* see anybody you have seen before. You do not have to pick anybody at all, and you should not just guess. Now look at these pictures, and tell me if you see anybody you have seen before." There was a separate set of six photographs for each medical staff member. Instructions for identifying the clinic room in which the child had been seen from the photo array paralleled those given for person identification.

Follow-Up Interviews

At the 1- and 6-month follow-up interviews, children were greeted by their interviewer with the welcome, "Hi ———! Remember the day when we talked before? I showed you a picture like this one [shows child elephant certificates]. Now I'm going to ask you some questions to see how much you can remember and tell me about that day. What happened to you the first time you talked to me?" On all follow-up interviews, each child was interviewed by the same person and received the same interview format as on the

TABLE 4

MEANS, STANDARD DEVIATIONS, AND RANGES OF THE
CONTINUOUS REGRESSION VARIABLES

	Mean	SD	Range
Age (in months)	59.2	13.6	37–83
Language age (in months)	57.2	14.2	31–108
Medical experience	4.2	2.1	0–8
Family stress	63.5	5.5	45–72
Health status	4.1	1.2	1–5
Physician rating of pain	1.2	1.4	0–5
Nurse rating of pain	1.9	1.6	0–5
Child total pain score	6.0	8.8	0–48
Negative feeling	3.4	4.4	0–12
No. of invasive procedures	1.7	1.1	0–5
No. of outpatient visits, 1 month	1.3	2.4	0–13
No. of inpatient visits, 1 month	.5	2.0	0–14
No. of outpatient visits, 6 months	7.0	10.2	0–55
No. of inpatient visits, 6 months	1.5	6.5	0–53

initial interview. Only the drawing interview was modified. On the second
and third follow-up interviews, the rogues' galleries of people and places were
added to the drawing interview in a manner parallel to their place and use
in all the doll interviews. That is, the photo arrays were introduced only after
the child had been asked to name and describe medical staff to establish the
child's identification.

Standardized Measures

In addition to age, gender, ethnicity, and mother's education, the following continuous variables were employed as potential moderators of children's
recall: children's language age, mother's report of children's past medical
experiences and family stress; medical staff ratings of children's health status
and distress; children's judgments of the relative painfulness of body touch
and ratings of their emotions; research team ratings of the number of invasive
medical procedures a child experienced during the pediatric visit; and the
number of intervening outpatient and inpatient visits between the clinic visit
and the follow-up interviews. (For a display of the means, standard deviations,
and ranges of the continuous variables introduced in the regression analysis,
see Table 4.) In addition, information was available on the likelihood of previous abuse, which was treated as a categorical variable.

Language

The language assessment administered to the children immediately prior
to their clinic visit was the TELD, the Test of Early Language Development

(Hresko, Reid, & Hammill, 1981). The TELD is appropriate for children aged from 3-0 to 7-11 and takes approximately 15 min to administer. Internal consistency and test-retest reliabilities are high, and validity has been established with other tests of language, reading, and intelligence. The TELD yields a number of scores, including a language age in months, a percentile score, and expressive and receptive language scores.

Medical Experience

A Medical Experience Index was created for this study to assess the child's past experiences with common medical procedures and illness in the family. Information was requested from the parent about the child's previous experience of blood sticks, blood draws, shots/vaccinations, bone marrow aspirations, spinal taps, hospitalizations, and surgeries and about family member illness and chronic pains. One point was given for each experience, and the scores ranged from 1 to 8.

Family Stress

The Family Inventory of Life Events (FILE; McCubbin, Patterson, & Wilson, 1981) was completed in the waiting room prior to the clinic visit by a parent from each family whose child was in the study. This instrument includes a list of 72 items: normative and nonnormative life events and changes experienced by a family unit (e.g., the birth of a new child, the divorce of the parents, the death of a family member). The parent was asked to circle all the events that his or her family had experienced in the past year. The reliability has been established employing Cronbach's alpha ($\alpha = .81$); construct and concurrent validity has been established with a number of family environment instruments. On this instrument, a high score means low stress, and scores could range from 72 to 0. For our sample, $M = 63.5$, and SD = 5.5.

Medical Staff Ratings of the Child's Health Status and Distress

At the end of the child's pediatric outpatient visit, the relative health of each child was rated by the medical staff person responsible for the child's care. The rating scale ranged from -5 to $+5$. The end points of the scale were anchored by the following descriptions: "serious health problems" and "very healthy, rarely ill." These data were transformed to a scale ranging from 1 to 5 for this study: $1 = -5$ and -4; $2 = -3$ and -2; $3 = -1$, 0, and 1; $4 = 2$ and 3; and $5 = 4$ and 5. Scores were available for 128 children and were distributed as follows: $1 = 4.7\%$; $2 = 7\%$; $3 = 11.7\%$; $4 = 19.5\%$;

and $5 = 57\%$. The modal health status score was 5; the mean health status score was 4.1, with a standard deviation of 1.2.

The medical staff personnel (physician, nurse, and/or physician's assistant) who administered the medical procedures during the clinic visit rated their judgment of how much distress the child experienced. Ratings were based on a six-point Likert-like scale, with 0 representing "no pain" and 5 representing "extreme pain."

Child Pain Rating

Children were asked to rate each body touch that they spontaneously reported. Children in the enhanced interviews were shown the first, third, fifth, and seventh faces from the Faces Pain Scale (Bieri et al., 1990). Unfortunately, children in the verbal interview were presented with only three rather than four choices: "not at all," "a little," or "a lot." A weighted pain score was created by assigning the neutral (first) face and the verbal choice "not at all" a weight of 0, the second (third) pain face and the verbal choice "a little" a weight of 3, the third (fifth) pain face a weight of 5, and the most extreme (seventh) pain face and the verbal choice "a lot" a weight of 7.

The weighted pain score was used in two ways: to develop a total pain score for each child and to identify a High Pain group of children. The total pain score was the sum of a child's pain ratings of all reported body touch. The High Pain group included every child who rated any body touch at the extreme (seventh pain face or "a lot"), in contrast to those children who did not rate any touch as that distressing.

Children's Rating of Emotions

Children in the enhanced interviews were shown the thermometers with five optional spaces, valued from 4 to 0. Children in the verbal interview were presented with four choices: "a lot," "some," "a little," or "not at all," valued 4, 3, 1, and 0, respectively. A total positive feeling score was created by summing the values given to three feelings: happy, safe, and relaxed. A total negative feeling score was created by summing the values given to three feelings: scared, angry, and sad.

Invasive Procedures

During the clinic visit, children in this study experienced a wide range of body touch and handling. Some touches, but not all, were considered invasive. For the purposes of this study, medical procedures that probed body orifices (e.g., otoscope in the ear) or that employed a needle (e.g., a shot or stitches) were considered invasive.

Intervening Outpatient and Inpatient Visits

Medical records were scanned for the number of outpatient and inpatient visits a child made to our medical center between the first and the second interview and between the second and the third interview. The number of intervening outpatient visits between the initial and the 1-month interview ranged from 0 to 13 (mode = 0, M = 1.3, SD = 2.4). The number of inpatient visits ranged from 0 to 14 (mode = 0, M = 0.5, SD = 2.0). At 6 months, the number of intervening outpatient visits from the first to the third interview ranged from 0 to 55 (mode = 0, M = 7.0, SD = 10.2); the number of intervening inpatient visits ranged from 0 to 53 (mode = 0, M = 1.5, SD = 6.5).

Abuse Experience

The Scales of Likelihood of Sexual Abuse (Leventhal et al., 1989) were used to rate the abuse experience of the 32 children recruited from the Child Protection Center. Following the clinic visit, the material from each child's medical record, including social history (including allegations of abuse), medical evidence of abuse, and the child's report of abuse, was reviewed and rated for likelihood of abuse by one of the authors, Michael Reinhart. A child was rated as "definitely abused" if the abuse was witnessed by an adult, if there was positive physical evidence, if there was evidence of a sexually transmitted disease, if repeated episodes had been reported, or if the child had given a clear description and demonstration of the abusive event. A child was rated as "probably abused" if there were a suspicious history and suggestive results from the physical examination and the child gave a demonstration and limited description of the abusive event. A child was rated as "possibly abused" if there were a suspicious history and suggestive physical examination results, a sibling had been abused, but there was no description by the child. A child was rated as "no evidence" if none of the evidence listed above was available. The scores ranged from 0 to 3.

Derived Measures

Both the clinic visits and the interviews were videotaped. It was therefore possible to code the child's individual spontaneous reports as either accurate or inaccurate by comparing the child's assertions during the spontaneous/prompted narrative portion of the core interview with the events that actually took place during the clinic visit (i.e., the touches the child experienced, the people present during the procedures and their descriptions, and the location and description of the clinic room). It was also possible to score each of the "events" that *did take place* during the clinic visit as being either reported or not reported spontaneously by the child. The spontaneous narratives yielded three types of responses: *accurate assertions, errors of commission,* or *errors of omission.*

The child's responses to the direct yes/no questions, on the other hand, elicited affirmations and denials, and, by comparing these with the events that actually took place during the clinic visit, it was again possible to code the child's individual responses as either accurate or inaccurate. Four types of responses could be discerned in evaluating the child's responses to the direct yes/no questions: *accurate affirmations, accurate denials, commission errors,* and *omission errors.* It should be noted that, when coding a child's spontaneous narrative, an error of omission was generally a silent "no response" or a failure to report, while following a direct inquiry a child who made an omission error usually did so by verbally denying a verifiable occurrence.

Coding the Videotapes

Two people coded the videotapes of all the children's interview and clinic visits. Both had completed a master's degree in child development, had research experience, and had worked with young children in early childhood programs and hospital settings. The coders did not work on site at the medical center, were not acquainted with any of the children in the study, and had no prior knowledge of what occurred during a child's clinic visit or interviews. They worked together with Margaret Steward and David Steward during the evolution of the coding system and then independently from one another after adequate interrater reliability with the final coding system had been established.

The coders began by reviewing the videotape of the first interview with a child, recording that child's spontaneous assertions during the open-ended narrative portion of the interview, the child's responses to direct yes/no questions, and the child's descriptions of medical staff and the clinic setting. Each response was also coded as being expressed verbally, nonverbally, or both verbally and nonverbally. Coders then moved on to review the videotape of that child's visit to the pediatric clinic, recording the events that did occur: where the child was touched, who was in the room, and the location and description of the room. Coding of accurate assertions and denials and errors of commission and omission was completed by comparing the interview record to the clinic visit record.

The Utilization of Medical Records to Resolve "Unverifiable" and "Questionable" Touch

The medical record of the pediatric visit was used to assist in clarifying the events that occurred during the clinic visit. The medical records of every child in the study were reviewed, and the notes and lab tests from the medical record were photocopied for the day of the child's visit to the pediatric clinic. We worked closely with our pediatric consultants to develop a "code book" to translate each common pediatric medical procedure noted in the medical record in terms of where the child's body is touched, with what it is touched (e.g., a gloved hand, a cotton swab), and how that touch is recorded. For example, in the medical record, "L & S not felt" means that the child's abdomen was touched with the doctor's hand and that neither the liver nor the spleen was found to be unusual in size, shape, or firmness. It does not mean, as a nonmedical person might believe, that the child's tummy was not touched.

The information in the medical record allowed us to determine the nature of the few procedures that were completed out of camera range. The most common example of an off-camera event was taking a blood-pressure reading with a blood-pressure cuff. Without confirmation from the medical record, some children's very elaborate reports of the "ribbon thing and the pump" would have been coded wrongly as commission errors.

The medical records were utilized in two specific instances. First, the medical record was reviewed for each child who reported a body touch during free recall or who answered the action questions that were scored "unverifiable" by the coders when examining the clinic visit videotape. Second, all reports of genital touch were double-checked. Two team members, Margaret Steward and a graduate student, independently reviewed the medical record in each of these cases. A total of 105 events, representing 3.6% of the pediatric touch and handling children experienced, were double-checked: 21 reported touches were clearly refuted by the medical record, 65 were confirmed, and 19 remained "unverifiable."

Rater Reliability

Interrater reliability was assessed at the level of accurate assertions and denials and errors of commission and omission. That is, the evaluation of the presence and accuracy of each child's response by one coder was examined to see whether the other coder agreed. Interrater reliability of the coding judgments of our two coders was sampled three times during the study: at the beginning, midway through, and at the end of the study. Each check included the records of six different children, with approximately 200 judgments on body touch and handling, 200 judgments on persons, and 18 judgments on place. The third check was on third-interview data and involved 486 judgments per child. Agreement on the first set of coding judgments for body touch, persons, and place averaged 94%, 97%, and 93%, respectively. Agreement on the second set averaged 96%, 92%, and 95%. Agreement on the third averaged 97%, 92%, and 99%. Throughout the study, the coders were in regular contact with one another and with Margaret Steward and David Steward to clarify coding decisions and resolve disagreements. In addition, they kept a running record of their individual rationales regarding "close judgment calls" that was reviewed regularly by Margaret Steward and David Steward.

Accuracy and Completeness Scores

In subsequent analyses to be reported shortly, the central issue was the comparison of the accuracy and completeness of children's reports across the four interview conditions. We have accepted the recommendation of Davies et al. (1989) to determine accuracy rates separately for each content area rather than creating a total reporting score that, by definition, masks reporting differences. Accuracy scores were therefore derived for each child in each of several domains. For the spontaneous narrative data, accuracies (for body touch and descriptions of persons and places) were computed as the number of accurate assertions over the total number of assertions. For the direct yes/no question data, accuracy was computed as the sum of accurate affirmations and accurate denials over the total number of questions asked. Completeness scores were derived only for total body touch and for the identification of persons present, as it was not deemed feasible to develop completeness scores for descriptions of either persons or place. Completeness was calculated as the number of touches reported over the total number of touches experienced and as the number of people reported present over the total number of people present.

Consistency

For both spontaneous narratives and the direct yes/no questions, consistency across interviews was also of central interest. Consistent accurate and consistent error scores were created by analyzing the content of each child's report of body touch, action questions, and persons at each interview. The proportion of information that was reported in only one interview, reported in two interviews, or reported all three times was calculated and the categories weighted to create consistency scores.

Dependent Variables

The dependent variables in this study, which measure the quality of children's reports, are those derived from the coding of the videotapes and the comparing of children's assertions, affirmations, and denials with the events and settings known to have been experienced during the clinic procedure. Accuracy, completeness, and consistency scores were computed in each of several domains summarized below.

The Reports of Body Touch

Children's reports of being touched by medical personnel were assessed in terms of (1) accuracy (the number of touches accurately reported divided by the sum of the number of touches accurately reported and the number of touches inaccurately reported), (2) completeness (the number of touches accurately reported divided by the number of touches actually received), and (3) consistency (the frequency with which reports of accurate and inaccurate touch were reliably repeated across interviews).[3]

The Identification and Description of People

Children's reports of the number of people present in the clinic room were assessed in terms of (1) accuracy (the number of persons accurately reported as being present divided by the sum of the number of people reported) and (2) completeness (the number of people accurately reported as being present divided by the number of people actually present).

Once the child identified a medical staff person, he or she was asked what that person looked like and was encouraged to describe the person. The child was asked to identify the sex, name, and role of each person described. Prompts were also given to elicit descriptions of hair color and clothing and to ask whether there was "anything special about the way he/she looked?" A relative accuracy score for person description was created to reflect the number of accurate descriptors compared to the total number of descriptors given. The majority of children described only one staff person, but some described two or even three. Only the accuracy score for the first person mentioned by the child was included in the analysis reported below.

A relative accuracy score for identification of medical staff was created for those children who were presented with the six-picture rogues' gallery of

---

[3] In addition, a Multiple Body Touch score was developed as another completeness score expanded to include reports of multiple touches to the same body part; however, the results paralleled the findings of the completeness score described above and thus will not be reported here.

medical staff, described above. A percentage accuracy score was created by dividing the number of correct selections by the total number of choices or pictures to which a child pointed, and the results were tested against the chance "hit rate" of 17%, which would be achieved by randomly pointing to the one correct picture out of the display of six.

A consistency measure was created from the children's descriptions of medical staff to determine the relative stability of person descriptions from the initial interview to the 1- and 6-month follow-up interviews.

The Identification and Descriptions of Settings

A relative accuracy score for place description was created to reflect the number of accurate descriptors that children gave of the clinic room or office where they saw the medical staff person compared to the total number of descriptors given. Children were given a number of prompts with respect to room description: where, look, color, smell, sound, things in room, anything special. (The children's responses to the question about unusual smells could not be coded for accuracy by viewing the videotape.)

A relative accuracy score for places was created for those children who were presented with the six-picture rogues' gallery of places, described above. A percentage accuracy score was created by dividing the number of correct answers by the total number of choices or pictures to which a child pointed, and the results were tested against the chance "hit rate" of 17% since one of the six pictures was always accurate.

Data Analysis

Data were analyzed employing the analysis of variance, regression, correlation, and, where appropriate, nonparametric procedures found in the Macintosh II edition of SYSTAT 5.1 (Wilkinson, 1989). The dependent measures of reporting accuracy, completeness and consistency of body touch, and accuracy of person and place descriptions were analyzed utilizing a 4 × 4 (interview strategy by age group) analysis of variance. The three degrees of freedom associated with interview strategy were partitioned into a series of three orthogonal contrasts: (1) the verbal interview was tested against the three enhanced interviews; (2) the doll interview was tested against the drawing and computer-assisted interviews to determine the efficacy of the three-dimensional as compared to the two-dimensional enhancements; and (3) drawing was tested against the computer-assisted interview to determine the efficacy of two modes of presenting the same graphic materials. The planned contrasts for age group tested mean differences among the four groups at the initial and the 1-month interview. At 1 and 6 months, repeated-measures analyses of variance were employed to assess the effect of changes in dependent measures as a result of interview type and age across the interview sessions.

Following the ANOVAs, a hierarchical multiple regression was conducted in order to examine the role of a large number of covariates available in this clinically derived pool of participants on children's report of body touch. Four sets of covariates were included in these models, with each set containing from two to four variables. Set 1 included two personal variables: the child's age in months and gender. Set 2 included four demographic variables: the mother's education, ethnicity, family stress (FILE), and the mother's report of the child's past medical experiences. Set 3 included four experiential variables: a physician's rating of the child's current health status, the number of body touches, the number of invasive procedures, and the child's pain ratings. Set 4 included two additional experiential variables: the number of intervening outpatient and inpatient visits to our medical center. This set was created for use in analyzing the 1- and 6-month follow-up interviews.

These covariates were grouped hierarchically to reflect differences in the ease and expense with which researchers could access the data. The information in the first set, the child's age and gender, could be provided by the child. The information in the second set, parents' education, ethnicity, family stress, and the child's health history, could be obtained from a parent in the clinic waiting room by means of an interview or a questionnaire. The information in the third set documents each child's unique experiences during the clinic visit. This set of variables is the most labor intensive and could be obtained only by videotaping the clinic visit, reviewing the medical record of the clinic visit, interviewing the child following the clinic visit, and obtaining medical staff judgments after the clinic visit. The child's medical record had to be reviewed (from the date of the first interview following the child's pediatric clinic visit to the date of the final interview) to obtain the information required in the fourth set.[4]

In the analysis of each dependent variable, hierarchical regressions (Cohen & Cohen, 1975) were conducted with all the variables in a set entered one at a time in all possible orders to understand their redundancy and suppression effects. Any and all significant covariates in that set were then retained as successive sets were added. After all covariates were assessed and significant predictors retained, three dummy variables capturing interview type were entered: one representing the contrast between the verbal and the enhanced interview formats, one contrasting the doll interview with the drawings and computer-assisted interviews, and one contrasting the drawings and the computer-assisted interviews. As a final step, variate-covariate interactions

[4] We thank Calvin P. Garvin, Department of Psychology, University of Nebraska, Lincoln, for recommending this four-step organization to analyze the contributions of the covariates.

were examined (i.e., interactions between the significant covariates and the dummy-coded interview format variables).

In the preliminary analyses, each of the covariate and dependent variables was reviewed for homogeneity of variance, skew, and kurtosis. In order to reduce skew and kurtosis to acceptable levels, the percentage accuracy and completeness scores were subjected to arcsine transformations.

The results reported in Chapters III, IV, and V are complex. It may be helpful to keep in mind two basic features of the study design when reading and interpreting the findings. First, not all 130 children participating in the initial interview were available for follow-up interviews. Second, not all children interviewed during any one session responded to every question.

The results of the initial interviews with 130 children, conducted immediately after their pediatric visit, will be reported in Chapter III. The results of the first follow-up interview with 124 of the initial group of 130 children, conducted 1 month later, will be reported in Chapter IV. These children were interviewed twice (immediately following their pediatric visit and 1 month later). The results of the second follow-up interview with 74 of the initial group of 130 children, conducted 6 months later, will be reported in Chapter V. These children were interviewed three times (immediately after their pediatric visit and 1 and 6 months later). (For the distribution of children at the initial and follow-up interviews, see Table 3 above.)

One should not compare the absolute mean values of the dependent variables from Chapters III, IV, and V because, in Chapters IV and V, values for the initial and 1-month interviews are based only on children participating in those interviews, not on the total pool of 130 children initially interviewed and reported in Chapter III. The repeated-measures analyses presented in Chapter IV compare reports of the children at the 1-month follow-up interview only with their own responses at the initial interview. The repeated-measures analyses presented in Chapter V compare reports of children at the 6-month follow-up interview only with their own responses at the initial and 1-month interviews. This allows longitudinal retrospective analysis of each of the dependent measures. Changes over time in children's responses to the interviewers' requests for information about the different facets of their experience during a pediatric visit can be seen clearly in these longitudinal retrospective analyses. For example, for the 74 children interviewed all three times, data reported in Chapter V reveal that spontaneous report of body touch dropped from the initial to the 1-month interview, then remained stable at the 6-month follow-up.

Analyses of multiple dependent variables are reported within each interview session. Each analysis draws on the total pool of children interviewed during the session being reported. Sample size varies depending on the number of children who responded to the item analyzed. For example, in the initial interview, 116 children spontaneously reported body touch. Their data provide the source for the analysis reported. The remaining 14 children from the total group of 130 are not included in this analysis because they offered no spontaneous description of body touch. The number of children who responded to a specific stimulus will be reported at the beginning of each analysis.

We have chosen to report the results of the study by interview session—initial, 1-month follow-up, and 6-month follow-up—with the constraints of investigative interviewing in mind. The investigative interviewer may be interested in the tables at the end of each results section that summarize the personal, demographic, and experiential variables that positively and negatively influenced children's reports of a complex, personally salient event at three different points in time. To assist those interested in the longitudinal patterns of change or stability of individual memory variables, we report the results of comparative analyses at 1 and 6 months.

III. RESULTS:
INTERVIEWING CHILDREN
IMMEDIATELY AFTER AN EVENT

We report the results of the initial interview in four sections, with brief summaries at the end of each section. First, we present the relative accuracy and completeness of children's spontaneous reports for information about body touch and handling. Second, we present children's spontaneous and cued descriptions of person and place. Third, we focus on the accuracy of children's yes/no answers to direct questions about events and the "double-check" direct questions about body touch assisted by anatomical cues. Finally, we offer a detailed description of children's use of medical props and anatomical cues.

SPONTANEOUS REPORT OF BODY TOUCH AND HANDLING

In this section, we present the accuracy and completeness of children's spontaneous reports of body touch and the accuracy of their reports of what they were "touched with" during the medical visit. Children's reports of body touch and "touch with" are analyzed initially employing a 4 × 4 (interview strategy by age group) ANOVA. These analyses are followed by an exploration of the positive and/or negative influence on the reporting variables of the three sets of personal, demographic, and experiential variables.

Accuracy and Completeness of Reports of Body Touch

Accuracy

The relative accuracy of the 116 children who spontaneously reported body touch was high ($M = .94$). In fact, 105 children (81%) made no errors in reporting body touch. The range and frequency of commission errors (false positives) were quite limited: 17 children made only one error, one made three errors, one made five errors, and two made six errors.

TABLE 5

MEANS AND STANDARD DEVIATIONS OF ACCURACY OF BODY TOUCH AND "TOUCH WITH"
AND COMPLETENESS OF BODY TOUCH BY AGE AT INITIAL INTERVIEW

	3 YEARS		4 YEARS		5 YEARS		6 YEARS	
	Mean	SD	Mean	SD	Mean	SD	Mean	SD
Accuracy:								
Body touch	.97	.08	.90	.18	.96	.09	.94	.12
"Touch with"	.55	.43	.67	.38	.79	.26	.80	.32
Completeness:								
% body touches	.17a	.16	.26b	.15	.26b	.18	.37c	.23

NOTE.—Means that do not share a common letter designation are significantly different ($p < .05$).

A 4×4 ANOVA (interview strategy by age group) revealed neither main effects nor interaction (all p's > .10). (For a display of the mean accuracy scores for each of the four age groups, see Table 5.) Accuracy was positively related to the number of invasive medical procedures administered ($r = .24$, $p < .001$) and the total number of touches a child received ($r = .23$, $p = .01$) and negatively related to the total number of body touches a child reported ($r = -199$, $p < .05$). These three variables accounted for 16.8% of the variance in the prediction of the accuracy of body touch, as displayed in Table 6. Inspection of the raw data revealed that some children were 100% accurate across the full range of none to five invasive medical procedures, and, while accuracy was depressed for some children who reported multiple body touches, everything said by the child who reported the largest number of

TABLE 6

EVENT FEATURES THAT PREDICT ACCURACY AND COMPLETENESS
OF SPONTANEOUS REPORT OF BODY TOUCH AND "TOUCH WITH"
FOR THE INITIAL INTERVIEW

	β	t	R^2
Accuracy of:			
Body touch:			
No. of invasive procedures	.159	1.633	
No. of touches reported	−.327	−3.514	
No. of total touches	.279	2.685	.168*
"Touch with":			
Age	.259	2.584	
No. of total touches	−.216	−2.155	.107*
Completeness of:			
Body touch:			
Age	.331	4.540	
Child pain rating	.484	6.536	
No. of total touches	−.253	−3.424	.354*

* $p < .001$.

TABLE 7

Total Body Touch during the Clinic Visit and Spontaneous
Report during Initial Interview

	Mean	SD	Range
Total body touch	13.69	5.44	2–23
Spontaneous report	3.63	2.89	0–15
Accurate	3.35	2.64	0–15
Error	.28	.71	0–5
Omission	10.34	4.97	0–21

body touches (15) was accurate. There were no contributions to the prediction of accuracy from any of the other covariates.

Completeness

Videotapes of the clinic visits confirm that every child in the study was touched by medical staff; however, only a small proportion of that body touch was spontaneously reported ($M = .26$). The typical child reported 3.4 of the touches that he or she received but failed to report an additional 10.3 body touches from medical staff. (For a summary of the occurrence and reporting of body touch, see Table 7.)

A 4×4 ANOVA (interview strategy by age group) revealed a main effect for age (M's = .17, .26, .26, and .37, $F[3, 114] = 5.875$, $p = .001$). A post hoc contrast revealed that 3-year-old children disclosed less than 4- and 5-year-old children and that 6-year-old children disclosed the most information ($F[1, 114] = 17.462$, $p < .001$). (See the age group differences reported in Table 5 above.) Although the main effect for interview strategy did not reach significance, a planned contrast revealed that children in the verbal interview disclosed less information than did those in the enhanced interviews (M's = .20 and .28, respectively, $F[1, 114] = 4.548$, $p < .05$), a difference that equaled the report of touch to one additional location. There was no age by interview interaction. The regression analysis demonstrated that, in addition to the child's age ($r = .327$, $p < .01$), completeness of disclosure of body touch was influenced by two variables reflecting the quality and quantity of events that occurred during the pediatric visit: the child's judgment of the relative painfulness of the touch ($r = .396$, $p < .01$) and the total number of touches the child experienced ($r = -.221$, $p = .01$). These three variables accounted for 35.4% of the variance in the prediction of completeness of body touch, as displayed in Table 6 above. Children's own pain ratings did not correlate with doctors' or nurses' ratings of children's pain (r's = .04 and −.01, respectively), and only children's ratings were related to how much children told us about the touch and handling of their bodies. Completeness of report was not influenced by any of the other demographic or experiential variables.

Because empirical data from the lives of young children on the relation of stress to memory and reporting are scarce, we chose to look more closely at what children told us about how they felt during their clinic visit, in the light of their pain judgments. A High Pain group was created composed of children who reported at least one body touch as being very painful (by selecting the most extreme pain face in the enhanced interviews or by describing the touch as hurting "a lot" in the verbal interview). The 47 children (21 boys and 26 girls) in the High Pain group did not differ from the rest of the children in the sample in terms of age, medical experience, health status, or number of invasive medical procedures experienced. However, they did receive an average of two more body touches by medical staff than did the other children (M's = 15.1 vs. 12.9, $t[128] = 2.288$, $p < .05$).

The High Pain group's ratings of eight feelings about their pediatric visit were compared with those of the rest of the children in the study. There were no differences in the two groups' ratings of the four positive emotions: happy, safe, relaxed, and surprised. The absence of a difference in the rating of positive emotions may reflect parents' and health care professionals' desire that a child's clinic visit be a reasonably pleasant experience and their effective communication that whatever painful medical procedure a child must experience is "for their own good." But children's responses were more complex than that. In addition to feeling relatively good, those who reported high pain also told us that they were significantly more angry (M's = 2.00 vs. 1.44, $t[101] = 2.786$, $p < .01$), sad (M's = 2.08 vs. 1.58, $t[102] = 2.294$, $p < .05$), scared (M's = 2.49 vs. 1.59, $t[100] = 3.950$, $p < .001$), and sleepy (M's = 2.64 vs. 1.84, $t[101] = 3.086$, $p < .01$) than their counterparts.

Accuracy of Report of "Touch With"

Seventy percent of the children reported that they were "touched with" something—ranging from "a hand [of the medical staff person] in a glove" to a medical instrument such as a needle or a courtesy item such as a soft blanket covering their body. Their overall accuracy rate was .72. A 4 × 4 ANOVA (interview strategy by age group) revealed no main effects or interaction. (For a display of mean age group scores, see Table 5 above.) A planned contrast for interview strategy comparing the reports of children who had access to the box of props to children in the other three interviews revealed no advantage for those with the props (M's = .72 and .73, respectively, $p > .10$). Although there was no main effect when age was grouped by years, a data set in which age was grouped by months documented a significant positive correlation between children's age and the accuracy of "touch with"

($r = .25$, $p < .05$). There were also trends for child's pain ($r = .20$, $p < .10$) and total touch ($r = -.20$, $p < .10$). The regression analysis demonstrated that age and total touch contributed to the prediction of "touch with" and accounted for 11% of the variance in the prediction of the accuracy of "touch with," as displayed in Table 6 above. Older children and those who experienced fewer touches were more likely to report accurately what they were "touched with."

Summary: Spontaneous Reports of Body Touch

The 3–6-year-old children's spontaneous descriptions of body touch were highly accurate (94%), and their reports revealed no developmental differences, as displayed in Table 5. For each age group, inquiry about what children were touched with yielded generally lower accuracy (72%), with only about half the reports from 3-year-old children accurate. Children's reports about the number of body touches were incomplete (26%), the amount of information children offered increased with age, and the reports from 3-year-old children were especially sparse. Interview strategy did not influence either of the accuracy measures (e.g., there was no advantage for children with access to props in reporting what they were touched with), but children with access to anatomical doll/drawing cues reported, on average, touch to one more body location. As can be seen in Table 6, the features of the event itself differentially influenced accuracy and completeness. Distress was important: children who experienced more invasive procedures were more accurate, and those who judged body touch to be more painful gave more complete reports. Total touch was negatively correlated with completeness but positively correlated with accuracy of body touch, suggesting that, if the event involved multiple touches and handling, children may not report it all but that what they say is likely to be accurate. However, increased amount of touch dampened the accuracy of children's reports of what they were touched with, suggesting that, in more complex events, children attended less closely to the stimulus with which they were touched than to the experience of body touch itself.

REPORT OF PERSONS AND SETTING

There are three sets of data that reflect children's responses to the requests for information about the persons in the clinic with them and the setting in which they were seen. The accuracy and completeness of the number of persons reported by the children are presented first. Children's descriptions of medical staff based on a set of specific prompts and recognition of staff on the basis of photographs are presented next. Then we present the

TABLE 8

Mean Accuracy of Persons Present, Person Description, and Setting and Mean
Completeness of Persons Present by Age at Initial Interview

	3 Years		4 Years		5 Years		6 Years	
	Mean	SD	Mean	SD	Mean	SD	Mean	SD
Accuracy:								
Persons present	.71a	.39	.83b	.22	.88b	.25	.82b	.31
Person description	.83	.20	.85	.17	.84	.21	.89	.13
Setting description	.83	.26	.85	.21	.84	.26	.92	.13
Completeness:								
% persons present	.32a	.27	.52b	.29	.52b	.28	.58b	.27

Note.—Means that do not share a common letter designation are significantly different ($p < .05$).

accuracy of children's description of setting and setting recognition. Inquiry and verbal prompts were identical in all four interviews. Therefore, data on description of persons and setting were combined across interviews, and one-way analyses of variance were employed to assess potential differences among the four age groups. None of the demographic or experiential covariates was significantly correlated with children's reports of persons or setting, and none contributed to the prediction of reporting accuracy, completeness, or medical staff description. Only the children in the doll interview were presented with the rogues' gallery photographs to identify medical staff and setting, and the relative accuracy of their responses was compared with chance.

Accuracy and Completeness of Number of Persons Present: Spontaneous Report

Accuracy

Children were accurate 81% of the time in their reports of the number of persons who were with them in the clinic. A one-way ANOVA demonstrated no main effect for age group; however, a planned contrast revealed that 3-year-old children were less accurate than the older children (M's = .71, .83, .88, and .82, respectively, $F[1, 119] = 4.065$, $p < .05$). Children were most accurate when reporting their mother's presence (98.9%)! They were 84% and 81% accurate when reporting the presence of a sibling and their father, respectively. Children were more accurate in reporting the presence of nurses than of doctors (95% and 74.5%, respectively). (For a display of accuracy of person identification by age group, see Table 8.)

Completeness

While children's reports about the people who were with them in the clinic room were quite accurate, they were far from complete. There were from two to nine persons in the room with a child during the medical visit. On average, children told us about only half (51%) the people who were present with them. A one-way ANOVA revealed a main effect for age group ($F[3, 126] = 5.541$, $p < .001$). A planned contrast revealed that 3-year-old children gave less complete reports than the older children (M's $= .32, .52, .52,$ and $.58$, respectively, $F[1, 126] = 15.577$, $p < .001$). (For a display of completeness of persons reported present by age group, see Table 8.)

Family members were identified more frequently than were medical staff. Children reported their mother's presence 79.3% of the time, their father's presence 85% of the time, and sibling presence 67% of the time. Medical staff fared less well. The presence of the doctor was spontaneously reported 47% of the time, that of the nurse 19.6% of the time.

Accuracy of Description of Medical Staff: Verbal Prompt

Children were asked about the sex and name of the medical staff persons who touched them. Children's identifications of the sex of the medical staff were 93.9% accurate. But, when asked to identify staff by name, 32.8% responded accurately, 10.3% responded incorrectly, and 56.9% responded that they did not know. Children usually referred to doctors by their last names and to nurses by their first names. There were no age or sex differences found in children's accuracy of reporting either sex or name. Although the 43 children who described a second staff person were quite clear about the person's sex (95.3%), they were less likely to remember the person's name (21.4%). Identification by either sex or name of the second staff person was not reported differentially when analyzed in terms of age or sex.

In response to the questions, "What did he/she look like?" "What was he/she wearing?" "What color was his/her hair?" and "Was there anything special about the way he/she looked?" the number of accurate descriptors that children used ranged from zero to nine, the number of inaccurate descriptors from zero to three. A relative accuracy score for person description was created for the first medical staff person a child mentioned. The score included information from the verbal prompts and children's spontaneous descriptions. The average relative accuracy of person descriptors was 85.5%. A one-way ANOVA revealed that there were no differences in reporting accuracy as a result of age group, as displayed in Table 8.

When we examined the content of children's spontaneous descriptive characteristics, we found four clusters of responses: role, facial hair, glasses, and ethnicity. When asked the name of the medical staff member, some children replied, "I don't know," but then spontaneously mentioned the medical staff person's role directly ("He looks like a doctor") or implied it by describ-

TABLE 9

CHILDREN'S VERBALLY CUED DESCRIPTION OF MEDICAL STAFF
AT INITIAL INTERVIEW

Item	% Accurate[a]	% Complete[b]
Color of clothing:		
Skirt/blouse	97	41
Pants/skirt	97	45
Dress/shirt	62	68
Coat/jacket	96	38
Shoes	100	6
Tie/jewelry	100	3
Hair color	98	89
Facial hair	88	29
Glasses	78	27
Ethnicity	71	5
"Doctor clothes"	83	96

[a] % accurate = (number of accurate reports/number of accurate reports +
number of error reports).

[b] % complete = (number of accurate reports/number of features of staff described).

ing distinctive clothing ("She gots on a white doctor suit"). Children were
65.5% accurate assigning a role to the first person identified and 54.1% accurate identifying the role of a second person. Role was coded separately for
nurse and doctor; had we defined *role* more broadly as "medical staff," children would have been nearly 100% accurate. No child inaccurately referred
to any of the medical staff, for example, as a teacher, a judge, or a priest,
although one child said that the nurse looked like one of her hospital teachers. Twenty-four children were seen by a medical staff member who had a
beard, a mustache, or both: seven children accurately reported and one child
erroneously reported facial hair. Twenty-six children were seen by staff members with glasses: seven children accurately and two children erroneously reported that feature. Five children accurately and two children erroneously
reported ethnicity. Only one child mentioned that the medical staff member
wore a badge with his or her picture and name on it—a feature that one
might expect children to notice and comment on.

The relative accuracy of children's descriptions of the color of the medical staff members' clothing and other personal characteristics and the number of persons noted by our coders as possessing those characteristics are
displayed in Table 9. It should be noted that, in order to estimate the relative
accuracy of "reasonable responses" that might be pursued by an investigative
interviewer, the set of "I don't know" responses was removed from the pool
and percentage relative accuracy scores were based only on accurate and erroneous answers.

Recognition of Medical Staff: The Rogues' Gallery

In addition to the open-ended and direct questions about persons present, 31 children in the doll interview responded to at least one set of six rogues' gallery pictures (which were created uniquely for every child from pictures of women and men in our files). Of the 31 children, 21 made only one selection. We analyzed the data to determine whether making a single choice would be a useful clue to accuracy and to see whether the accuracy of that selection differed from chance. Of the 21 children who pointed to only one picture to identify the key medical staff person, 86% were accurate. Of the 15 children who selected a single photograph of a second medical staff person, 80% were accurate. Three of the four children who accurately identified a third person did so on their first and only selection. The relative proportions of children who made accurate selections with their only choice on the first and second person are significantly higher than an expected chance rate of 17% ($z = 8.043$, $p < .001$, and $z = 7.159$, $p < .001$, respectively). Thus, response pattern was a useful cue for identifying children who were correct. There was a trend for children who made a single selection to be older than those who made multiple selections (M's = 61 and 53 months, respectively, $t[29] = 1.68$, $p = .10$).

The accuracy with which a child selected a photograph was examined by organizing the data according to the number of photograph selections made because, while some children were technically accurate in pointing to the correct staff picture, they did so only in the process of pointing to several pictures. In fact, two children, a 42-month-old boy and a 51-month-old girl, pointed to all six photographs. The responses of these two children were not likely to be useful at all in an investigative interview, and any information gleaned from their data would probably be discarded were this a forensic investigation.

Description of the Setting: Verbal Prompt

When the children were prompted by the interviewer to describe "where," "what did it look like," "colors in the room," "sounds," "things in the room," and "anything special," the number of accurate descriptors ranged from 1 to 16. The number of inaccurate descriptors ranged from 0 to 4. The relative accuracy of children's descriptors was 86%. A one-way ANOVA revealed no significant main effects for age group, as displayed in Table 8. Most often, children mentioned items found in the room, such as the toy box, rather than information about the location or features of the room itself, although one child said she could find the room again because she could hear her doctor's voice next door.

Children's descriptions of the clinic settings were esoteric and often charming, but they lacked the specificity that might allow an investigator actually to identify the setting. Many of the descriptions included large, sweeping gestures indicating a sequence of turns and stairs (which were difficult to code for accuracy) or vague location cues (such as "by the other room by the other door"). In fairness to the children, and to provide a closer approximation to the investigative process, the interviewer should have asked the children to "show me."

Recognition of the Setting: Rogues' Gallery

The rogues' gallery for setting was offered to 28 children in the doll interview, 15 of whom made a single selection. Nine of 15 children (60%) were accurate, a rate that was significantly higher than chance ($z = 4.886$, $p < .001$). There were no differences in relative accuracy as a function of the child's age.

Summary: Spontaneous and Cued Reports of Person and Setting

Immediately after a clinic visit, the 4-, 5-, and 6-year-old children told us about approximately half the people who were present with them in the clinic, and their reports were more than 80% accurate. Three-year-old children told us about approximately one-third of the persons and were significantly less accurate (70%) than the older children when they mentioned a person present with them during the clinic visit. The verbally cued descriptions of person and setting were highly accurate and revealed no developmental differences, as can be seen in Table 8. Accuracy of photograph identification of medical staff (86%) and setting (60%) was significantly higher than chance when the responses of children who made a single selection, from the set of six, were coded. Photographs were used effectively by some children across the full age range to identify medical staff and setting, although there was a trend for children who made only a single choice to be older than those who made multiple choices.

DIRECT INQUIRY ABOUT BODY TOUCH AND HANDLING

In this section, we focus on children's accuracy in response to a set of direct questions about clinic events and on the efficacy in the enhanced interviews of follow-up yes/no questions assisted by anatomical doll/body outline cues to "double-check" touch to selected body locations, including the genitals. Then we present a closer look at the responses of the reports of genital touch by allegedly abused children.

Accuracy of Answers to the "Action Questions"

An "absent event" score, reflecting the total number of action questions that had *not* occurred during a pediatric visit, was created for each child to test the frequency of occurrence/nonoccurrence of the action questions (Ornstein et al., 1992). Although for eight of the nine questions we had no way of knowing which would be true for each child (all children participating in the study were videotaped), our pediatric colleagues anticipated that 3–6-year-old children would experience about half the events, and they were right ($M = 4.3$, SD $= 1.2$). There were no differences in absent event scores by interview strategy, age group, or sex of child (all F's < 1).

A total accuracy score was created for each child on the basis of eight action questions,[5] and age and gender differences were explored employing a 4×2 ANOVA. The overall average accuracy rate on the action questions was 70.5%. There was a main effect for age group ($F[3, 126] = 2.708$, $p < .05$), there was no main effect for gender, and there was no age by gender interaction. Planned contrasts demonstrated that the three groups of younger children were significantly less accurate than were 6-year-old children (M's $= 69\%$, 66%, 71%, and 78%, respectively, $F[1, 126] = 6.634$, $p = .01$). The relation between the relative accuracy of children's spontaneous reporting of body touch and their accuracy in response to the yes/no action questions was low and insignificant ($r = .076$).

The relative accuracy of each question summed across all children was compared with a 50% chance expectation elicited by the yes/no format to determine whether children were differentially responsive to the questions by content. Children answered seven of the nine action questions accurately at a significantly higher than chance rate (all p's $< .01$): "Did anyone . . . hold you down, take your clothes off, put something in your mouth, in your ears, take pictures of you, wrap anything around your arm, wrap anything around your head, hit you with a hammer?" Each question was also analyzed for possible sex and age group differences. No sex differences were found. A developmental difference was found only for the report that "pictures" had been taken (M's $= .38$, $.26$, $.52$, and $.78$, respectively, $\chi^2[3] = 19.6$, $p < .001$). Only the reports of the 6-year-old children were significantly more accurate than chance ($z = 2.167$, $p < .05$).

Differences in the pattern of omission and commission errors between

---

[5] Because the question, "Did anyone put anything in your ear?" was not included in the computer interview, responses to this question were not included in the total accuracy score.

TABLE 10

PERCENTAGE RESPONSE TO DIRECT ACTION QUESTIONS ON INITIAL INTERVIEW

| | TOUCHED | | NOT TOUCHED | | ACCURATE: |
QUESTIONS	AA	OM	AD	COM	AA + AD[a]
Pictures	46	54	N.A.	N.A.	46
3-year-olds[b]	38	62			
4-year-olds	26	74			
5-year-olds	52	48			
6-year-olds	78	22			
Clothes off	51	18	28	3	79*
Body	13	47	37	3	50
Ear[c]	30	33	33	3	63*
Arm	39	16	35	10	74*
Hold down	19	10	56	14	75*
Mouth	14	13	67	6	81*
Hammer	6	2	83	8	89*
Head	1	2	87	10	88*

NOTE.—AA = accurate assertion; OM = error of omission; AD = accurate denial; COM = error of commission; N.A. = not applicable.

[a] Accuracy rate (AA + AD) tested against 50% chance response.

[b] Difference among age groups ($p < .001$).

[c] $N = 130$ for all except this question, where $N = 98$.

* $p < .01$.

the younger (3- and 4-year-old) and the older (5- and 6-year-old) children were explored in a series of χ^2 analyses, and only two differences were found. Younger children were more likely than older children to make errors of omission (false negatives) in response to the question, "Did anyone hold you down?" ($\chi^2[1] = 6.19$, $p < .05$). Older children were more likely than younger children to make commission errors (false positives) in response to the question, "Did anyone wrap anything around your arm?" ($\chi^2[1] = 4.95$, $p < .05$). There was an inverse relation between the frequency of occurrence of an event and the accuracy of the report such that the less commonly occurring events were likely to be reported more accurately than the more commonly occurring events ($r = -.826$, $p < .01$). This held for both the younger and the older groups of children (r's $= -.79$ and $-.75$, respectively). (For a display of the type of accurate or incorrect response to action questions, see Table 10.)

Accuracy and Completeness as a Result of the "Double-Check"

In order to test the efficacy of multiple cues in the enhanced interviews, the interviewers were instructed to ask a yes/no question to "double-check" children's report of touch to the ear, belly button, genitals, buttocks, or anus. Interviews were personalized so that children were not repeatedly asked about body touches they had already reported during free recall, only about touch to body locations they had not yet mentioned. The "double-check" was a doll/drawing-assisted direct question that provided double cues as each child was cued with a yes/no question while the interviewer pointed to the appropriate location on the anatomical outline or doll. (Children with access to the body outlines were questioned about touch to the buttocks, while children with access to the anatomical doll were questioned about anal touch.) The "double-check" allowed a child to deny as well as confirm touch; thus, the proportion of accurate responses elicited by the "double-check" for each body part (accurate assertions plus accurate denials/total responses to direct questions) was tested against the fifty-fifty chance of answering a direct question correctly. Each child in the enhanced interview was asked about touch to at least one of the four body locations. Chi square analyses revealed that there were no differences among the four age groups in the proportion of children who spontaneously reported as opposed to those who required a "double-check" for each of the different body locations (all p's > .10).

The accuracy rates of the children who were initially silent about body touch to each of the specific locations were calculated following the "double-check" inquiry. The accuracy of reports of touch to the anus (75%, $z = 3.03$, $p < .01$), the penis/vagina (70%, $z = 2.45$, $p < .05$), and the belly button (69%, $z = 3.467$, $p < .01$) was significantly higher than chance, while the accuracy rate of reports of touch to the ear (54%) and the buttocks (48%) was not above chance level. When presented with the direct question, 3-year-old children were significantly more likely to err in reporting touch to the genitals than were the 4-, 5-, and 6-year-old children ($\chi^2[3] = 9.00$, $p < .05$). Of the eight errors made by 3-year-old children, seven were errors of omission, one an error of commission. There were no developmental differences found on the relative accuracy of the double-check for the other four body locations.

Table 11 allows the comparison of the reports of children in the verbal interview who were asked only open-ended questions, the responses of children with access to anatomically detailed cues in the enhanced interviews, and the additional disclosures by children in the enhanced interviews who responded following the yes/no "double-check" questions. There are two things to note especially from the display. First, the yes/no "double-check" question elicited a higher percentage of accurate denials than of accurate assertions. Second, for each body location, the errors of omission continued to be greater than the errors of commission. These silent children were more likely to respond no than yes to a direct question; they were more likely to deny touch than falsely to report it. As a result of the "double-check," five additional children accurately reported genital touch; however, the "double-check" was ineffective in eliciting new reports of touch to the buttocks or

TABLE 11

PERCENTAGE OF CHILDREN REPORTING BODY TOUCH AS A FUNCTION OF CUES AT INITIAL INTERVIEW

BODY PART	TOUCHED			NOT TOUCHED		
	N^a	AA	OM	N^a	AD	COM
Ear:						
Verbal	17	.35	.65	16	N.A.	.06
Enhanced	68	.46	.54	26	N.A.	0
Enhanced and double-check	68	.60	.40	26	.92	.08
Belly button:						
Verbal	9	.12	.88	23	N.A.	0
Enhanced	35	.20	.80	58	N.A.	.05
Enhanced and double-check	35	.34	.66	58	.90	.10
Genitals:						
Verbal	11	.27	.73	22	N.A.	0
Enhanced	55	.62	.38	39	N.A.	.03
Enhanced and double-check	54	.73	.27	38	.92	.08
Buttocks:[b]						
Verbal	17	.06	.94	16	N.A.	0
Enhanced	36	.39	.61	26	N.A.	0
Enhanced and double-check	36	.39	.61	26	.88	.12
Anus:[b]						
Verbal	4	0	1.00	29	N.A.	0
Enhanced	9	.33	.67	22	N.A.	.09
Enhanced and double-check	9	.33	.67	22	.82	.18

NOTE.—AA = accurate assertion; OM = error of omission; AD = accurate denial; COM = error of commission; N.A. = not applicable. Verbal = data from children in the verbal interview; enhanced = data from children in the three enhanced interviews who reported spontaneously; double-check = data from children in the enhanced interviews who responded spontaneously plus data from children who responded after being cued with a direct question.

[a] The decrease in cell size from enhanced cues to enhanced and double-check cues reflects uncodable responses or failure to question the child about that body location.

[b] Only children with access to body outlines were questioned about touch to the buttocks, while only children with access to the doll were questioned about anal touch.

anus. Two additional children reported genital touch erroneously, and two erroneously reported anal touch.

Report of Genital Touch by Abused Children

Because of our interest in understanding the reports of genital touch from sexually abused children, we looked specifically at the influence of abuse status on and the role that the anatomically detailed and direct question cues from the enhanced interviews played in the reports of genital touch. Of the 66 children (35 girls and 31 boys) who experienced genital touch by medical staff during the clinic visit, 20 children (18 girls and 2 boys) were seen in the Child Protection Center and met the criteria for identification as "definitely sexually abused" (Leventhal et al., 1989). By chance, all these children were in the enhanced interviews. (They were all identified after the completion of the study; thus, there was no way to have distributed them randomly across the four interview conditions.)

The spontaneous reporting rate of genital touch by the "definitely abused" children in the enhanced interviews was 95%, compared to 43% for the other/nonabused[6] children in the enhanced interviews and 27% for the other/nonabused children in the verbal interview group ($\chi^2[2] = 15.502$, $p < .001$). In the "definitely abused" group, the single nonreporting child denied the genital touch during the "double-check" inquiry, while five of the 19 of the other/nonabused touched children in the enhanced interviews, four boys and one girl, responded to the "double-check," thereby raising the reporting rate for other/nonabused children in the enhanced interviews from 43% to 57%. Two boys had access to the doll; two boys and one girl had access to the drawing or the computer. Following the "double-check," twice as many of the other/nonabused children in the enhanced interviews as children in the verbal interviews reported genital touch ($\chi^2[1] = 2.986$, $p < .10$).

When sex differences in reporting genital touch were examined, it was found that all 18 girls and one of the two boys in the "definitely abused" group reported genital touch. In the group of other/nonabused children, 14 of 24 boys (58%) and 6 of 11 girls (55%) reported genital touch in the enhanced interview, while two of five boys (40%) and one of six girls (17%) reported it in the verbal interview.

Summary: Response to Direct Questions about Body Touch and Handling

Children interviewed immediately after the clinic visit were significantly more accurate than chance when asked direct yes/no action questions, but their answers were comparatively less accurate than when they reported spontaneously (70% vs. 94%). Developmental differences were found in accuracy related to question content: only 6-year-old children reliably answered the question about pictures having been taken, probably reflecting both cognitive and linguistic competence. Doll/drawing-assisted direct questions elicited accurate reports of genital touch from five initially silent children, although no additional children reported touch to the anus when asked directly. Direct questions yielded commission errors from two children about genital touch

[6] There is no way to guarantee that none of the remaining children had not been abused. Some of the children from the Child Protection Center received "probable" or "possible" ratings, and some of the children from the other six clinics might have been abused— although medical chart review revealed no referrals for abuse-related medical assessments, underreporting of child abuse in young children is a common phenomena (Besharov, 1990). However, it seemed that the conservative estimate employing the Leventhal group's definitions gave us some confidence in the "definitely abused" group as being a unique group of youngsters.

TABLE 12

Relative Accuracy of Names for "Bottom Touch" in Enhanced Interviews (%)[a]

	ACCURATE			
BODY PARTS	Label	Nickname	ERROR	NO NAME
Penis (boys, $N = 49$)	14	63	5	18
Vagina (girls, $N = 48$)	6	58	9	27
Anus ($N = 33$)[b]	0	53	9	38
Buttocks ($N = 97$)	5	75	7	13

[a] All ages combined.
[b] Only children in the doll interview were asked to label anus.

and from two children about anal touch. Age-related errors were seen most strikingly when doll/drawing-assisted direct questions were employed. Every 3-year-old failed to report genital touch when asked directly. When children who had not experienced genital or anal touch were asked a doll/drawing-assisted direct question, more than 90% of them were able accurately to deny genital touch, and more than 80% of them were able accurately to deny anal touch. However, previously abused children with access to the doll/drawing cues spontaneously reported genital touch at a very high rate and did not benefit from doll/drawing-assisted direct questioning.

CHILDREN'S USE OF STIMULUS MATERIALS

In this section, we provide a detailed description of children's use of the stimulus materials from the enhanced interviews, including the anatomically detailed drawings and dolls, the pain faces, the box of props, the feeling thermometers, and the rogues' gallery photographs of persons and places.

Anatomically Detailed Drawings and Dolls

How well did the children in the enhanced interviews understand and use the anatomically detailed stimulus materials? The anatomical drawings and dolls were used twice: first, to elicit children's names of common body parts as the interviewer pointed them out on the body outline or doll or as individual body parts were highlighted sequentially on the body outline displayed on the computer screen; second, to assist the child in reporting body touch. A coding scheme drawn from Sivan (1987) was employed that discriminated among accurate names, nicknames, errors, and no response. Children used proper anatomical names at the 90% level of accuracy or better for most body parts, but, as can be seen in Table 12, children frequently used nicknames for what one child called "the front half and the back half of the bottom" (i.e., genitalia and anus/buttocks). No gender differences were found in the naming of same-sex genitalia when data from the accurate labels and nicknames were combined ($\chi^2[1] = 2.05$, $p > .10$). Six children in the 3–4-year-old group, two boys and four girls, made errors labeling genitalia; none were made by the 5–6-year-old children. Children from the 5–6-year-old group were more likely to refuse to label the genitals ($\chi^2[2] = 9.63$, $p < .01$).

Among the group of children who had experienced genital touch, the subsequent reporting rate of genital touch by those who initially refused to name the genitals was as high as the reporting rate by those who named the genitalia ($\chi^2 < 1$), and this finding held for both boys and girls. Of the 10 children (five boys and five girls) who had refused to name the genitals, six (three boys and three girls) subsequently spontaneously reported genital touch by pointing to the genitals of the doll/body outline when asked about location of body touch later in the interview.

Fifty-nine of the 64 children (92%) across the full age range who had access to the anatomical body outlines in the drawing and computer-assisted interviews spontaneously pointed to relevant body locations when reporting body touch. All the children responded to the interviewer's use of the body outlines to "double-check" the children's reports of touch to the ears, genitals, and buttocks. Of the 31 children who reported genital touch, four reported it verbally, 11 reported it verbally and demonstrated by pointing to the appropriate place on the body outline, and 16 responded nonverbally by nodding or pointing.

Twenty-eight children in the doll interview (85%) used the anatomical dolls to demonstrate the location of body touch. Of the five children who did not use the dolls, three erroneously claimed that they had not been touched, and two (one boy and one girl) only demonstrated touch on their own bodies. Six of the children (five girls and one boy) who used the doll did so after first pointing to places on their own bodies that were touched, then demonstrating a second time with the doll. Not all the children's reports of body touch demonstrated on the doll were accurate: some of the places on the doll touched by five of the children were erroneous. Only one child made an error when pointing to herself. Of the 14 children who reported genital touch, four only pointed to the doll's genitals, while 10 children verbally reported and demonstrated the genital touch with the dolls. Children with access to the dolls were also asked about anal touch. Three girls accurately reported anal touch, while four boys made commission errors by pointing to the doll's anus. Again, there were no reporting errors with respect to genital touch by children who had access to the anatomically detailed dolls and no reporting errors with respect to anal touch by children with access to the drawings.

Did the two sets of anatomically detailed cues—doll and drawing—differ-

entially stimulate children to make commission errors with respect to genital touch? In the doll interview, no child who had not been genitally touched made a false report of genital touch. Three of the 40 children (7.5%) in the drawing and computer-assisted interviews who had not received genital touch but who were cued by anatomical body outlines made commission errors: one (a 77-month-old boy) pointed spontaneously, and two (a 66-month-old boy and a 43-month-old girl) erroneously nodded only during the "double-check" in which the interviewer asked the child directly about genital touch while pointing to the genitals. Therefore, all three commission errors were limited to nonverbal pointing or nodding with no verbal description or explanation of the purported genital touch.

We have already reported that the anatomically detailed cues in the enhanced interviews effectively elicited a 73% reporting rate of genital touch, in striking contrast to a rate of 27% for children in the verbal interview. However, the two- as opposed to three-dimensional presentation of the anatomical cues did not appear to be differentially effective as eight of the children in the enhanced interviews who failed to report genital touch had access to the drawings and seven had access to the dolls.

Medical and Nonmedical Props

Props were used in the doll interview by 27 of the 31 children (87%) to demonstrate what they were touched with during the clinic visit (unfortunately, the interviewers failed to offer the box of props to two children). Of those who did not use the props, one child initially reported several body touches but failed to identify any items with which he was touched when he sorted through the box. The three children who claimed that they had not been touched by anyone or anything were not enticed by the props to report body touch. Summing across all use of the medical equipment props, 21% were used by children on their own bodies, 77% were used with the dolls, and two children demonstrated the use of the medical equipment on the interviewer.

Prop use was coded into four categories: (1) accurate replay of the use of the medical props that the child had experienced during the preceding medical visit; (2) irrelevant medically scripted play, where the use of the medical equipment (e.g., a blood pressure cuff or syringe) was accurate but the child had not had that particular experience during the clinic visit; (3) playful but inaccurate use of the medical equipment (e.g., use of the reflex hammer for hitting objects); and (4) play with nonmedical props (props that were irrelevant with respect to the children's clinic visit). When children used the medical props on themselves, 48% of their demonstrations accurately replicated their experience during the medical visit, 33% were medically scripted, and 19% represented "playful" but inaccurate use of the medical equipment. Although children demonstrated on the dolls far more often than on themselves, when medical equipment was used with the dolls, the proportions of accurate, "medically scripted," and "playful" but inaccurate use were similar to the use of props on themselves: 42%, 28%, and 30%, respectively. Thus, whether the children used medical props on themselves or on dolls, they actually demonstrated their clinic visit experience less than half the time.

Children who made no errors selecting and using medical equipment were significantly older than those who used the material inaccurately ($M = 72$ vs. 58 months, $t[27] = 2.05$, $p < .05$). Accurate children were typically boys (four of five). Children who made the most frequent medical script errors were typically girls (7 of 10, $M = 60.6$ months). Children who chose most often to play with the medical equipment inaccurately were typically girls (six of nine, $M = 56.7$ months). Three young children (two boys and one girl, $M = 50$ months old) selected and played with the irrelevant nonmedical equipment in the box. The stethoscope, blood pressure cuff, and syringe were the props used most frequently for accurate demonstration of body touch. But the blood pressure cuff was also selected most frequently when medical play errors were made, as were the reflex hammer, tongue depressor, and syringe. The interviewer was subject to the medically scripted play of two children.

Pain Faces

Children were asked to describe a past experience to anchor each end of the Faces Pain Scale and thereby ensure that they could make the association between the pain faces and their own experience of pain/distress. Eightyeight of the 97 children (91%) were able to do this task immediately. The "neutral" face elicited descriptions from children of positive, happy events in their lives or those that reflected comparatively minor distress such as "a little tiny owie" or "kind of sad." The extreme pain face elicited descriptions of psychological distress as well as physical pain. The interviewers helped nine children (five boys and four girls) use the scale appropriately by asking which face showed how you might feel "if you skinned your knee." The children who needed assistance ranged in age from 37 to 78 months.

Feeling Thermometers

Most children (75 of 97, or 77%) were able to label how they were feeling during the interview, use a thermometer to rate that feeling, and then rate how they felt about eight feeling states during the pediatric visit. Those who failed the pretest by being unable to name and/or rate how they were feeling at the time of the interview were significantly younger than the children who could use thermometers successfully ($M = 49$ and 62 months, respectively, $t[95] = 4.287$, $p < .001$). There was a trend revealing that more boys than girls were able to use the thermometers to rate their feelings ($\chi^2[1] = 3.165$, $p < .10$).

Rogues' Gallery Photographs of People and Places

Each child was introduced to the rogues' gallery by first being shown a set of six pictures in which the interviewer had inserted his or her own photograph before reading the standard instructions. Of the 33 children in the doll interview, 19 immediately identified the interviewer accurately, while 14 needed expanded instructions that included pointing out to them the interviewer's picture. Although some children seemed to need more practice with the picture-selection format than did others, age was not the critical variable. Indeed, some of our 3-year-old children were able to select the medical staff who touched them, as did the 3-year-old abuse victim reported by Jones and Krugman (1986). Only two children, a 52-month-old girl and a 58-month-old girl, did not meet the criterion established as a pretest to demonstrate successful use of the rogue's gallery, pointing to all six pictures in a playful, nondiscriminating manner. As noted above, two other children passed the pretest but, when asked to select the photograph of the medical staff person, touched all six pictures.

Summary: Children's Use of Stimulus Materials

Most, but not all, of the children who had access to the stimulus materials in the enhanced interviews made use of them. Although there was no significant reporting advantage for children with access to the props, there are three clusters of interesting observations: (1) some props were used accurately and effectively by children across the age range from 36 to 84 months (e.g., the anatomically detailed dolls and drawings, the pain faces, and the photographs); (2) some were used more appropriately by older than by younger children (medical equipment and the feeling thermometer); and (3) boys seemed to use some of the props (e.g., medical equipment and the feeling thermometer) more skillfully than did girls of the same age.

What Just Happened: Children's Responses Immediately after an Event

What were children able to tell us when they were interviewed immediately after experiencing a salient, personal event in which their bodies were

TABLE 13

SUMMARY OF THE MEAN ACCURACY AND COMPLETENESS OF THE REPORTS OF CHILDREN
WHO PARTICIPATED IN THE INITIAL INTERVIEW

Variables	Initial Interview	Variables	Initial Interview
Body touch:		No. of persons present:	
Accuracy	.94	Accuracy	.81
Completeness	.26	Completeness	.51
"Touch with":		Person description:	
Accuracy	.72	Accuracy	.86
Direct action questions:		Place description:	
Accuracy	.74	Accuracy	.86

touched and handled? Table 13 presents a summary of the mean accuracy and completeness of the reports from children who participated in the initial interview. Table 14 presents a summary of the interviewing and personal variables as well as features of the event that significantly influenced the accuracy and completeness of these children's reports.

Two facets of the initial interview stand out: access to anatomical cues and type of question used to elicit information. The anatomical cues in the enhanced interviews enabled children to report their experiences of body touch more completely, and the doll/drawing-assisted direct questions enabled more children to report genital touch accurately. So did past experience with sexual abuse. The anatomical cues did not interfere with the accuracy of reporting. Even within the narrow age range of 3–6-year-old children, we found age differences related to the type of question used to elicit information. When children were simply asked what happened, all children re-

TABLE 14

VARIABLES THAT SIGNIFICANTLY INFLUENCED THE ACCURACY AND COMPLETENESS
OF CHILDREN'S REPORTS DURING THE INITIAL INTERVIEW

Variables	Accuracy	Completeness
Positive influence:		
Enhanced interviews	Genital touch	Body touch
Age of child	"Touch with"	Body touch
	Action question	Persons present
	Double-check: genital	
	Prop use	
Abuse status	Genital touch	
Pain rating		Body touch
Invasive procedure	Body touch	
Total touch	Body touch	
Negative influence:		
Total touch	"Touch with"	Body touch
No. of touches reported	Body touch	

ported spontaneously and accurately. But, when direct questions were asked, accuracy dropped for all children. Younger children offered less accurate information in response to direct questions and specifically responded to direct questions about genital touch with omission errors. Not all events were equally memorable. Both the complexity (number of total touches and invasive procedures) and the relative painfulness of the event affected the accuracy of children's reports, but they reported more complex events less completely.

These young children knew who was with them during the medical visit and where the event occurred, but they were able to communicate that information better when they had access to photographs than when they had to generate descriptors themselves.

It is important to note the variables that did *not* influence either accuracy or completeness when children were interviewed immediately after a salient, personal event. There were no gender or ethnicity differences. Although children were being questioned about a pediatric visit, neither their current health status nor their past medical experience influenced their answers. Neither of the family variables, mother's education or family stress, influenced reporting.

IV. RESULTS:
FOLLOW-UP INTERVIEWS WITH CHILDREN
ONE MONTH AFTER AN EVENT

From the original group of 130 children initially interviewed, 124 children returned for a second interview 1 month later. The interview procedure and data analyses 1 month after each child's visit to the doctor generally paralleled the first interview, with the following exceptions: (1) The rogues' gallery person and place cues, which had been presented at the initial interview only to the children in the doll interview, were also presented to the children in the drawing interview group. (2) For all interview groups, two new independent variables—the number of outpatient visits and the number of inpatient visits to our medical center occurring between the initial interview and the 1-month follow-up—were added to the original set of 11 demographic and experiential variables in order to examine their relation to children's reports. (3) With the second interview, it was possible to add to *accuracy* and *completeness* a third measure of memory, *consistency,* in order to examine repeated as opposed to new information contained in children's reports.

In this chapter, we report the results of the children's responses at the 1-month follow-up interview and compare each child's results from the initial and 1-month interviews. There are four sections, each containing a brief summary at the end. Presentation generally parallels that of the results of the initial interview: (1) spontaneous reports of body touch and handling; (2) spontaneous and cued reports of person and setting; (3) reports following direct questions about clinic events and doll/drawing-assisted reports of body touch; and (4) analysis of cuing and multiple interviews.

SPONTANEOUS REPORT OF BODY TOUCH AND HANDLING

In this section, we present the accuracy, completeness, and consistency of children's spontaneous recall of body touch and the accuracy of "touch with" data. Children's reports of body touch and "touch with" will be analyzed initially employing a $2 \times 4 \times 4$ (interview session by interview strategy by age group) repeated-measures ANOVA. These analyses will be followed by

TABLE 15

MEANS AND STANDARD DEVIATIONS OF ACCURACY, COMPLETENESS, AND CONSISTENCY
OF BODY TOUCH AND "TOUCH WITH" BY AGE AT THE ONE-MONTH INTERVIEW

	3 YEARS		4 YEARS		5 YEARS		6 YEARS	
	Mean	SD	Mean	SD	Mean	SD	Mean	SD
Accuracy:								
Body touch	.74	.31	.82	.28	.87	.17	.73	.35
"Touch with"	.22a	.32	.56b	.41	.70b	.34	.60b	.36
Completeness:								
% body touches	.15a	.14	.21b	.17	.19b	.14	.28c	.17
Consistency:								
Body touch, accurate	1.23a	.29	1.38b	.28	1.40b	.24	1.50b	.32
Body touch, error	1.05	.14	1.11	.27	1.12	.23	1.05	.14

NOTE.—Means that do not share a common letter designation are significantly different ($p < .05$).

an exploration of the positive and/or negative influence on the reporting variables of the three sets of personal, demographic, and experiential variables. By definition, repeated-measures analyses will be limited in each instance to the children who have scores in both interview sessions.

Accuracy, Completeness, and Consistency of Reports of Body Touch

Accuracy

A 2 × 4 × 4 repeated-measures (interview session by interview strategy by age group) ANOVA revealed that there was a significant drop in the relative accuracy of the children's reports of body touch from the first to the second interview (M's = .94 and .79, respectively, $F[1, 97] = 31.490$, $p < .001$). There were no significant main effects for interview strategy or age, and none of the interactions was significant. (For display of mean accuracy scores by age group, see Table 15.) The number of invasive procedures ($r = .284$, $p < .01$) and the total number of body touches received ($r = .43$, $p < .001$) were positively correlated with accuracy, while medical history was negatively correlated with accuracy of report ($r = -.198$, $p < .05$). However, when entered into the regression equation, only the number of invasive medical procedures and total body touch contributed to the prediction of accuracy ($F[2, 106] = 12.779$, $p < .001$). These two variables accounted for 19.4% of the variance. (For a display of the event features that predict accuracy of body touch at 1 month, see Table 16.)

Completeness

A 2 × 4 × 4 (interview session by interview strategy by age group) repeated-measures ANOVA revealed a significant main effect for session, inter-

TABLE 16

EVENT FEATURES THAT PREDICT ACCURACY, COMPLETENESS, AND CONSISTENCY OF SPONTANEOUS
REPORT OF BODY TOUCH AND "TOUCH WITH" AT ONE MONTH

	β	t	R^2
Accuracy of:			
Body touch:			
No. of invasive procedures	.284	3.062	
No. of total touches	.379	3.868	.194**
"Touch with":			
Age	.287	2.615	.084*
Completeness of:			
Body touch:			
Age	.251	3.099	
Mother's education	.196	2.470	
Child pain rating	.313	3.822	
Verbal vs. enhanced interview	.802	2.908	
Mother's education $\times$ (verbal vs. enhanced)	−.633	−2.308	.280**
Consistency of accurate reports:			
Body touch:			
Age	.262	2.923	
No. of total touches	−.185	−2.067	.122**

* $p < .01$.
** $p < .001$.

view type, and age. None of the interactions was significant. There was a drop in the relative completeness of disclosure of body touch from the first interview to the 1-month follow-up (M's = .25 and .21, respectively, $F[1, 108]$ = 8.991, $p < .01$). A main effect for interview type was demonstrated ($F[3, 108]$ = 5.073, $p < .01$). A planned contrast revealed that children in the verbal interview reported significantly less information about body touch than children in the enhanced interviews (M's = .13, .22, .27, and .20 for the verbal and three enhanced groups, respectively, $F[1, 108]$ = 12.605, $p = .001$). There was also a main effect for age group ($F[3, 108]$ = 6.475, $p < .001$), and a planned contrast for a linear developmental trend was significant ($F[1, 108]$ = 7.87, $p < .01$). (For a display of mean completeness scores by age group, see Table 15.)

Three variables were significantly correlated with completeness: age (r = .212, $p < .05$), the child's judgment of the relative painfulness of body touch ($r = .335$, $p < .001$), and the child's total negative feeling score (r = .185, $p < .05$). The final regression equation included two of the three child variables: the child's age and pain judgment. In addition, mother's education ($r = .13$) and a binary variable, identifying whether a child received the traditional verbal interview or one of the enhanced interviews, made independent contributions. Finally, the interaction of mother's education and interview strategy added significantly to the regression equation ($F[5, 118]$ = 9.173, $p < .001$), with children in the verbal interview disclosing less information about body touch, except for one child of a highly educated mother. These five variables—age, pain, mother's education, verbal versus enhanced interview, and the interaction—accounted for 28% of the variance. (For a display of features that predict completeness of body touch at 1 month, see Table 16.) As in the initial interview, older children gave more complete reports, as did those who judged the touch to be painful.

Again, we examined the reports of feelings about the clinic visit through the lens of the High Pain group of children: those who reported on the first interview that at least one body touch was extremely painful. At 1 month, children in the High Pain group continued to report that they were significantly sadder (M's = 2.32 vs. 1.82, $t[95]$ = 2.134, $p < .05$) and more scared (M's = 2.38 vs. 1.68, $t[95]$ = 3.123, $p < .05$), and there was a trend for a report of feeling more angry (M's = 2.05 vs. 1.65, $t[95]$ = 1.800, $p < .10$). There were no differences in the reporting of positive feelings between the High Pain group and the other children.

Consistency

Three different facets of consistency of children's spontaneous reports were explored: (1) the proportion of repeated as opposed to new content in the second interview, (2) individual consistency scores based on accurate information from both the first and the second interviews, and (3) individual consistency scores based on erroneous information from both the first and the second interviews. First, pooling the data across all children, the content of the second interview was analyzed to identify information about body touch that was repeated from the initial interview and to identify information that was reported for the first time during the second interview 1 month after the clinic visit. Just over half (51%) the information in the second interview had been previously reported, and the overwhelming majority of that repeated information was accurate. That is, 49% of the data that children reported about body touch in the second interview was repeated from the first interview and was accurate, while only 2% of the repeated data was erroneous. Just under half (49%) the information in the second interview was new. While the ratio of accuracy to error in the information newly reported in the second interview still favored accurate reporting, it was much smaller than in the spontaneous reporting in the initial interview: 30% were accurate, 19% erroneous data. (For a display of the source and relative accuracy of the interview data on body touch at 1 month, see Fig. 2.)

Second, a consistency of accuracy score was created for each child by weighting each unique accurate report of body touch in either the first or the second interview by one and weighting each accurate report of body touch repeated in both interviews by two. The average consistency of accuracy

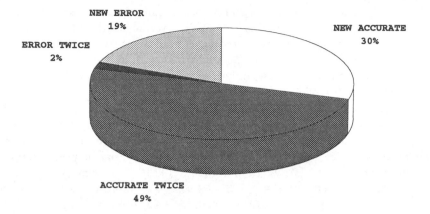

NEW ERROR
19%

NEW ACCURATE
30%

ERROR TWICE
2%

ACCURATE TWICE
49%

FIG. 2.—Percentage of new and repeated accurate and erroneous reports of body touch at a second interview after a 1-month delay.

score was 1.38, on a range from 1.00 to 2.00, suggesting that the 117 children who spontaneously reported accurate body touch in the first, the second, or both interviews were moderately consistent. No child received a score of 2.0, which would have reflected identical information reported on both the first and the second interviews. The 4 × 4 (interview strategy by age group) ANOVA revealed a significant main effect for age group ($F[3, 113] = 3.879$, $p = .01$). The planned contrast revealed that 3-year-old children were significantly less consistent in their accurate reporting than were children from the three older groups ($F[1, 113] = 8.939, p < .01$). (For mean consistency scores by age group, see Table 15 above.) Interview strategy did not enhance or detract from consistency of reporting, and the age by strategy interaction was not significant. Two variables, the child's age ($r = .39$, $p = .001$) and total touch ($r = -.24$, $p = .01$), were significantly correlated with the consistency of accurate reports, and both contributed to the prediction ($F[2, 114] = 7.902$, $p = .001$). These two variables accounted for 12.2% of the variance. (For variables that predict consistency of accurate reports of body touch at the 1-month follow-up interview, see Table 16 above.) Older children and children receiving fewer touches were more consistent in their reporting.

Third, a consistency of error score was created for each child by weighting each unique erroneous report of body touch in the first or second interview by one and weighting each erroneous report of body touch repeated in both interviews by two. The average consistency of error score was 1.08, on a range from 1.00 to 2.00, for the 57 children who spontaneously reported an error in the first, the second, or both interviews. A 4 × 4 (interview strategy by age group) ANOVA revealed no significant main effects and no interaction. None of the child, family, or experiential variables was significantly correlated with the consistency of inaccurate reports. The planned contrasts did not reveal any contribution to consistent error by interview strategy. The correlation between consistency of accuracy and error scores for those 57 children who spontaneously reported both accurate and inaccurate information about body touch was low and insignificant ($r = .139$, $p > .10$).

Accuracy of Report of "Touch With"

A $2 \times 4 \times 4$ (interview session by interview strategy by age group) repeated-measures ANOVA revealed that there was a significant drop in reporting accuracy from the first to the second interview (M's $= .74$ and $.60$, respectively, $F[1, 62] = 6.993$, $p = .01$). There was no main effect for interview strategy, but inspection of the data revealed a dramatic drop in relative accuracy of report of what children were touched with by those children who had access to the box of medical equipment in the doll interview—from 71% in the initial interview to 45% 1 month later. A t test for related means demonstrated a significant drop in reporting accuracy between the first and the second interviews for children who had access to the equipment box in both interviews ($t[26] = 3.98$, $p < .001$). In striking contrast, there was essentially no shift in the accuracy of reports from children who verbally described what they were touched with in the other three interview types ($M = 75$% and 68% on the first and second interviews, respectively). There was a significant main effect for age ($F[3, 62] = 5.140$, $p < .01$). A planned contrast demonstrated that 3-year-old children were significantly less accurate in reporting what they were touched with than children from the three older groups ($F[1, 62] = 15.337$, $p < .001$). (For a display of the mean accuracy of "touch with" scores by age group, see Table 15 above.) Although there was a trend for the number of invasive procedures to relate to the relative accuracy of "touch with" ($r = .184$, $p < .10$), the regression analysis demonstrated that only a child's age ($r = .29$, $p < .01$) contributed to the prediction of "touch with" and accounted for 8.4% of the variance. (For a display of variables that predict "touch with" at 1 month, see Table 16 above.)

Summary: Spontaneous Reports of Body Touch and Handling

One month after a clinic visit, 3–6-year-old children demonstrated significant forgetting about body touch, their accuracy dropping to 79% and completeness to 21%. Replicating the findings from the initial interview, neither age nor interview strategy significantly influenced the accuracy of children's reports of body touch, but older children gave more complete and consistent reports of body touch and reported more accurately what they were "touched with," as can be seen in Table 15. Children in the enhanced interviews with access to anatomical doll/drawing cues continued to give more complete reports, but, in sharp contrast, access to medical and nonmedical props at 1 month interfered with the accuracy of children's reports of what they were "touched with." Salient features of the pediatric visit also influenced children's reports. Children who experienced more invasive procedures and more total touch were more accurate, while children who rated the experience as more painful gave more complete reports, as can be seen in Table 16.

REPORT OF PERSONS AND SETTING

In this section, we present children's responses to the request for information about the persons in the clinic with them and the setting in which they were seen. The accuracy, completeness, and consistency of the number of persons will be presented first. Then children's descriptions of medical staff based on a set of verbal prompts and the recognition of staff photographs are presented. Finally, the accuracy of children's descriptions of the clinic setting and recognition of the setting are reported. Inquiry and verbal prompts were identical across all four interviews; thus, data were combined across interviews. A 2 × 4 (interview session by age) repeated-measures ANOVA was employed to analyze accuracy and completeness data. Children in the doll interview had access to the photographs of persons and setting from the rogues' gallery for the second time, while children in the drawing interview had access to the photographs for the first time during this 1-month follow-up. The relative accuracy of children's recognition of photographs was compared with chance. None of the demographic or experiential variables was significantly correlated with children's descriptions of persons or setting, and none contributed to the prediction of reporting accuracy. However, intervening outpatient visits did contribute to photograph recognition.

Accuracy, Completeness, and Consistency of Report of Persons Present: Spontaneous Report

Accuracy

A 2 × 4 (interview session by age) repeated-measures ANOVA demonstrated that the relative accuracy of children's report of the persons present dropped significantly from the initial interview to the 1-month follow-up (M's = .84 and .72, respectively, $F[1, 101] = 11.515$, $p = .001$). There were no significant main effects for age group and no significant interactions. (For

TABLE 17

MEAN ACCURACY OF PERSONS PRESENT, PERSON DESCRIPTION, AND SETTING DESCRIPTION AND
MEAN COMPLETENESS OF PERSONS PRESENT BY AGE AT ONE-MONTH INTERVIEW

	3 YEARS		4 YEARS		5 YEARS		6 YEARS	
	Mean	SD	Mean	SD	Mean	SD	Mean	SD
Accuracy:								
Persons present	.79	.31	.64	.40	.77	.33	.73	.33
Person description	.81	.20	.84	.22	.94	.11	.87	.15
Setting description	.64a	.44	.81b	.28	.85b	.25	.90b	.18
Completeness:								
% persons present	.28	.27	.36	.34	.45	.27	.46	.26

NOTE.—Means that do not share a common letter designation are significantly different ($p < .05$).

scores of mean accuracy of persons present by age group, see Table 17.)
Again, as in the initial interview, children's reports of their mother's presence
were more accurate than their reports of the presence of fathers or siblings
(94.8%, 71.4%, and 73.3%, respectively). Children were again more accurate
when reporting the presence of nurses (89%) than that of doctors (70%).

Completeness

A 2 × 4 (interview session by age) repeated-measures ANOVA revealed
that there was a significant drop in the report of the percentage of persons
who were in the room with the child (M's $= .49$ and $.40$, respectively) from
the first interview to the 1-month follow-up ($F[1, 120] = 11.426$, $p = .001$).
No differences were found for age of child, and the session by age interaction
was not significant. (For scores of mean completeness of persons present by
age group, see Table 17.) Children reported their mother's presence only
approximately two-thirds of the time (68.9%) and that of their fathers and
siblings half the time (52.6% and 51.2%, respectively). Fewer than half the
doctors were reported (40.2%), and reports of nurses were even more rare
(16.7%).

Consistency

More than half the children (59.6%) reported their mother as being
present in both interviews, 27.8% identified her as being present only once,
and 12.5% did not mention their mother's presence in either interview, although she had been present during the clinic visits. Again, more than half
the children (55.5%) reported their father as being present twice, 27.8% reported him as being present only once, and 16.7% failed to mention their
father's presence in either interview. Coding of the consistency of report of

medical staff was fairly liberal, with credit being given for the accurate name and also for an approximation, if the approximation were near enough to the actual name to make a clear identification; for example, "He has an apple in his name" qualified for Dr. Abildgaard, but "Dr. Something" was not sufficient. Children's responses were as follows: 23.4% reported the same staff person twice, 21.9% reported a staff person only once, and 54.7% did not name a staff member in either interview, although they may have described other characteristics of a staff member.

Accuracy of Description of Medical Staff: Verbal Prompt

A 2 × 4 (interview session by age) repeated-measures ANOVA revealed that children's person descriptors maintained a high level of accuracy with no significant shift from the initial to the 1-month interview (M's = .86 and .87, respectively, $F[1, 90] < 1$). There were no age differences found in reporting accuracy, as shown in Table 17, and the session by age interaction was not significant. Children's identification of the sex of medical staff was 96.4% accurate; as for identification of medical staff by name, 24.3% responded accurately, 12.6% incorrectly, and 63.1% that they "didn't know." It should be noted that several children named and/or described different staff members on the second interview than they did on the first. Therefore, while the accuracy of descriptors continued to be high, the persons being described were sometimes different from those described in the initial interview. Children's descriptions of the color of staff members' clothing were all above 90% accuracy for shirt/blouse, pants/skirt, and shoes. The descriptions of coat/jacket were 89%, a "doctor suit" 85%, and dress/suit 50% accurate. All the children who mentioned hair color, facial hair, glasses, or ethnicity were 100% accurate.

Recognition of Medical Staff: Rogues' Gallery

The rogue's gallery was presented to 60 children from the doll and drawing interviews during the 1-month follow-up interview. Children's data were examined to determine whether making a single choice would continue to be a useful clue to accuracy and whether the proportion of those who made only one selection differed from chance. Of the 47 children who pointed to only one picture to identify the key medical staff person, 80.1% were accurate. Of the 34 children who selected a single photograph of a second medical staff person, 62% were accurate. Neither child who identified a third person was accurate, and each made two selections. The relative proportions of the children who made accurate selections with their only choice on the first and second person are significantly higher than an expected chance rate of

17% (z = 12.62, p < .001, and z = 7.627, p < .001, respectively). Thus, a child's response pattern continued to be useful in identifying children who were correct.

As on the initial interview, there were no differences in accuracy of photograph selection by age or gender of child. No practice effect was found for the children who had used the photograph technique on both interviews as their accuracy was comparable to that of those children using the photographs for the first time at 1 month. We also examined the relation between recognition accuracy and two measures of familiarity: return visits to the medical center either to the outpatient clinic or for inpatient hospitalization between the initial and the 1-month interview. The data from each variable were dichotomized into no intervening visits and one or more intervening visits, and a series of chi square analyses was conducted. The relative accuracy of recognition of the first staff member was not significantly related to either outpatient or inpatient visits. However, familiarity did make a difference if children identified a second staff person; children who had returned for an outpatient visit in the 1-month interim made significantly fewer errors (χ^2 = 3.821, p < .05). There was no advantage to children who made inpatient visits during the interim.

Description of the Setting: Verbal Prompt

A 2 × 4 (interview session by age) repeated-measures ANOVA revealed that the relative accuracy of children's descriptions of the pediatric clinic room dropped significantly from the first to the second interview (M's = .86 and .80, respectively, F[1, 84] = 4.592, p < .05). There was a trend for age group (F[3, 84] = 2.474, p < .10). A planned contrast on the 1-month interview data revealed that 3-year-old children's reports were significantly lower than those of the older children (M's = .64, .81, .85, and .90, F[1, 84] = 6.47, p < .01), as reported in Table 17. The session by age interaction was not significant.

Recognition of the Setting: Rogues' Gallery

The rogue's gallery continued to be useful for identifying the location of the pediatric clinics. Sixteen of the 25 children (64%) who made only one selection were accurate, a rate that is significantly higher than the chance rate of 17% (z = 6.87, p < .001). There were no differences in setting identification as a function of age or sex of child, familiarity as a result of return outpatient or inpatient visits, or experience with the photograph selection technique.

Summary: Spontaneous and Cued Reports of Persons and Setting

The accuracy of children's reports of who was with them in the clinic dropped significantly from 81% at the initial interview to 73% at the 1-month follow-up interview. Mothers and fathers were mentioned in both interviews about half the time, while staff were mentioned only one-quarter of the time. The accuracy of persons and setting descriptors continued to be high, as seen in Table 17. There are two interesting caveats: the persons being described after a 1-month delay were sometimes different from those whom children identified in the initial interview, and the 3-year-olds' descriptions of the clinic room were less accurate than those of the older children. Although rare, all mentions of hair color, facial hair, glasses, and ethnicity were accurate. As noted above, access to props interfered with children's reports of what they were touched with, but photographs continued to assist children in identification of staff (80%) and setting (64%). The only influence of return clinic visits in the interim between the initial and the 1-month interview that could be detected in this data set was to increase the accuracy of photograph identification for those children who named two staff members.

DIRECT INQUIRY ABOUT BODY TOUCH AND HANDLING

First, we focus on children's accuracy in response to the set of direct questions about clinic events. Then we present the comparative efficacy within the enhanced interviews of the direct inquiry "double-check" on children's reports of a selected set of body locations. Next we explore the potential influence of direct questions from the initial interview on the children's responses during the second interview. Finally, we contrast the reporting of genital touch by abused and nonabused children.

Accuracy of Answers to "Action Questions": Direct Inquiry

A $2 \times 4 \times 2$ (interview session by age group by gender) repeated-measures ANOVA revealed that there was a significant drop from the initial to the 1-month interview in the total accuracy score (M's = 70% and 64%, respectively, $F[1, 116] = 13.388$, $p < .001$). There was also a significant main effect for age ($F[3, 116] = 3.563$, $p = .01$). A planned contrast demonstrated that the 3-year-old children had significantly lower scores than did the 6-year-old children, while the 4- and 5-year-old children did not differ from either (M's = 56%, 62%, 66%, and 71%, respectively, $F[1, 116] = 8.799$, $p < .01$). There were no gender differences and no significant interactions. The correlation between children's accuracy on spontaneous reporting of body touch

TABLE 18

PERCENTAGE RESPONSE TO DIRECT ACTION QUESTIONS AT ONE-MONTH INTERVIEW

| | TOUCHED | | NOT TOUCHED | | ACCURATE: |
QUESTIONS	AA	OM	AD	COM	AA + AD[a]
Pictures	41	59	N.A.	N.A.	41
Clothes off	43	28	24	5	67**
Body	12	47	35	6	48
Ear	23	41	32	4	55
Arm	24	29	36	11	61**
Hold down[b]	12	20	55	13	67**
Mouth	11	16	62	11	73**
Hammer	8	3	80	9	88**
Head	N.A.	2	91	7	91**

NOTE.—AA = accurate assertion; OM = error of omission; AD = accurate denial; COM = error of commission; N.A. = not applicable.

[a] Accuracy rate (AA + AD) tested against 50% chance response.

[b] Difference among age groups.

** $p < .001$.

and their accuracy in response to direct inquiry about action was low but significant ($r = .201$, $p < .05$).

Looking at the content of the action questions, the rate of accuracy of children's answers had dropped on all questions but remained higher than the 50% chance expectation at the $p < .01$ level for six of the nine questions, as reported in Table 18. The rate of response to the questions about putting something in the ear or in the body and about picture taking was not different from chance. Age differences were found on only one question: the report of being held down ($\chi^2[3] = 12.83$, $p < .01$). Only 41% of the 3-year-old children reported this accurately. They were the only age group who did not report this at a rate reliably greater than one might expect by chance, as compared to 68% of 4-year-olds ($z = 2.142$, $p < .05$), 72% of 5-year-olds ($z = 2.650$, $p < .01$), and 85% of 6-year-olds ($z = 3.638$, $p < .01$).

Accuracy and Completeness as a Result of the "Double-Check"

Children in the enhanced interviews who initially remained silent about touch to specific body locations were asked a direct question as a follow-up in the "double-check." The accuracy rate (accurate assertion + accurate denial/total response) of responses to direct inquiry about touches to those body locations was as follows: anus (86%, $z = 3.30$, $p < .001$) and belly button (67%, $z = 2.906$, $p < .01$) were significantly higher than chance; there was a trend for a higher than chance reporting of buttocks (64%, $z = 1.75$, $p < .10$) and penis/vagina (62%, $z = 1.71$, $p < .10$); while the responses to ear (50.8%) were not above chance level. Again, as in the initial interview, the

TABLE 19

PERCENTAGE OF CHILDREN REPORTING BODY TOUCH AS A FUNCTION
OF CUES AT ONE-MONTH INTERVIEW

| | TOUCHED | | | NOT TOUCHED | | |
BODY PART	N^a	AA	OM	N^a	AD	COM
Ear:						
Verbal	17	.24	.76	16	N.A.	.06
Enhanced	66	.35	.65	26	N.A.	.12
Enhanced and double-check	65	.52	.48	26	.84	.16
Belly button:						
Verbal	9	0	1.00	22	N.A.	0
Enhanced	34	.24	.76	54	N.A.	.13
Enhanced and double-check	34	.35	.65	54	.83	.17
Genitals:						
Verbal	11	.18	.82	20	N.A.	0
Enhanced	52	.69	.31	39	N.A.	.05
Enhanced and double-check	50	.74	.26	39	.85	.15
Buttocks:[b]						
Verbal	17	.06	.94	14	N.A.	0
Enhanced	31	.55	.45	25	N.A.	.08
Enhanced and double-check	31	.61	.39	25	.88	.12
Anus:[b]						
Verbal	5	0	1.00	26	N.A.	0
Enhanced	8	.62	.38	23	N.A.	.22
Enhanced and double-check	8	.88	.12	23	.70	.30

NOTE.—AA = accurate assertion; OM = error of omission; AD = accurate denial; COM = error of commission; N.A. = not applicable. Verbal = data from children in the verbal interview; enhanced = data from children in the three enhanced interviews who reported spontaneously; double-check = data from children in the enhanced interviews who responded spontaneously plus data from children who responded after being cued with a direct question.

[a] The decrease in cell size from enhanced cues to enhanced and double-check cues reflects uncodable responses or failure to question the child about that body location.

[b] Only children with access to body outlines were questioned about touch to the buttocks, while only children with access to the doll were questioned about anal touch.

"double-check" elicited a higher percentage of accurate denials than of accurate assertions. Second, the errors of omission were greater than the errors of commission for ear, belly button, genitals, and buttocks, but not for anus. Third, the "double-check" was helpful in increasing the number of children accurately reporting touch to the ear. Age differences in reporting were examined for each of the five body locations. Only the report of genital touch revealed age differences ($\chi^2[3] = 8.05$, $p < .05$). Three-year-old children were significantly more likely to err in reporting genital touch than were older children; the errors were predominantly errors of commission (six) rather than errors of omission (two).

Reporting rates from the verbal interview, the enhanced interviews, and the double-check at the 1-month follow-up interview are displayed in Table 19. The genital reporting rate for children with access to the anatomically detailed dolls was 80%, while the reporting rate for those with access to the anatomically detailed drawings was 60%, a difference that was not significant ($p > .10$). The surcharge for direct inquiry that followed children's opportunity for free recall of body touch included additional errors of commission and omission. No children with access to the dolls made spontaneous genital touch commission errors, although two did do so following the "double-check" inquiry; two children with access to the body outlines made spontaneous commission errors, and an additional two children made commission errors following the "double-check" inquiry. Children who made commission errors reporting genital touch ranged in age from 43 to 77 months.

Anal touch was not reported by any of the 60 children with access to the anatomically detailed body outlines—nine children who had and 51 children who had not been touched—and, beyond the invitation to freely recall body touch, they were not questioned further. Five children with access to the dolls accurately reported anal touch spontaneously; however, seven children with access to the dolls made commission errors when reporting anal touch, five spontaneously and an additional two when asked directly during the "double-check." Children who made commission errors reporting anal touch ranged in age from 44 to 68 months.

Report of Genital Touch by Abused Children

The spontaneous reporting rate of genital touch by the "definitely abused" children (all of whom were in the enhanced interviews) was 83%, compared to the reporting rate (62%) of the other/nonabused children in the enhanced interviews and that (18%) of the other/nonabused children in the verbal interview ($\chi^2[2] = 11.95$, $p < .01$). In the enhanced interviews, the "double-check" elicited only one additional, previously unreported accurate response from the 16 children who had been touched. The child who reported after the "double-check" was an other/nonabused child, thereby raising the reporting rate for other/nonabused children in the enhanced interview to 65%. The other/nonabused children in the enhanced interviews with access to anatomically detailed cues were more likely to report genital touch than were the other/nonabused children in the verbal interview ($\chi^2[1] = 6.236$, $p < .05$). During the "double-check," three "definitely abused" and 10 other/nonabused children all denied touch, thereby making errors of omission; unfortunately, the interviewers failed to "double-check" two additional children.

In the group of other/nonabused children, girls reported genital touch more frequently than boys (82% vs 56%), although, owing to the small numbers, that difference was not significant ($p > .10$). Fifteen of the 16 girls but neither of the two boys in the "definitely abused" group reported genital touch.

Effect of the Initial Interview "Double-Check" on Spontaneous Responses in the One-Month Interview

Data from the children who were initially silent about touch to the ear and/or to the penis/vagina on the first interview, and were therefore subject to a direct question about touch to those body locations during the double-check, were explored to determine the possible effect of that cuing on subsequent spontaneous reports of body touch in the second interview. We found some continuity in children's response style. There were no age differences among children in the enhanced interviews who were initially silent and had to be cued by doll/drawing-assisted direct questions in the first interview. These children were less likely to report touch to the ear or the penis/vagina spontaneously in the second interview than were children who reported the touch spontaneously in the first interview ($\chi^2[1]$ = 13.83, $p <$ .001, and $\chi^2[1]$ = 6.91, $p <$ .01, respectively). Thus, the children who required cuing on the first interview continued to need the cues to elicit information about those body locations when interviewed a month later.

The cuing led to different results with respect to the two body locations: those children who required cuing about ear touch in the first interview were significantly less likely to respond accurately on the second interview than those who spontaneously reported ear touch ($\chi^2[1]$ = 3.98, $p <$ .05), while the accuracy of the children's reporting of touch to the penis/vagina was not differentially influenced by whether the child reported the event spontaneously in the first interview or was cued by a direct question. The accuracy rate in the second interview of those children who accurately reported touch to the ear in the first interview was 47%, while that same rate for children who accurately reported touch to the penis/vagina was 84%. We speculate that the doll/drawing-assisted direct question cue elicited more false reports of ear than of genital touch because children were paying differential attention to touch and handling by medical staff of those two body locations.

Summary: Response to Direct Questions about Body Touch

There was a significant drop in the overall accuracy rate of children in response to the action questions to 64%, an accuracy rate that continues to be lower than the rate of spontaneous responses at the 1-month follow-up (79%). However, question content reflected differential forgetting of some

TABLE 20

SUMMARY OF THE MEAN ACCURACY AND COMPLETENESS OF THE REPORTS
OF CHILDREN WHO PARTICIPATED IN THE INITIAL INTERVIEW
AND IN THE ONE-MONTH FOLLOW-UP INTERVIEW

Variables	Initial	1 Month	p
Body touch:			
Accuracy	.94	.79	<.001
Completeness	.25	.21	<.01
"Touch with":			
Accuracy	.74	.60	<.01
Direct action questions:			
Accuracy	.70	.64	<.001
No. of persons present:			
Accuracy	.84	.72	<.001
Completeness	.51	.40	<.001
Person description:			
Accuracy	.86	.87	N.S.
Place description:			
Accuracy	.86	.80	<.05

but not the majority of the events. The 3-year-old children's score on the action questions was no better than chance, and again, when asked a doll/drawing-assisted direct question about genital touch, most remained silent, thereby making an omission error. Doll/drawing-assisted direct questions did yield new information about genital touch from one child and about anal touch from two children, but they also elicited commission errors from four children about genital touch and from two children about anal touch. Following a doll/drawing-assisted direct question, 85% of the untouched children were able to deny genital touch, and 70% were able to deny anal touch. One process observation was made: children who required direct questions on the initial interview to elicit information about touch to body locations continued to need cuing at the 1-month follow-up, but the relative accuracy of the answers reflected differential forgetting of ear but not genital touch.

What Happened One Month Ago: Children's Responses One Month after an Event

What were children able to tell us when they were interviewed for a second time 1 month after experiencing a salient, personal event in which their bodies were touched and handled? Table 20 presents a summary of the accuracy and completeness of the reports of children who participated in both the initial interview and the 1-month follow-up. Table 21 presents a summary of the interviewing and personal variables and features of the event that sig-

TABLE 21

VARIABLES THAT SIGNIFICANTLY INFLUENCED THE ACCURACY, COMPLETENESS, AND CONSISTENCY
OF CHILDREN'S REPORTS FOLLOWING A ONE-MONTH DELAY

Variables	Accuracy	Completeness	Consistency
Positive influence:			
Enhanced interviews	Genital touch	Body touch	
Age of child	"Touch with"	Body touch	Body touch
	Action question		
	Double-check: genital		
Abuse status	Genital touch		
Mother's education		Body touch	
Pain rating		Body touch	
Invasive procedure	Body touch		
Total touch	Body touch		
Negative influence:			
Interview strategy	Prop use		
Event/interview delay	Body touch	Body touch	
	"Touch with"	Persons present	
	Persons present		
		Action question	
Total touch			Body touch

nificantly influenced the accuracy, completeness, and consistency of children's reports. Three facets of the 1-month follow-up interview stand out: the effect of the time delay, access to anatomical cues, and type of question used. Quite simply, over time, children forgot. After a 1-month delay, their responses were less accurate about where they were touched, what they were touched with, and who was present. And their responses were even more sparse. Spontaneously given information continued to be more accurate than that elicited by direct questions. As in the initial interview, anatomical cues in the enhanced interviews enabled children to report their experiences of body touch more completely, and the doll/drawing-assisted direct questions enabled more children to report genital touch accurately. Children who had past experience with sexual abuse continued to provide the most accurate reports of genital touch.

Neither anatomical cues nor age of the child interfered with the accuracy of reporting. However, for children in the verbal interview, mother's education provided a scaffolding that resulted in more complete reports of body touch when children did not have access to anatomical cues. Older children were more complete and more consistent in their reports of body touch and more accurate in their reports of genital touch and what they were touched with. Both the complexity (number of total touches and invasive procedures) and the relative painfulness of the event continued to make events more memorable and more accurately reported, but more complex events were reported less consistently.

Descriptive accuracy of persons and settings was high, but, pragmatically, photographs continued to be more useful in identifying both medical staff and setting. In sharp contrast, medical props interfered with children's reports of what they were touched with.

The variables that did *not* influence accuracy, completeness, or consistency when children were interviewed 1 month after an event included gender, ethnicity, current health status, past medical experience, family stress, and intervening outpatient or inpatient visits.

V. RESULTS:
FOLLOW-UP INTERVIEWS WITH CHILDREN
SIX MONTHS AFTER AN EVENT

From the original group of 130 children initially interviewed, 80 families were contacted for a 6-month follow-up interview. A total of 74 children returned for their third interview. There were no significant differences between the children in the 6-month follow-up and those in the original group on any of the demographic or experiential variables (all p's > .20). There was nearly an equal number of participants returning across the four interview types (see Table 3 above). Owing to the smaller subject pool, two age groups, rather than four, will be entered into the analyses: the 41 3- and 4-year-old children will be designated as the younger group ($M = 48$ months), the 33 5- and 6-year-old children as the older group ($M = 73$ months). The number of outpatient and inpatient visits to our medical center occurring between the original interview and the 6-month follow-up was added to the experiential covariate set.

The results of each child's responses at the 6-month interview will be reported and compared with his or her responses from the initial and 1-month interviews. There are three sections, each ending with a brief summary: (1) spontaneous reports of body touch and handling, (2) spontaneous and cued reports of person and setting, and (3) reports following direct yes/no questions about clinic events and doll/drawing-assisted direct yes/no questions about body touch.

SPONTANEOUS REPORTING OF BODY TOUCH AND HANDLING

In this section, we present the accuracy, completeness, and consistency of children's spontaneous reports of body touch and the accuracy of their reports of what they were "touched with." Data will be analyzed employing a 3 × 4 × 2 (interview session by interview strategy by age group) repeated-measures ANOVA, followed by the results of the regression analysis with the 6-month data. By definition, repeated-measures analyses will be limited in each instance to the children who have scores in all three interview sessions.

TABLE 22

MEANS AND STANDARD DEVIATIONS OF ACCURACY, COMPLETENESS,
AND CONSISTENCY OF BODY TOUCH AND "TOUCH WITH"
BY AGE AT SIX-MONTH INTERVIEW

	3–4 YEARS		5–6 YEARS	
	Mean	SD	Mean	SD
Accuracy:				
Body touch	.76	.27	.68	.34
"Touch with"	.33	.35	.46	.32
Completeness:				
% body touches	.23a	.18	.28b	.23
Consistency:				
Body touch, accurate	1.54a	.41	1.79b	.49
Body touch, error	1.27	.48	1.20	.29

NOTE.—Means that do not share a common letter designation are significantly different ($p < .05$).

Accuracy, Completeness, and Consistency of Reports of Body Touch

Accuracy

Fifty-six children reported body touch in all three interviews. A $3 \times 4 \times 2$ (interview session by interview strategy by age group) repeated-measures ANOVA revealed that accuracy of reporting body touch stabilized after the significant change noted from the first to the second interview (M's $= .94$, .71, and .72, $F[2, 96] = 19.126$, $p < .001$). There were no differences in reporting accuracy as a result of interview strategy or age group, and none of the interactions was significant. (For mean scores of accuracy of body touch by age group at the 6-month follow-up interview, see Table 22.) For the first time in this study, the child's judgment of the painfulness of the body touch was significantly related to accuracy of report at the 6-month interview ($r = .26$, $p < .05$), while the total number of touches a child experienced was again related to accuracy ($r = .46$, $p < .001$). None of the other personal, experiential, or interview strategy variables was significantly correlated with reporting accuracy. When entered into the regression, pain and total touch accounted for 23.4% of the variance. (For a display of the event features that predict accuracy of body touch at the 6-month follow-up interview, see Table 23.)

Completeness

The $3 \times 4 \times 2$ (interview session by interview strategy by age) repeated-measures ANOVA revealed that there was a significant shift in the relative completeness of spontaneous disclosure of body touch across the three interview sessions ($F[2, 128] = 4.255$, $p < .05$). But the pattern of shift was not

TABLE 23

EVENT FEATURES THAT PREDICT ACCURACY, COMPLETENESS, AND
CONSISTENCY OF SPONTANEOUS REPORT OF BODY TOUCH AT SIX MONTHS

	β	t	R^2
Accuracy:			
Child pain rating	.261	2.143	
No. of total touches	.428	3.763	.236**
Completeness:			
Child pain rating	.233	2.037	.055*
Consistency of accurate reports:			
Age	.411	3.691	
Verbal vs. enhanced	.199	1.784	.191**

* $p < .05$.
** $p < .001$.

all "downhill," as one might anticipate (M's = .26, .20, and .25). A post hoc
cubic contrast revealed that the report of completeness at the second interview session was significantly lower than at the initial or 6-month interviews
($F[1, 64] = 11.395$, $p = .001$). A trend was found for interview strategy ($F[3,
64] = 2.303$, $p < .10$). The planned contrast with respect to interview strate-
gies revealed that children disclosed less in the verbal interviews than in the
enhanced interviews (M's = .18, .26, .27, and .23, respectively, $F[1, 64] =
6.376$, $p = .01$). A main effect for age group revealed that younger children
disclosed body touch less completely than did older children (M's = .23 and
.28, respectively, $F[1, 64] = 7.114$, $p = .01$). (For the mean scores for completeness of reports of body touch by older and younger children, see Table
22 above.) There were no significant interactions among interview session,
interview strategy, and age group. Pain was the only variable that was significantly related to the prediction of completeness at the 6-month interview ($r
= .23$, $p < .05$), as displayed in Table 23.

Again, we examined the reports of feelings about the clinic visit by children in the High Pain group: those children who reported at least one body
touch as being extremely painful during the initial interview. At the 6-month
interview, the 26 children in the High Pain group continued to report more
negative feelings about their clinic visit than did the other children. They
told us that they were significantly more angry (M's = 2.25 vs. 1.44, $t[54] =
2.682$, $p = .01$), and there were trends in their reports that they were sadder
(M's = 2.33 vs. 1.75, $t[55] = 1.791$, $p < .10$) and more scared (M's = 2.10
vs. 1.56, $t[54] = 1.757$, $p < .10$).

Consistency

During the 6-month interview, as noted above, 72% of the information
that children spontaneously reported about body touch was accurate and 28%

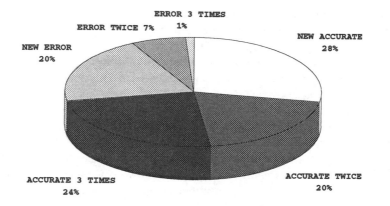

FIG. 3.—Percentage of new and repeated accurate and erroneous reports of body touch at a third interview after a 6-month delay.

in error. Figure 3 displays the sources of the accurate and erroneous information. Twenty-four percent of the accurate information about body touch in the 6-month interview was reported at all three interviews, 20% was also reported at either the first or the second interview, and 28% was new, accurate information reported for the first time. The source of the error data included 1% of information that was reported in all three interviews, 7% that had been previously reported at either the first or the second interview, and 20% that was reported for the first time at the 6-month interview.

Consistency scores were created for each of the 69 children who spontaneously reported body touch in at least one of the three interviews by weighting each unique accurate report by one, weighting reports repeated in two of the three interviews by two, and weighting reports in all three interviews by three. A 4 × 2 (interview strategy by age group) ANOVA revealed no main effect for interview strategy. There was a significant main effect for age, with younger children receiving lower consistency scores than older children (M's = 1.54 and 1.79, respectively, $F[1, 61] = 6.015$, $p = .017$). (For mean consistency scores of older and younger children, see Table 22 above.) The interview strategy by age group interaction was not significant. Because at the 1-month interview the accurate reports of body touch of 3-year-old children were found to be significantly less consistent than those of the older children, a post hoc analysis was conducted to examine the difference within the younger group between 3- and 4-year-old children. Again, 3-year-old children were significantly less consistent than 4-year-old children (M's = 1.27 and 1.72, respectively, $t[36] = 3.816$, $p < .001$); thus, their scores were responsible for the age group difference reported above. Children's age was the only variable that was significantly correlated with the consistency of accurate response ($r = .389$, $p = .001$), as displayed in Table 23. None of the other personal or experiential variables contributed to the regression, but the planned contrast between the verbal and the enhanced interviews entered into the regression and, together with age and interview strategy, accounted for 19% of the variance. Younger children and children in the verbal interview with no access to anatomical body cues were less consistent than their peers in reporting body touch.

Consistency scores were also created for the 50 children who spontaneously erroneously reported a body touch in at least one of the three interviews. The average consistency of error score was 1.23. A 4×2 (interview strategy by age group) ANOVA demonstrated that neither of the main effects nor the interaction was significant. There were two covariates that correlated with consistency of error scores, number of outpatient days ($r = -.154$, $p < .10$) and number of inpatient days ($r = .249$, $p < .05$), and both these variables contributed to the prediction of consistent error, accounting for 12.5% of the variance. Inspection of the raw data revealed that one child, who was very ill, could be considered statistically as an "outlier," having spent 48% of the past 5 months at our medical center: 19 days as an outpatient and 53 days as an inpatient. (For the whole sample, the average number of outpatient days was 6.5 and of inpatient days was 1.6; the mode for outpatient and inpatient days was 0.) When his data were removed from the analysis, neither the measures of intervening medical experience (p's $> .10$) nor any of the other covariates contributed to the prediction of consistent error.

Accuracy of Report of "Touch With"

There were 40 children who in all three interviews described what they were touched with. A $3 \times 4 \times 2$ (interview session by interview strategy by age group) repeated-measures ANOVA revealed that there was a significant decrease across the three interview sessions in the accuracy of children's reports of what they were touched with (M's = .78, .60, and .41, respectively, $F[2, 72] = 12.848$, $p < .001$). There were no differences in relative accuracy as a result of interview type or age group, and none of the interactions was significant. (For mean scores of accuracy of "touch with" by age group, see Table 22 above.) The significant drop in relative accuracy of report seen by children with access to the props in the doll interview from the first to the second session was examined again on the 6-month follow-up with a planned contrast. However, children in the doll interview were not significantly less accurate than children in the other three interview types. None of the demographic or experiential variables contributed to the prediction of children's reports of what they were touched with.

Eighteen children had access to the box of props during the third interview. Summing across all use of the medical equipment props, 14% of the touches were demonstrated by children using the equipment on their own bodies, 86% of the touches were demonstrated with the dolls, while none of the children demonstrated the use of the medical equipment on the interviewer. Unlike the initial interview, in which the modal use of the equipment with both self- and doll touch was accurate, during this third interview, when children used the props on themselves, only 25% of their demonstration accurately replicated their experience during the medical visit; the modal use of the equipment (44%) was defined as irrelevant "medically scripted," and 31% of the demonstrated touches were "playful" but inaccurate use of the medical equipment. Although children demonstrated with the dolls far more often than on themselves, when medical equipment was used with the dolls, the proportions of accurate use (30%), irrelevant "medically scripted" use (40%), and "playful" but inaccurate use (30%) were similar to that of use on the self. Children who demonstrated medically scripted play were nearly a year older than those who played randomly with the equipment (M's = 58.5 and 49.8 months old, respectively). Furthermore, all children made at least one error in their selection and use of medical equipment; the average age of the children who made only errors was 45.5 months. The stethoscope, otoscope, and syringe were the props used most frequently for accurate demonstration of body touch. Most errors were made when children selected the blood pressure cuff, stethoscope, reflex hammer, and otoscope for medical play.

Summary: Spontaneous Reports of Body Touch and Handling

The relative accuracy of spontaneous reports of body touch (72%) was stable from 1 to 6 months, while completeness increased significantly (to 25%). Replicating findings from the two previous interviews, accuracy was independent of both age and interview strategy. However, age and access to the doll/drawing cues in the enhanced interviews supported more complete and consistently accurate reporting about body touch. (For a summary of developmental comparisons for accuracy, completeness, and consistency of body touch, see Table 22 above. For event features that predict spontaneous reporting at the 6-month follow-up interview, see Table 23.) Analysis of the interview content revealed that the information that children consistently reported about body touch in all three interviews was 24 times more likely to be accurate than erroneous while information reported at least twice was nearly three times more likely to be accurate as erroneous. However, only about half the information reported for the first time at the 6-month interview was accurate. Only half the children spontaneously mentioned what they were touched with. The relative accuracy of their reports was very low (41%), and these reports no longer reflected developmental differences or prop access. Children's judgment of the relative painfulness of body touch was a salient event feature that influenced both the accuracy and the completeness of their spontaneous reports, and accuracy continued to be bolstered for children who experienced more touch.

REPORTS OF PERSONS AND SETTING

In this section, we present children's responses to the request for information about the persons who were in the clinic with them and the clinic setting where they were seen. The accuracy, completeness, and consistency of the number of persons will be presented first, followed by children's descriptions of medical staff based on a set of verbal prompts and, for the children in the doll and drawing interviews, the accuracy of their photograph identification of medical staff. Next we report the accuracy of children's setting descriptions and their photograph recognition of the setting. A 3 × 2 (interview session by age) repeated-measures ANOVA was employed to analyze accuracy and completeness data. During this 6-month follow-up, children in the doll interview had access to the photographs of persons and places from the rogues' gallery for the third time, children in the drawing interview for the second. None of the demographic or experiential variables was significantly correlated with children's descriptions of person, and none contributed to the prediction of reporting accuracy. As in the 1-month interview, intervening outpatient visits contributed to photograph recognition.

Accuracy, Completeness, and Consistency of Reports of Persons Present: Spontaneous Reports

Accuracy

Fifty-seven children reported persons present in all three interviews. The relative accuracy of children's reports about who was with them was stable from the second to the third interview, and the 3 × 2 (interview session by age) repeated-measures ANOVA revealed no significant change across the three interviews (M's = .82, .73, and .74, respectively). The main effect for age group was not significant. The interaction was not significant. (For the mean accuracy scores of younger and older children, see Table 24.)

Children who reported that their mothers were present were highly accurate (93%), as were those who reported the presence of a nurse (79%) and a doctor (62%). Children's reports of the presence of their father (56%) or of siblings (53%) were less accurate. (For a summary of the reports of persons

TABLE 24

MEAN ACCURACY OF PERSONS PRESENT, PERSON DESCRIPTION, AND
SETTING DESCRIPTION AND MEAN COMPLETENESS OF PERSONS
PRESENT BY AGE AT SIX-MONTH INTERVIEW

	3–4 YEARS		5–6 YEARS	
	Mean	SD	Mean	SD
Accuracy:				
Persons present	.74	.32	.73	.30
Person description	.84	.22	.92	.13
Setting description	.80a	.31	.88b	.18
Completeness:				
% persons present	.37	.30	.44	.24

NOTE.—Means that do not share a common letter designation are significantly different ($p < .05$).

across the three interview sessions, see Table 25.) Only the spontaneous reporting of mother's presence did not decline.

Completeness

A 3×2 (interview session by age) repeated-measures ANOVA revealed that the reporting of percentage of persons in the room with the child had stabilized from the second to the third interview, following the initial drop from the initial interview to 1 month (M's = .51, .40, and .40, respectively, $F[2, 132] = 6.794$, $p < .01$). There was no main effect for age group. The interaction was not significant. (For the mean completeness scores of younger and older children, see Table 24 above.)

Although children who did report their mothers present were highly accurate, by 6 months only two-thirds included their mothers in their descrip-

TABLE 25

ACCURACY OF SPONTANEOUS REPORTS OF PERSON PRESENT
ACROSS THREE INTERVIEWS

	INITIAL		1 MONTH		6 MONTHS	
	%	N[a]	%	N[a]	%	N[a]
Person report:						
Mother	99	89	95	77	93	46
Father	81	21	71	14	56	9
Sibling	84	32	73	30	53	19
Doctor	75	55	70	50	62	29
Nurse	95	22	89	19	79	14

[a] N = number of children spontaneously identifying person.

tion of the clinic visit. Approximately half reported their fathers (55.6%) and siblings (58.8%). Medical staff were forgotten as well, with only 37.5% remembering their doctors and 19.6% their nurses.

Consistency

Forty-eight percent of children reported their mothers as being present at every interview, 27% as being present twice, and 18% as being present only once. Four children never spontaneously mentioned that their mothers were present. Although far fewer fathers brought their children to the clinic visit, the consistency of identification paralleled that of the mothers: 56% mentioned their father's presence at every interview, 33% at two interviews, and 11% at only one.

The consistency of children's identification of medical staff across the three interviews was determined by review of the staff named. Again, as in the review after the 1-month interview, coding of children's names for staff was fairly liberal. Children's responses were as follows: 16.2% consistently named the same medical staff person as being present at every interview, 23% named a staff person twice, 20.3% named a staff person only once, and 40.5% did not give the name of any medical staff member at any interview.

Accuracy and Consistency of Description of Medical Staff: Verbal Prompt

Accuracy

Children's descriptions of medical staff were highly accurate and stable for the group of 54 children who reported in all three interviews (M's = .86, .88, and .90, respectively). A 3×2 repeated-measures ANOVA revealed no main effects for interview session or age, and the session by age interaction was not significant. Again, it should be noted that children were not necessarily offering descriptions of the same individuals at each of the three interviews.

At the six-month interview, children's identification of the sex of medical staff was 98.3% accurate; as for identification of staff by name, 37.1% were accurate, 9.7% were in error, and 53.2% responded that they "didn't know." Although few children offered descriptions of staff members' clothing, those who did were all above 90% accuracy for the color of shirt/blouse, pants/skirt, dress/suit, and shoes. The descriptions of the color of coat/jacket were 86% accurate. All the children who described the staff member as wearing a "doctor suit" were accurate, as were all the children who mentioned hair color, facial hair, glasses, or ethnicity. The average relative accuracy of de-

TABLE 26

MEDICAL STAFF DESCRIPTIONS AT INITIAL, ONE-, AND SIX-MONTH INTERVIEWS

| | INITIAL | | 1 MONTH | | 6 MONTHS | |
ITEM	% Acc	% Comp	% Acc	% Comp	% Acc	% Comp
Sex[a]	93.9	100.0	96.4	93.8	98.3	89.1
Name[a]	76.0	32.8	65.9	24.5	79.3	37.1
Clothing[a,b]	93.4	43.8	88.5	36.0	92.3	32.4
Hair color[a]	98.0	88.5	100.0	71.7	100.0	79.4
"Doctor clothes"[c]	83.3	95.2	84.6	100.0	100.0	100.0
Facial hair[d]	87.5	29.0	100.0	50.0	100.0	47.3
Glasses[e]	78.0	26.9	100.0	13.8	100.0	11.0
Ethnicity	71.4	4.6	100.0	6.5	100.0	12.2

NOTE.—$N = 116$ in initial interview, 113 in 1-month interview, and 65 in 6-month interview. % acc = (no. of accurate reports/no. of accurate reports + no. of error reports); % comp = (no. of accurate reports/no. of features of staff described).

[a] Direct question.

[b] Includes description of at least one article of clothing.

[c] Twenty-one children described staff wearing "doctor clothes" at the initial interview, 22 at 1 month, and 11 at 6 months.

[d] Twenty-four children described staff with facial hair in the initial interview, 20 at 1 month, and 19 at 6 months.

[e] Twenty-six children described staff with glasses in the initial interview, 29 at 1 month, and 9 at 6 months.

scriptors was 90%. (For a summary of the children's descriptions of medical staff across the three interview sessions, see Table 26.)

Consistency

The verbatim descriptions of medical staff were reviewed to determine the extent to which children repeated characteristics that might be useful in identifying people, for example, "He had on red high-top tennis shoes," or, "She had a black pony tail." A score was created for each child weighting each descriptive characteristic of each medical staff person who was correctly identified on the first, second, or third interview by one, weighting descriptors of each medical staff person who was correctly identified in two interviews by two, and weighting descriptors of each medical staff person who was correctly identified in three interviews by three. The average consistency of descriptors was 2.040, on a range from 1.00 to 3.00. A 2×2 (sex by age group) ANOVA of these weighted relative consistency of accuracy scores demonstrated no main effects or interactions. The characteristics most consistently reported were "doctor suits," hair color, and facial hair.

Recognition of Medical Staff: Rogues' Gallery

Data from 38 children were examined to determine whether making a single choice would continue to be a useful clue to accuracy. Of the 32 children who pointed to only one picture to identify the key medical staff person, 81.2% were accurate. Of the 15 children who selected a single photograph of a second medical staff person, 73% were accurate. The relative proportions of the children who made accurate selections with their only choice on the first and second person are significantly higher than an expected chance rate of 17% ($z = 10.596$, $p < .001$, and $z = 6.34$, $p < .001$, respectively). Thus, response pattern continued to be useful in identifying children who were correct.

Again, there were no differences in accuracy on the basis of age or sex of child or experience with the technique. The relation between recognition accuracy and two measures of familiarity was examined: return visits to the medical center either to the outpatient clinic or for inpatient hospitalization between the initial and the 6-month follow-up interview. The data from each variable were dichotomized into no intervening visits and one or more intervening visits, and a series of chi square analyses with Yates corrections was conducted. The relative accuracy of recognition of the first and second staff member was significantly related to outpatient but not to inpatient visits. Significantly more children who made an accurate selection of both the first and the second staff member had returned for an outpatient visit during the 6-month interim ($\chi_c^2[1] = 4.103$, $p < .05$, and $\chi_c^2[1] = 4.188$, $p < .05$, respectively).

Description of the Setting: Verbal Prompt

Forty-seven children described the pediatric clinic room on all three interviews. A 3 × 2 repeated-measures analysis of the relative accuracy of their reports revealed no significant change across the three interview sessions (M's = .88, .83, and .87, respectively). There was a main effect for age group ($F[1, 43] = 6.013$, $p < .05$). Although the session by age group interaction did not reach significance, inspection of age by interview session revealed that, while there were no differences in the 6-month data, younger children's descriptions on the initial and 1-month interview were less accurate than older children's.

Recognition of the Setting: Rogues' Gallery

The rogues' gallery was used by 37 children to identify the room in the pediatric outpatient clinic where they had been seen. Nineteen of the 21 children (90.5%) who chose only one photograph were accurate, a proportion that is significantly different from the chance rate ($z = 9.939$, $p < .001$). There were no differences as a result of age or sex of child, experience with the photograph technique, or intervening outpatient or inpatient visits.

Summary: Spontaneous and Cued Reports of Persons and Setting

Six months after children were seen on a clinic visit, they reported only 40% of the persons who were with them, with family members more likely to be mentioned than medical staff. Parents were also more consistently mentioned than medical staff across the three interviews, as can be seen in Table 25. For a summary of the relative accuracy and completeness of children's descriptors of medical staff across the three interviews, see Table 26; for the mean accuracy and completeness of person description and the accuracy of setting description by age group, see Table 24. As might be anticipated, children who returned to the clinic sometime between the initial and the 6-month interview were more likely to make an accurate photograph identification of medical staff than those who had not returned. Recognition of medical staff (81%) and clinic (90%) continued at high levels.

DIRECT INQUIRY ABOUT BODY TOUCH AND HANDLING

Accuracy of Answers to "Action Questions"

At the 6-month interview, the children's average response rate to action questions was 63.3%, a rate that is significantly higher than chance ($z = 2.282$, $p < .05$). A $3 \times 2 \times 2$ (interview session by age group by gender) repeated-measures ANOVA revealed a significant main effect for interview session (M's = 73.8%, 62%, and 63.3%, $F[2, 138] = 15.712$, $p < .001$). The significant drop from the initial to the 1-month interview is demonstrated again, but there was no further change between the 1- and the 6-month interviews. There were no differences between the scores of older and younger children. In fact, the average scores of each of the four age groups fell in a narrow range between 60% and 66%. No gender differences were found, and none of the interactions was significant.

Looking at the content of the action questions, the rate of accuracy of children's answers had dropped on all questions but remained higher than the 50% chance expectation at the $p < .01$ level for five of the nine questions, as displayed in Table 27. The rate of response to the questions about putting something in the ear or in the body or of having something wrapped around the arm was not different from chance. The accuracy rate for the question about picture taking dropped to 31%. Unlike the earlier interviews, there were no significant age differences found on any of the nine questions.

Accuracy and Completeness as a Result of the "Double-Check"

Children in the enhanced interviews who initially remained silent about touch to specific body locations were followed up on with a doll/drawing-

TABLE 27

Percentage Response to Direct Action Questions at Six-Month Interview

| | Touched | | Not Touched | | Accurate: |
Questions	AA	OM	AD	COM	AA + AD[a]
Pictures	31	69	N.A.	N.A.	31
Clothes off	37	26	33	4	70**
Body	14	49	36	1	50
Ear[b]	16	31	34	19	50
Arm	19	32	30	19	49
Hold down	12	20	54	14	66**
Mouth	11	11	67	10	78**
Hammer	7	3	81	9	88**
Head	3	4	83	10	86**

Note.—AA = accurate assertion; OM = error of omission; AD = accurate denial; COM = error of commission; N.A. = not applicable.

[a] Accuracy rate (AA + AD) tested against 50% chance response.

[b] $N = 74$, except for this question, where $N = 54$.

* $p < .01$.

assisted direct question. The accuracy rate (accurate assertion + accurate denial/total response) of responses to direct inquiry for reporting of those body locations was as follows: penis/vagina (84%, $z = 3.82$, $p < .01$) was the only touch reported significantly higher than chance; the responses to the anus (69%), buttocks (65%), ear (63%), and belly button (62%) were not above chance level (all p's > .10). Again, as in the first two interviews, the direct question elicited a higher percentage of accurate denials than of accurate assertions. Second, for each body location, the errors of omission were greater than the errors of commission for ear, belly button, and genitals and equal for buttocks; but errors of commission were greater than errors of omission for the anus. Third, the direct question was helpful in eliciting an accurate assertion from at least one child with respect to each of the body locations. There were no age differences in patterns of reporting accuracy or error on any of the five body locations.

The free recall responses of the children in the verbal interview were contrasted to the responses of the children in the enhanced interviews, who were presented with anatomically detailed cues, and to the responses of the children who required a direct question in addition to the anatomically detailed cues. The results are displayed in Table 28. When we focus on the information that was elicited from the "double-check," four children accurately reported genital touch, while one child erroneously reported both genital and buttocks touch. Two children accurately reported anal touch, while four children erroneously reported anal touch. There was no difference in the efficacy of the anatomically detailed dolls over the drawings in eliciting genital touch reports, as 11 of 13 of the children with the dolls reported while

TABLE 28

PERCENTAGE OF CHILDREN REPORTING BODY TOUCH AS A FUNCTION
OF CUES AT SIX-MONTH INTERVIEW

	TOUCHED			NOT TOUCHED		
BODY PART	N^a	AA	OM	N^a	AD	COM
Ear:						
Verbal	7	0	1.00	12	N.A.	.42
Enhanced	35	.40	.60	19	N.A.	.32
Enhanced and double-check	34	.65	.35	19	.64	.36
Belly button:						
Verbal	4	0	1.00	15	N.A.	0
Enhanced	20	.25	.75	35	N.A.	.11
Enhanced and double-check	20	.40	.60	35	.80	.20
Genitals:						
Verbal	6	.33	.67	13	N.A.	0
Enhanced	29	.72	.28	25	N.A.	.08
Enhanced and double-check	29	.86	.14	25	.88	.12
Buttocks:[b]						
Verbal	10	0	1.00	9	N.A.	.11
Enhanced	17	.47	.53	17	N.A.	0
Enhanced and double-check	17	.53	.47	17	.94	.06
Anus:[b]						
Verbal	3	0	1.00	16	N.A.	0
Enhanced	5	.40	.60	14	N.A.	.07
Enhanced and double-check	5	.80	.20	14	.74	.36

NOTE.—AA = accurate assertion; OM = error of omission; AD = accurate denial; COM = error of commission; N.A. = not applicable. Verbal = data from children in the verbal interview; enhanced = data from children in the three enhanced interviews who reported spontaneously; double-check = data from children in the enhanced interviews who responded spontaneously plus data from children who responded after being cued with a direct question.

[a] The decrease in cell size from enhanced cues to enhanced and double-check cues reflects uncodable responses or failure to question the child about that body location.

[b] Only children with access to body outlines were questioned about touch to the buttocks, while only children with access to the doll were questioned about anal touch.

14 of 16 of the children with access to the drawings reported. One child with access to the body outline and two children with access to the dolls made commission errors about genital touch. All five children who made commission errors about anal touch had access to the dolls.

Reporting of Genital Touch by Abused Children

The spontaneous reporting rate of genital touch by our medical staff, alleged by the "definitely abused" children at the 6-month interview, was 83%. The spontaneous reporting rate of the other/nonabused children in the enhanced interviews at the 6-month interview was 65%, while that of the other/nonabused children in the verbal interview was 33%. Four of the nine touched children who did not report genital touch spontaneously did so when asked directly, one abused child and three other/nonabused children.

113

The added report from direct questions raised the reporting rate for abused children to 92% and for other/nonabused children in the enhanced interviews to 82%. Chi square analysis revealed that touched, other/nonabused children in the verbal interview were less likely to report genital touch than were the other/nonabused children in the enhanced interview $(\chi^2[1] = 5.179, p < .01)$. In the group of other/nonabused children, girls reported genital touch less frequently than boys (50% vs. 73%), although the differences were not significant $(p > .10)$. Nine of the 10 girls and both of the boys in the "definitely abused" group reported.

Summary: Response to Direct Questions about Body Touch and Handling

Six months after the clinic visit, children answered the direct action questions accurately at a rate significantly higher than chance (63%), essentially unchanged from the 1-month interview and lower than the spontaneous reporting rate (72%). Neither total scores nor individual questions reflected differences in accuracy among the four age groups. Answers to five of the nine questions remained above chance. However, fewer than one-third of the children remembered that we had filmed them. When silent children were asked directly about body touch, 84% of the reports of genital touch were accurate. The genitals were the only one of five body locations to elicit accurate reports higher than chance. In contrast to the finding that 3-year-old children at the initial and 1-month interviews were significantly more likely than older children to underreport genital touch when asked directly, their high rate of accurate response (assertions and denials), 87%, paralleled the older children, possibly reflecting their own maturation during the intervening time period. Doll/drawing-assisted direct questions yielded accurate reports from four additional children about genital touch and two additional reports about anal touch; however, one child made a commission error about genital touch, and four children made commission errors about anal touch. Direct doll/drawing-assisted questions to untouched children yielded 88% accurate denial of genital touch and 74% accurate denial of anal touch.

What Happened Six Months Ago:
Children's Responses Six Months after an Event

What were children able to tell us when they were interviewed for a third time 6 months after experiencing a pediatric visit? Table 29 summarizes the accuracy and completeness of the reports of the children who participated in all three interviews. Table 30 summarizes the interviewing and personal variables and features of the event that significantly influenced the accuracy, completeness, and consistency of children's reports at the 6-month follow-up

TABLE 29

SUMMARY OF THE ACCURACY AND COMPLETENESS OF THE REPORTS OF CHILDREN
WHO PARTICIPATED IN THE INITIAL INTERVIEW AND IN THE ONE-MONTH AND
SIX-MONTH FOLLOW-UP INTERVIEWS

Variables	Initial	1 Month	6 Month	p
Body touch:				
Accuracy	.94a	.71b	.72b	<.001
Completeness	.26a	.20b	.25a	<.05
"Touch with":				
Accuracy	.78a	.60b	.41c	<.001
Direct action questions:				
Accuracy	.74a	.62b	.63b	<.001
No. of persons present:				
Accuracy	.82	.73	.74	N.S.
Completeness	.51a	.40b	.40b	<.01
Person description:				
Accuracy	.86	.88	.90	N.S.
Place description:				
Accuracy	.88	.83	.87	N.S.

NOTE.—Means in the same row that do not share a common letter designation are significantly different ($p < .05$).

interview. Information in Table 30 is drawn from two sources: the repeated-measures ANOVAs and the regression analysis.

Three facets of the 6-month follow-up interview stand out: the effect of the time delay, access to anatomical cues, and type of question used. For those children who participated in all three interviews, reports of body touch after a 6-month delay were as accurate as they had been at 1 month but less accurate than at the initial interview. Their responses about what they were touched with were less accurate and about who was present were less complete. Spontaneously given information continued to be more accurate than that elicited by direct questions. As in the initial and 1-month interviews, ana-

TABLE 30

VARIABLES THAT SIGNIFICANTLY INFLUENCED THE ACCURACY, COMPLETENESS, AND
CONSISTENCY OF CHILDREN'S REPORTS FOLLOWING A SIX-MONTH DELAY

Variables	Accuracy	Completeness	Consistency
Positive influence:			
Enhanced interview	Genital touch	Body touch	Body touch
Event/interview delay		Body touch	
Age of child		Body touch	Body touch
Abuse status	Genital touch		
Pain rating	Body touch	Body touch	
Total touch	Body touch		
Negative influence:			
Event/interview delay	"Touch with"		

TABLE 31

SUMMARY OF MEAN ACCURACY, COMPLETENESS, AND CONSISTENCY OF CHILDREN'S REPORTS
BY AGE AT INITIAL, ONE-MONTH, AND SIX-MONTH INTERVIEWS

Variables	3 Years	4 Years	3 and 4 Years	5 Years	6 Years	5 and 6 Years
Body touch:						
Accuracy:						
Initial	.97	.90		.96	.94	
1 month	.74	.82		.87	.73	
6 months			.76			.68
Completeness:						
Initial	.17a	.26b		.26b	.37c	
1 month	.15a	.21b		.19b	.28c	
6 months			.23a			.28b
Consistently accurate:						
1 month	1.23a	1.38b		1.40b	1.50b	
6 months			1.54a			1.79b
"Touch with":						
Accuracy:						
Initial	.55	.67		.79	.80	
1 month	.22a	.56b		.70b	.60b	
6 months			.33			.46
Action questions:						
Accuracy:						
Initial	.69a	.66a		.71a	.78b	
1 month	.56a	.62b		.66b	.71c	
6 months			.63			.63
No. of persons present:						
Accuracy:						
Initial	.71a	.82b		.88b	.82b	
1 month	.79	.64		.77	.73	
6 months			.74			.73
Completeness:						
Initial	.32a	.52b		.52b	.58b	
1 month	.28	.36		.45	.46	
6 months			.37			.44
Person description:						
Accuracy:						
Initial	.83	.85		.84	.89	
1 month	.81	.84		.94	.87	
6 months			.84			.92
Setting description:						
Accuracy:						
Initial	.83	.85		.84	.92	
1 month	.64a	.81b		.85b	.90b	
6 months			.80a			.88b

NOTE.—Means in the same row that do not share letter designations differ at $p < .05$.

tomical cues in the enhanced interviews enabled children to report their experiences of body touch more completely, and the doll/drawing-assisted direct questions enabled more children to report genital touch accurately. Children who had past experience with sexual abuse continued to provide the most accurate reports of genital touch.

Older children were more complete and more consistent in their report of body touch. Information that children continued to repeat was very likely to be accurate, while new information this far removed from the event was as likely to be wrong as right. More complex (number of total touches and invasive procedures) and painful events continued to be more memorable and more accurately reported.

Children's verbal descriptions of persons and setting remained highly accurate across all three interviews, but photographs continued to be more useful in identifying both medical staff and setting. Medical props offered no support for children's reports of what they were touched with.

No personal variables besides the child's age influenced reporting after a 6-month delay. The variables that did *not* influence accuracy, completeness, or consistency when children were interviewed 6 months after an event included gender, ethnicity, current health status, past medical experience, mother's education, family stress, and intervening outpatient or inpatient visits.

Readers interested in a summary of the effect of developmental differences on study variables over the three interviews are referred to Table 31. This table displays accuracy, completeness, and consistency by four age groups at the initial and 1-month follow-up interviews and by younger and older children at the 6-month follow-up interview.

VI. DISCUSSION

This study was initiated by our research team because we had worked with young abused children at the interface of the education, health, and mental health systems and the courts and were critical of these systems' apparent lack of awareness about the capacities and limitations of young children. We were able to videotape children during a visit to our outpatient pediatric clinics and then interview them three times over a 6-month period about their experiences of body touch and handling. By comparing the video replay of the events that children actually experienced to their reports, it was possible to assess three different reporting variables—accuracy, completeness, and consistency. We contrasted the relative efficacy of different anatomical cues, photographs, and props in the three enhanced interviews to a traditional verbal interview and explored the differential contributions of a rich set of covariates to children's reports. We anticipate that the findings gleaned from observing and following young children through an experience that offers an ecologically valid analogue to critical features of sexual and physical abuse will have implications for the process of investigative interviewing and will focus attention on the product, children's testimony.

What do our data indicate about the capacities and limitations of young children to report as participant eyewitnesses? Three to six-year-old children provided highly accurate reports of experiences of body touch and handling—some of which was coercive, painful, and highly emotionally charged—findings that are compatible with children's data from other, autobiographical researchers (Fivush, 1993). Over time, children forgot, but touches that children found distressing owing to pain and/or personal experience were not forgotten randomly over a 6-month period of time, extending the findings of Bearison and Pacifici (1989), Goodman et al. (1995), and Merritt et al. (1994). As anticipated, the free recall reports of all children were sparse, with younger children reporting less information than older children, a finding compatible with previous research (Baker-Ward et al., 1993; Goodman & Reed, 1986; Ornstein et al., 1992; Saywitz et al., 1991), but children who experienced enhanced interview formats were able to communicate more completely and more consistently what had happened to them than were children who experienced the traditional verbal interviews (Goodman et al., 1995; Saywitz et al., 1991). While accuracy and completeness were influenced by both question format and props, not all cues were equally useful (DeLoache & Marzolf, 1995; Pipe, Gee, & Wilson, 1993), and accuracy varied according to the specific features of the event on which children were asked to report (Davies et al., 1989). In the discussion below, we focus initially on young children's responses to the investigative interview process. We then discuss the relative efficacy of the stimulus materials that were introduced in our enhanced interviews and the issue of repeated interviewing. Next we comment on the role of pain and distress in reporting. Finally, we note the role of child and family variables.

YOUNG CHILDREN AND THE INVESTIGATIVE INTERVIEW PROCESS

Do young children understand the purpose of the investigative interview? Coolbear (1992) found that none of the legal or human service professionals in his study would explain the reason for an investigative interview to a child. To parallel investigative interviewing strategies (Myers, 1992) and avoid unduly influencing the children with leading questions (Ceci & Bruck, 1993, 1995), our interviewers opened with a broad invitation to children to tell us, "What did you do today? What has happened to you?" During the initial interview, children had a hard time understanding just what it was that we wanted them to talk about, an observation also made by Fivush and Shukat (1995) when they offered no prompts or cues beyond general open-ended questions. Only 26.9% of the children began immediately to tell us about the medical visit. Many children began with details of breakfast and preparation for school, while a few children began their narrative even further back in time with descriptions of their bedtime rituals the night before. This strategy that young children employ of anchoring their responses in familiar, routine events has also been described by Fivush and Hammond (1990). A second prompt, "What else happened to you today?" brought another 10.8% on board. It was not until the third, very direct question, "Did you visit the doctor today?" that the majority of children understood what the topic of conversation was to be. In response to the direct question, seven children denied that they had visited the doctor, notwithstanding that the fact that they were still on the grounds of the medical center obviously contradicted their statements. When the interviewer pursued, asking them to describe who was with them etc., all children cooperated and eventually spoke about some features of their medical visit.

Walker (1993) asserts that legal interviewers rarely test whether a child understands their specific questions. We explored the role of developmental differences in the ease with which children began to relate their experiences of pediatric touch and handling. A post hoc analysis of language age scores (used originally as a screening tool prior to the interview) gave us a better understanding than did chronological age of the child's capacity to understand the purpose of the interview and to get on board quickly (Eiser, Eiser, & Lang, 1989). The average language age of those children who required a direct question before beginning to report the details of their pediatric visit was more than 1 year lower than the average language age of those who began to report after the first or second open-ended question (M's = 52.3 vs. 65.3 months, $t[127] = 5.62$, $p = .001$). This points to the advantage of brief developmental screening prior to or at the beginning of the interview to tailor the interview to the child's level of understanding (Boat & Everson, 1986, 1993; Keary & Fitzpatrick, 1994; Saywitz, Jaenicke, & Camparo, 1990).

At the 1-month follow-up interview, individual differences even among children with similar language and communication skills were apparent. Some children found the task of coping with our free recall format frustrating and fatiguing. Other children who had a lot to tell us skillfully wove their own agenda into the interview. For example, on a follow-up interview, one child began to rehearse his clinic visit by telling our interviewer, "I got something in my arm before when we talked. I got hurt on my knee. [What else happened to you?] Um. . . . The needle came out, and it hurt me a lot, and I started crying. [Did anything else happen before you saw me?] My brother caught a fish . . . my grandpa caught two, a blue gill." This child later anchored the fourth pain face with the experience, "I got cut right here with the thing that caught fishes." Another child on her 1-month follow-up interview explained that what she remembered was the first interview: "We was playing with the computer. . . . Um, we was talking about touching people in private places. [Who was talking about that?] . . . Me and you." We found that children's response styles were distinctive and stable from one interview to the next. For example, if they needed increasingly specific questions to get them "on board" regarding the topic for discussion in the initial interview, they did in the second as well ($r = .424$, $p < .001$); if they needed doll/ drawing-assisted direct questions in the first interview to elicit information about touch to body locations, they also needed it in the second and third interviews.

In order to understand the relative accuracy of young participant eyewitnesses, it is important to consider the specific features of the event (Christianson, 1992; Davies et al., 1989; Merritt et al., 1994), the question format (Ceci & Bruck, 1993, 1995; Fivush & Schwarzmueller, 1995; Howe et al., 1994; Poole & White, 1991), and the consistency of children's responses over time (Fivush, 1993; Fivush & Hammond, 1990; Fivush et al., 1991; Fivush & Shukat, 1995). Inspection of our data reveals that, if one were to construct a set of concentric circles, centered in the child's sensation and perception of body touch and emanating out to the four corners of the room, one would note that the accuracy of children's reports dropped circle to circle—from body touch (greater than 90%), to what the child was touched with (greater than 70%), to notice of other persons present (50%), to awareness of our video camera suspended from the ceiling in one corner of the room (less than 50%). These data reflect the dominance of central over peripheral events in the children's reports and parallel the findings of Cassel and Bjorklund (1995), Goodman and Reed (1986), and Howe et al. (1994).

Ornstein, Larus, and Clubb (1991) noted that it is a difficult task to interview young children well and that over time one needs to modify interview strategies and question formats in order to enable children to report what they remember (Baker-Ward et al., 1993; Ornstein et al., 1992). All four of the interview protocols in this study included free recall and specific and direct questions. In general, reports based on free recall were more accurate than those based on specific or direct yes/no questions, replicating findings by Dent (1982), Dent and Stephenson (1979), and Howe et al. (1994), and the drop in relative accuracy over time maintained the differences in accuracy among the three types of questions. In this study, inspection of individual direct questions revealed that, contrary to expectations, some direct questions were answered repeatedly at a high level of accuracy across the 6-month time span and that some were rarely or never answered at a rate better than chance.

We have selected from our data set three examples of the interplay of question content and question format that carry implications for the assessment of the accuracy of allegations of physical and sexual abuse. First, our children did not find touch to all body locations equally memorable even when asked directly about them, replicating the findings of Saywitz et al. (1991) that reporting of back touch was at a rate no higher than chance while reporting of genital touch was at high levels and accurate. This is not surprising, given that tactile qualities in various body locations differentially affect individual perceptual abilities for sensory discrimination (for a review, see Barnard & Brazelton, 1990) and that touch to various body locations carries different social and emotional values and taboos (Everson & Boat, 1994; Friedrich, Grambsch, Broughton, Kuiper, & Beilke, 1991; Jourard, 1966; Saywitz et al., 1991; Secord & Jourard, 1953). In our study, although some of the body touches had been forgotten by 6 months, the spontaneous reporting of genital touch remained at high levels and accurate. In response to the double-check, in which we pursued with doll/drawing-assisted direct questions children who had told us nothing about touch to five specific body locations, only the reporting rate for genital touch was above chance. The highly accurate reporting of genital touch at 6 months in response to both open and direct questions is an important finding, for there is often a striking time lag between sexually abusive incidents and investigative interviewing (Perry & Wrightsman, 1991; Sauzier, 1989; Sorenson & Snow, 1991).

Second, children's responses to our direct questions about touch to the head and mouth were at high levels and stable across the three interviews. Worlock, Stower, and Barbar (1986) reported that injuries to the head and neck are seen significantly more often following abuse than following accidental injuries. Head and facial injuries are typically seen in 17% of 1½–3-year-old children following accidents but in 60% when nonaccidental injury is suspected (Robertson, Barbar, & Hull, 1982). The head, neck, and face are highlighted in a graphic display used by the St. Louis police department for identifying the location of typical accidental as opposed to abusive injuries (Besharov, 1990). When children believe that they have been hurt, our data suggest that they are likely to report the incident. The combination of the physical symptoms and a child's accurate narrative report should provide a coherent and compelling presentation to the court (DeJong & Rose, 1991; Lipovsky et al., 1992).

Third, and in sharp contrast to the high reporting rate elicited by direct questions about genitalia, head, and mouth, children's erroneous responses to the direct questions about whether photographs had been taken or whether something had been put in their body raise our concern. The question about the camera was included as a control question because we anticipated that every child would get it right! Even in the first interview session, fewer than half the children understood not only that we had taken pictures of them in the doctor's office but also that their picture was being taken at the very moment they were being questioned. In fact, in the initial interview, only 6-year-olds reported reliably that pictures had been taken—an important issue especially for pornography investigations. Six months later, fewer than a third of the children remembered this accurately.

The children's essentially passive role in the filming (Baddeley, 1972; Saywitz, 1989) may have contributed to the high error rate. Goodman, Rudy, Bottoms, and Aman (1990) found that 72% of their 4-year-olds remembered that they had been lifted onto a table and had posed for several pictures in a playful sequence. In addition, the three groups of younger children may have been less likely than 6-year-olds to notice a videocamera or may have associated picture taking with instant cameras that produce an immediate product in light of the fact that Ornstein et al. (1992) reported that 90% of the 3-year-olds and 92% of the 6-year-olds in their study remembered a Polaroid picture being taken during a visit to their pediatrician's office.

In our study, the Child Protection Center Clinic had a very visible 35-mm camera mounted on a tripod that was utilized in the colposcope exam as well as the videocamera mounted on the wall for our study, yet, in response to a direct question, the reporting rates of neither the younger children

(32%) nor the older children (50%) seen in that clinic were reliably higher than chance. More flexible questioning might have clarified whether the critical variable contributing to such a high error rate for our children was semantics, type of camera, or the fact–to tap the imagery of concentric circles—that what was happening (or might happen) to their bodies was more salient than peripheral features of the clinic environment (Goodman, Hirschman, et al., 1991; Slackman, Hudson, & Fivush, 1986; Yuille & Tollstrup, 1992).

Because multiple interviews are the rule, not the exception, during the investigation and prosecution of child abuse allegations, one set of important findings from our study is the relation between the consistency and the accuracy of children's spontaneous reports of body touch. Conte et al. (1991) documented that reporting consistency is highly valued by professionals who work with abused children, although Terr (1983, 1990) has warned that consistent data are not necessarily accurate data. This is particularly true if coercive strategies or interviewer bias confounds and influences a child's narrative over time (Ceci & Bruck, 1993, 1995). A series of studies by Fivush and her colleagues (Fivush & Hammond, 1990; Fivush et al., 1991; Fivush & Shukat, 1995) reveals that the spontaneous reports of young children were quite inconsistent. Interviewed about personally salient but pleasant "special events that children greatly enjoyed," the children essentially reported different facets of their past experiences at each interview. In fact, the researchers found that 2–5-year-olds repeated on subsequent interviews only 10%–25% of the information they had given initially. They also found, however, that both the repeated information and the new information (e.g., both consistent and inconsistent data) were confirmed by parents as being highly accurate.

In our study, children's initial reports of body touch were highly accurate. In subsequent interviews, a discrepancy began to emerge in the accuracy of consistent and inconsistent reports. When the children in our study repeatedly reported body touch and handling, the information was more likely to be true than false. Like the children in the Fivush studies, our children told us new information during each of the subsequent interviews, but the more time that had passed since the pediatric visit, the less likely the new information was to be accurate. In fact, after 6 months, information repeated at each of the three interviews was 24 times more likely to be true than false, while there was little better than a fifty-fifty chance that the new information was true. The factors that contributed to accurately consistent responses make sense: older children and children who had access to the anatomical cues were able to report more consistently. In contrast, we were able to identify no factors that predicted consistent error; it was rare and idiosyncratic. Howe et al. (1994) found that young children's spontaneous and cued recall reports of central features of their experience as patients at a hospital emergency room continued to be highly accurate at 6 months, while the accuracy of their report of peripheral features dropped. In the case of child abuse, the core set of data is the report of body touch and handling. In sum, we believe that attorneys, judges, and juries should be more skeptical of new information reported late in the process but that they could rely on repeated information about body touch and handling as being both more accurate and more important.

STIMULUS MATERIALS IN THE ENHANCED INTERVIEWS

A young child's accurate but often brief narrative response rarely provides sufficient information for a forensic investigation (Saywitz & Snyder, 1993). Hulse-Trotter and Warren (1990) point out that young children often believe that adults already know the answer to the question they have just posed and that they therefore do not need to tell everything they have observed or know to be true about an event. We contrasted a traditional verbal interview to three interviews enhanced with stimulus cues in order to support children's memory and reporting. Did the enhanced interviews work? The answer is complex and varies, depending on which of the stimulus cues one is focusing on: anatomical cues, photographs, or medical props. Not all cues were equally effective.

Anatomically Detailed Materials

The spontaneous reports about body touch by children in the enhanced interviews with access to anatomically detailed materials were more complete at all three interviews than reports by children in the verbal interviews, and, after a 6-month delay, the anatomical cues enabled children to give more consistent reports as well. Since details offered in children's reports were sparse, the advantage for children in the enhanced interviews was the reporting of touch to one or two additional body locations. This becomes very important for investigative interviewing since anatomical cues were helpful especially in eliciting high rates of and accurate spontaneous reports of genital touch across 6 months, in contrast to the consistently low reporting rate for genital touch by children in the verbal interview. Goodman et al. (1995) also found a striking increase in reporting of genital touch when 3–10-year-old children, initially interviewed in a free recall condition, had access to dolls. In our study, no child with access to the dolls made a spontaneous commission error when reporting genital touch at the initial or the 1-month interview, and only one child did so at 6 months. However, the dolls did elicit spontaneous erroneous reports of anal touch at all three interviews. No child with access to the drawings made an erroneous report of anal touch, although the drawings elicited spontaneous erroneous reports of genital touch.

As anticipated (Katz et al., 1995; Saywitz et al., 1991), the direct question increased the reporting of genital touch in the initial interview and of genital and anal touch in the 1- and 6-month interviews. Commission errors in the reporting of genital and anal touch also increased as a result of direct questioning, but the majority of children who had not been touched were able to deny touch accurately, even when confronted with a doll/drawing-assisted direct question. It is important to note that, when our silent 3-year-olds were asked directly about genital touch, they went underground during the initial and 1-month interviews, making omission errors when asked directly. Never did the 3-year-olds in our study reach the 50% commission error rate found by Bruck, Ceci, Francoeur, and Renick (1995), but our interviewers did not ask leading questions or encourage children's use of props with the dolls. Although Poole and White (1991) noted that adults have a penchant for asking children direct questions, a conservative practice for investigative interviewers would be to give children access to the dolls or drawings as anatomical models and demonstration aids but not ask a doll/drawing-assisted direct question since previously abused children consistently reported genital touch spontaneously at a high rate with little or no increase in reporting when directly questioned. We believe that anatomically detailed materials help the child understand that the purpose of the interview is to discuss body touch and may function like a visual multiple-choice test—giving the child possibilities to consider and report or reject. Given the reticence of many children to use either the proper label or a nickname for genitalia, anatomically detailed materials give them the option of a silent, nonverbal response that may then open the way for further narrative (Jones & McQuiston, 1988; Leventhal et al., 1989).

We presented anatomical cues in three different formats: doll, drawing on paper, and drawing on computer. All three formats were effective in eliciting spontaneous reports of body touch. All formats could be used by boys and girls across the 3–6-year-old age range, although none were error free. In some communities, anatomical drawings, presented on paper or via computer graphics, may be judged less offensive than anatomically detailed dolls. The drawings leave no room for the chance that a nonabused but curious young child's exploration of the genital or anal openings will be misinterpreted (Ceci & Bruck, 1995; Koocher et al., 1994), and some older children may be more willing to use them (Saywitz et al., 1991; White, Strom, Santilli, & Halpin, 1986). However, children have more difficulty demonstrating vaginal and anal penetration or unusual sexual acts when they are working with the two-dimensional drawings than when dolls are available. In addition, interviewers may have more difficulty inquiring about such touch and penetration when working with the anatomical drawings. Another strategy might be to combine the use of anatomically detailed drawings with access to regular dolls. Goodman and Aman (1990) found that 5-year-olds reported more information

125

about an activity in which they had participated when they could demonstrate with dolls, whether or not the dolls had genitalia, than did children who were in the free recall condition. This suggests that ordinary dolls, which can provide a body outline and an orientation, can allow young children to demonstrate to investigative interviewers what has happened to them.

Photo Lineups

Photo displays of people and places offered a useful technique to supplement the limited descriptive skills of our young participants since very few, if any, of their verbal descriptions alone would have resulted in a definitive and accurate identification of a stranger or an unfamiliar location. Our children did offer descriptive details of the medical staff when prompted for specific descriptors, often using their own clothes and hair as referents or comparing the person to a parent, for example, "pockets like these," or "hair like mine," or "taller than my daddy." It was very helpful to have access to videotapes of the interviews when coding children's descriptions. One child reported that the doctor had a "moustache right here" while cupping her chin in her hand. The request for color offered other examples. One child pointed to her own red slacks and said, "Blue." When one coded the actual color of the referent and not the color word uttered, the report was accurate. Yet the information that children provided was rarely unique enough to guarantee identification in a university training hospital, where on any day at least 200–300 persons could fit the description, "He looked like a doctor with pens in his pocket." Davies et al. (1989) found sparse descriptive detail of a "health visitor" from school-age children, yet children as young as 6 years were able to use both a photo lineup and the "Photofit" technique (a face reconstruction kit) as ably as 10–12-year-olds and adults. It would be interesting to determine the feasibility of asking preschoolers to assemble the components of a face using "Photofit" as some children in our study did attend to specific details with considerable accuracy.

By monitoring the child's selection process, we were able to determine that the child who made "one and only one" choice of a photograph was likely to be accurate. One little girl offers an example of the relative usefulness of allowing children to select a photograph rather than providing only a verbal description. The child's verbal description of a medical staff person was "a ugly girl"—nearly identical to that of the child in the study by Hulse-Trotter and Warren (1990) who described the confederate employed in their study as "big and ugly." However, she correctly pointed to the picture of that medical staff person with one quick move. Indeed, some of our 3-year-olds were able efficiently and accurately to select the medical staff member who touched them, as did the 3-year-old abuse victim reported by Jones and Krugman (1986).

In retrospect, we might have used photograph cues more aggressively and more interactively to stimulate children's narrative descriptions had the photographs been introduced earlier in the interview session. For example, we wonder whether a child's memory would have been refreshed and whether the descriptions of persons and events offered would have been qualitatively different had pictures of the medical staff been available in the rogues' gallery from the beginning.

Goodman, Bottoms, Schwartz-Kenney, and Rudy (1991) have suggested that photo displays may be useful, not only for stranger identification, but even more so for identification of people whom children know. We agree. It is well documented that child abuse allegations frequently occur within intact, blended, and/or multigenerational families and that the perpetrator is therefore known to the child. The fact that a child knows a perpetrator does not necessarily mean that he or she can give a verbal description that is adequate for purposes of identification (Leippe et al., 1991).

Photographs could be used, not only during initial interviews, but also when a child serves as a witness in court. After reviewing court transcripts, Brennan and Brennan (1988) and Walker (1993) found that children do not always understand about whom an investigator or attorney is speaking when referring to the alleged perpetrator, even if they are familiar with that person. Questioning about a familiar person is usually put in terms of that person's personal relationship to the child or other family members. Saywitz (1990) has argued that children develop an understanding of kinship relationships and designations very slowly—often not mastering until age 10 the fact that "your mother's brother," "your grandma's son," and "your uncle" are one and the same person. So the differentiation, for example, between "big Daddy" and "Daddy Bill" or between multiple "uncles" may be accomplished more clearly with photographs. There needs to be a brief teaching session prior to using photograph identification, possibly using a photograph of the child as well as one of the investigator in an initial practice photo lineup. Davies (1993) suggests the introduction of the use of a "Mr. Nobody" as well so that a child can default out of any particular photo lineup if the alleged perpetrator is not represented therein. Given our experience with abusive families, we would strongly discourage the use of photographs of a child's mother or of any other family member in the practice set, for the child may need to identify that person subsequently as one of the perpetrators.

Props and Cues

There were two findings that deserve note with respect to children's use of the box of props when reporting their medical visit. First, props were used more accurately by older children, who actually had less need for them than did the younger children. Second, with repeated interviewing, the error rate with regard to reports of what a child was "touched with" escalated faster for children who were given props than for those who were not.

It may be that, when young children are asked to recall events that are familiar or scripted (Hudson & Nelson, 1986; Nelson, 1993; Nelson & Hudson, 1988), props detract from rather than enhance their ability to sort out the particular events from one specific time period. Miniature props have been found to be helpful to young children remembering novel events (Price & Goodman, 1990), and the actual objects were more helpful than verbal labels of the objects (Wilson & Pipe, 1989). Although we anticipated that, by selecting real, life-size equipment and objects as cues, we might avert the problems that young children have demonstrated with miniature or scale-model props (DeLoache, 1991; DeLoache et al., 1991; Price & Goodman, 1990; Salmon, Bidrose, & Pipe, in press; Saywitz et al., 1991), the error rate still increased over time. Pipe et al. (1993) and Smith et al. (1987) also found that repeated interviewing with cues increased the amount of information that children offered but depressed the accuracy of prompted recall.

In our study, the children who had access to props were as accurate, complete, and consistent in their reporting of body touch as children in the other enhanced interviews. Only in their reporting of what they were "touched with" was their accuracy significantly lower. There was no doubt that children enjoyed looking at and handling the props, and, during the first interview session, they demonstrated a good bit of appropriate medical play with such items as the blood pressure cuff and the stethoscope in the process of explaining their medical experience. However, in subsequent interviews, the feather and the curling iron proved to be much too fascinating, and the accuracy of the reports of what children were touched with fell abysmally.

Pipe et al. (1993) have suggested that props may be more useful if they can be seen but children are not allowed to handle them. It was our observation that, when children have the opportunity to manipulate props, they are likely to change the assigned task themselves from remembering the past to playing with a specific prop or demonstrating their knowledge of its use. The early laboratory study by Kobasigawa (1974) found that access to picture cues was not sufficient to enhance the recall of first or third graders. They needed a "directive cue" procedure that encouraged them to attend to and use the cues throughout the task. When they got that help, they did as well as fifth graders. It may be that the combination of the visual, but not tactile, availability of cues and the instruction to look at them as a memory aid would be a useful strategy to use with young children.

Pipe et al. (1993) noted that, unlike researchers, investigative interviewers will not know which items and objects are relevant to the events a child is being asked to recall. Davies (1991) suggested that, in abuse investigation, interviewers may be able to make available only "approximate cues" for children. The results of our study and others suggest caution in the use of props in investigative interviews. Our caution is based on the worry that the irrelevant items may mislead children and contaminate their reports by eliciting a playful response—random or thematic, depending on the child's developmental level.

The problem of just how to ask about "touch with" should not be dropped even though it is difficult. For example, in a 10-year follow-up study, Stein and Lewis (1992) found that questions about whether boys had ever been hit with specific objects (e.g., belt buckles, whips, extension cords) or punished in particular ways elicited reports of physical abuse from boys who had previously denied or minimized abuse by family members. The authors also found that being provided with a list of objects enabled their participants to reveal having been assaulted with objects that were not on the list.

In retrospect, a photo display of props might have been a useful antidote to the deterioration of children's accuracy in relating what they were touched with. Jones et al. (1988) found that, for 3-year-olds, object cues (including the original and two distractor items) aided same-day and 1-week but not 8-week recognition; however, photographs of the objects continued to be useful. In investigative interviews, a photo array of possible items might be less likely to stimulate irrelevant play than real items, which in our study seemed to pull a child off track.

One distinctive feature of the enhanced interviews in our study is that they took longer to complete than the verbal interviews. In a study of children's memory of a schoolyard sniper event, Pynoos and Nader (1989) observed that directing the children to go over an event "in slow motion" enabled them to fill in gaps, sequence events correctly, add details, and elaborate on their emotional responses. Haugaard, Reppucci, Laird, and Nauful (1991) found differences in the ability of seven interviewers to elicit information from children justifying their responses about a videotaped event that they had watched. The most effective interviewer was observed to employ a "patient but persistent nonthreatening" style of questioning that allowed a child 1 or 2 min more time to "search for the justification in her own mind" and to report relatively complex beliefs. Review of the videotapes in our study shows that it took extra time for the interviewer and the child to handle the materials in the enhanced interviews. The advantage of the enhanced interviews may lie both in the role the appropriately selected stimulus materials play in providing retrieval cues to aid children's memory and in the slowing down of the interview process. MacFarlane and Krebs (1986) remind us that competent, sensitive assessment takes time and that, when we encourage children to disclose abuse, we must take into consideration their own sense of timing.

In summary, we believe that selected stimulus materials can be used ef-

fectively in investigative interviews with young children to enhance the retrieval of memories and support the reporting of experiences—with the caveat that the materials be used conservatively, that is, to clarify spontaneous
narrative, to stimulate memories of people and actions, and to slow down the
pacing of the interview.

REPORTS OF PAINFUL AND DISTRESSING EVENTS

In a recent review of laboratory and real-life research on emotional stress
and eyewitness memory, Christianson (1992) asserted that the relation between negative emotional events and eyewitness reporting is not a simple,
unidimensional matter related to the intensity or degree of emotional
arousal. He identified complex interactions among the type of event, the cen-
trality of the information reported, and the timing of interview and retrieval
conditions. Stein and her colleagues (Stein, Trabasso, & Liwag, 1992; Stein,
Wade, & Liwag, in press) have focused on the cognitive and situational complexity of emotional experiences in which an individual interprets events on
the basis of prior knowledge and weighs the possibilities for goal attainment.
While there is no doubt that intensity of affect may make an experience more
distinctive and more personally salient (Easterbrook, 1959; Howe et al., 1994;
Slackman et al., 1986), there is no easy one-to-one correspondence between
an event and a specific emotion. In addition, comparable medical procedures
can be experienced as more or less painful depending on the physical and
psychosocial settings (Blount, Davis, Powers, & Roberts, 1991; Neisser, 1978).
Two major contributions of our research have been the demonstration of the
role of children's own estimates of pain and emotional distress in increasing
the prediction of both the accuracy and the amount of information that children report about past events and the documentation that, for a small group
of children, the task of coping with their own emotional reaction to a painful
medical procedure interrupted their ability or willingness to report their experience.

Christianson (1992) found empirical support for preferential initial sensory processing of emotionally laden events and later conceptual review and
elaboration in his review of laboratory and field research on the relation between emotional stress and eyewitness memory. Stein et al. (in press) note
that, because emotionally laden events have personal consequences, they
draw notice, require attention, and often provoke rumination. In our study,
we asked children, not only to judge the relative painfulness of touch, but
also to rate how they felt about the clinic experience, a task that Stein et al.
(in press) found that the majority of children can do.

When we compared the feeling ratings of the children in the High Pain
group (47 children who reported at least one body touch as being very pain-

ful) to the feeling ratings of the other children in the study across three interviews spanning 6 months, there were no differences in the two groups' ratings of four positive emotions—happy, safe, relaxed, and surprised—possibly reflecting the desire of parents and health care professionals that a child's clinic visit be a reasonably pleasant experience and their effective communication of the idea that whatever painful medical procedure a child experienced was "for your own good." But, in the initial interview, children who reported high pain rated themselves as significantly more sad, angry, and scared than their counterparts. In addition, High Pain children reported a significantly stronger endorsement of sleepy, one of a very limited number of ways in which a young child in a medical setting can escape a body in pain (Altshuler & Ruble, 1989).

At the 1-month follow-up interview, children in the High Pain group continued to report that they were significantly sadder, more scared, and more angry. At 6 months, children in the High Pain group were more angry, sadder, and more scared. Thus, not only did the children in the High Pain group believe that they had been hurt physically, but they also reported that they continued to feel badly about it. Although repeated measurement increases the possibility of chance rather than reliable, replicable findings, by chance one would anticipate that a difference in positive feelings would have surfaced, and it would be unlikely that the trilogy of negative feelings would be selected all three times. It is important to note that the children in this High Pain group did not differ from the other children on variables that might explain their differences: age, medical experience, health status, or number of invasive medical procedures they experienced. However, the High Pain group did receive an average of two more body touches by medical staff than did the other children, and thus they experienced an event that was more complex as well as more painful.

We submit that both their personal appraisal of the event and their feelings about it maintained the review (possibly rumination, as Stein et al., in press, suggest) that bolstered subsequent reporting, whereas, over time, the other children simply forgot. This interpretation is also supported by Peterson et al. (1993), who found that even small increases in children's fear, guilt, fatigue, or hunger were associated with more frequent recall of injury. As for the children who did not experience painful touch, we believe that their less complete reporting of body touch was a result of what Brainerd (1985) has called a memory storage problem, not a memory retrieval problem. This may alert us to the underreporting of young children who have been victims of sexual fondling, an experience that may be innocuous enough that the child does not even select it for storage. In the case of fondling, as in the case of benign pediatric touch, the young child may not be sufficiently attentive or interested to tuck the information away in the first place.

Several research teams have documented children's high rate of reporting and highly accurate reporting of painful touch to specific body locations—for example, back touch following spinal taps (Bearison & Pacifici, 1989) and genital touch following VCUG (Goodman et al., 1995; Merritt et al., 1994). We examined, post hoc, whether children's judgments of pain played a role in the consistently high reporting rate of pediatric genital touch by previously abused children. We found that the pediatric genital touch was not judged to be more painful by the abused children than by the nonabused children who also reported genital touch ($t[41] = .348$, $p > .10$). In a recent study (Steward et al., 1995), we verified that abused children are alert to potential pain. Child patients at our Child Protection Center recommended that we prepare other child patients for the colposcope exam by telling them, "The doctor was very gentle; it didn't hurt." Terr (1991) suggested that children who have experienced repeated trauma develop a greater sensitivity or hyperalertness that is meant to protect them from potentially traumatic encounters. Thus, the striking contrast for the abused children in the current study between the anticipated painful pediatric touch and the actual benign touch may have made the experience memorable for them.

We had originally planned to create another pain scale using an underlying dimension such as relative tissue damage (McGrath, 1991) to recalibrate children's descriptive anchoring of their most severe pain experiences and then recode and reanalyze the pain data. However, we came to appreciate that to do so would have vitiated the unique importance of pain as experienced by the children themselves. Pain is an individual experience, and the integrity of children's own calibrations served well as a predictor of both the completeness and the accuracy of their responses. The child who anchored the extreme pain face with the experience of catching a fishhook in his finger was able to calibrate his clinic vaccination as less painful. Beyer et al. (1991) found that one cannot estimate a child's pain by the procedure involved alone. In our study, children gave the highest pain rating to experiences ranging from a simple blood stick to a complex bone marrow aspiration, and they often judged that the most painful site was related, not to the location of the needle entry, but to the physical restraint involved. Although both shots and blood draws were seen by our skilled medical colleagues as straightforward and accompanied by only brief pain, these procedures are high on children's list of medical fears (Broome & Hellier, 1987). For some young children, the anticipation of a "needle" may have contributed to the judgment of how painful a procedure was (Eland & Anderson, 1977).

While children's judgments of pain contributed to the predictions of both completeness and accuracy, adult eyewitness estimates of child trauma should be viewed with caution and skepticism. This is especially true if the witness is the individual responsible for administering or causing the distress—as was the case with medical staff in our study and in Ornstein et al.

(1992), and as is the case with the perpetrator in child abuse cases. Our results replicate both the low correlations found when children's reports of their own actions and feelings with regard to accidental injury at home were compared to the "objective" reports of their parents when both were questioned about the children's injuries (Peterson et al., 1993) and the independence of children's ratings from those of their parents and teachers in other behavioral realms (Achenbach, McConaughy, & Howell, 1987).

CHILD AND FAMILY VARIABLES

A recent review of the epidemiological literature by Finkelhor (1993) reveals that there are no identifiable personal, demographic, or family characteristics of a child that may be used to exclude the possibility that a child has been sexually abused, and we find none that should automatically exclude a child's testimony from being carefully attended to. Data from our study were analyzed to compare the responses of children grouped traditionally according to gender and age. There were no significant differences between boys and girls in reporting accuracy, completeness, or consistency. Ours is the first study to demonstrate that boys could use the anatomically detailed materials and photographs as well as the girls could, and we found that the boys had a slight edge over the girls in the effective use of props. These findings are particularly important since Finkelhor and Baron (1986) report that boys are underrepresented in clinical samples, possibly because of their greater reluctance to disclose abusive events.

Many research teams have identified the relative vulnerability of the 2½–3-year-old in short-term memory studies (e.g., Baker-Ward et al., 1993; DeLoache & Marzolf, 1995; Goodman & Aman, 1990; Ornstein et al., 1992). Fivush and her colleagues (Fivush, 1994; Fivush & Hammond, 1990; Fivush & Shukat, 1995) have found very young children highly accurate but inconsistent because they are more dependent than older children on the interviewer's questions when attempting to access past experiences. We, too, found the reports of 3-year-olds less complete and less consistent than those of the older children, but they were rarely less accurate. Also, inspection of some discrepancies in the 3-year-olds' responses across the 6-month longitudinal study revealed normal developmental mastery rather than error. Preschool children are not "on hold" cognitively or linguistically during longitudinal research studies (or while the wheels of the legal, social service, or health care systems grind slowly on). Bjorklund (1987) has identified the critical role of age-related changes in the knowledge base that affects memory. The accessibility that an individual child has to specific information, the effort that he or she is required to expend in order to activate the relation among sets of information, and the ability to use retrieval strategies deliberately all change with age.

An example of age-appropriate shift in language from our study was the child who on the initial interview reported that the doctor had "green" hair but pointed accurately to the interviewer's black hair when asked to point to something in the room that was green. One month later, the same child offered the correct color label. During the same monthlong interval, another child shifted from the general, childish description "a ugly man" to the role description "my doctor." One final example of a response shift that we believe to be a result of normal development comes from the group of 3-year-olds who at the initial and the 1-month interviews made errors of omission rather than report genital touch. At 6 months, these children were able accurately to assert that touch, a response bringing them into line with the older children. As noted above, language age did make a difference in helping children get into the flow of the interview. One further developmental difference deserves note. When younger children had access to the box of props, their play was less sophisticated and thematic than was that of older children. Our findings support the recent trend in the legal community allowing the young child to report without setting arbitrary age criteria and urging the fact finder to listen to the child without age prejudice (Melton et al., 1987).

None of the demographic or family variables influenced the accuracy or consistency of children's reports, while only mother's education enhanced completeness for young children in the verbal interview. We were somewhat surprised that family stress neither enhanced nor exacerbated reporting (Long & Jackson, 1991). A more sensitive measure of family functioning, as opposed to a stressful life events checklist, and a broader range of family and caretaking units might have revealed the link that we believe to be there. There are also undoubtedly great individual differences in how children cope with dysfunction in their families—some may retreat into their own world to protect themselves from chaos; others may become hypervigilant after repeated trauma, as Terr (1991) suggests. We would anticipate that the quality and quantity of the reporting of children employing the former strategy would be compromised when contrasted with the quality and quantity of the reporting of children employing the latter.

Kessen (1960) has argued that, while the work of developmental psychology goes on within the hypothesis-testing, probability-estimate world, nothing is more compelling than the single case study to inform our understanding of complex realities or help us make appropriate responses to complex circumstances. Our legal colleagues demonstrate an appreciation of Kessen's point, for they build case law one case at a time. We want to highlight the responses of two young children in our study that invite special consideration.

First, one 4-year-old boy required care by either our clinic or hospital staff nearly half the time between the 1- and the 6-month interviews. His situation affected the study statistically and clinically. Statistically, he was identified as an "outlier" because of his extreme scores on the intervening visits variable. When we removed his data from the statistical analysis, we found no influence of intervening visits to the medical center on children's recall. However, his data, which influenced the significant negative correlation between intervening visits and accuracy of recall, are important, for they remind us that, when a child must deal with extreme conditions, these experiences do in fact impinge on cognitive and emotional processes.

In order to understand the negative relation between intervening visits and later recall, not only the content of the visits but also just how many visits are too many needs to be clarified. We suspect that there are both redundancies and great individual differences in the set of experiences offered on return visits, both of which make it difficult for the child to keep everything straight. The reporting of our "outlier" child, initially 100% accurate, deteriorated over time. Nelson (1988) would note that his increasing inaccuracies were a result of "slot-filler errors" reflecting a general script of a medical visit accurately but not the specific details of the visit we videotaped. Scripted or confused reports in child abuse cases may result from multiple experiences of victimization (Terr, 1991). We do not yet know how many experiences of abuse contribute to a merging or loss of detail in children's reports.

Second, we reviewed the videotape of the clinic visit of a 5-year-old boy in our study, the only child who persisted in falsely reporting three times that the pediatrician touched his penis. This child appeared frightened and protested vigorously during his physical exam when the doctor attempted to check him. In fact, he was so agitated that the doctor did not touch him, later writing in the medical record, "Genitalia not examined, patient refused." Three times during the clinic visit his mother accused the child of setting a fire, and she angrily followed him into the interview room—leaving only after several requests by the interviewer. In reviewing the tape, we were struck with the fact that the mother did not seem to be aware of the child's distress in response to the attempted genital exam. The medical record further noted that he was a child with multiple minor health problems and several fears and that he came from a chaotic home environment.

We report these cases to remind the reader and ourselves that children do not enter our research studies as blank slates. Whether we study children in laboratory or in field settings, our schedule of data collection establishes arbitrary beginning and ending points, while in reality the children we study are in the midst of complex feelings and experiences about which we may know little. For the investigative interviewer, another message is clear. The first case shows that, even when the initial interview presents highly accurate information, over time other forces may intervene that interrupt access to the original experience. By 6 months, this child's scripted report of a medical visit was compelling, but inaccurate. The second case speaks to the need for a multidisciplinary approach to the eliciting of information from a child. Communication between the pediatrician and the interviewer might have resulted in sending the pediatrician to pursue gently but persistently the child who refused examination. In addition, the investigator might be sent to speak with the child's mother, siblings, and other family members to seek corroboration of his allegations (Myers, 1994). This child may well have been accurate in reporting genital touch but fearful of the consequences of disclosing the identity of the perpetrator, so he erred by naming our pediatrician (Bussey, Lee, & Grimbeek, 1993).

VII. CHILD AND INTERVIEWER BEHAVIORS IN DRAWING AND COMPUTER-ASSISTED INTERVIEWS

David S. Steward, Lisa Farquhar, Joseph Driskill,
and Margaret S. Steward

Ross and Ross (1984b) have urged researchers investigating childhood pain to consider the importance of the type of question, psychological climate, and subject set when interviewing children. They believe that children should feel free to take as long as they want to answer a question or to come back to it later if they wish. Silences must be handled carefully, giving the children ample time to sort out their ideas. Feelings of disapproval should not be expressed by the interviewer. Subject set is assisted when the child is viewed as expert and can feel confident that he can function effectively during the interview. Research (e.g., Brainerd & Ornstein, 1991; Ceci, 1991; Johnson & Foley, 1984; Perry & Wrightsman, 1991) supports attention to the way in which investigative interviews are conducted with children. Although question type was held constant in our comparison of the drawing and computer-assisted interviews, we were eager to test how the presence of a computer might affect the interview climate and subject set. Specifically, the task was to document the character of the interviews and to determine whether there were significant variations in child and interviewer affect, relationship, behavior, or task management between the two interview formats.

METHOD

Participants

The behaviors of 24 child-interviewer dyads, 12 from the drawing interviews and 12 from the computer-assisted interviews, were analyzed by coding videotapes of the first interview. The participants were selected from a list that ordered the total pool of 130 children sequentially as they were enrolled

137

in the study. Sampling occurred so that gender and age groups were equally represented (i.e., three younger and three older boys and three younger and three older girls) from each type of interview.

The tapes were prepared by recording a signal every 15 sec on one of the two audio channels of the videotapes. Four different event samples, each 3 min long, were selected for coding from the complete interview: (1) the first 3 min of the interview, to observe the establishment of the interviewer-child relationship; (2) the naming of body parts, to observe the interaction of the child and the interviewer with graphic materials; (3) the report of body touch; and (4) the final 3 min of the interview, when fatigue could be expected. Each of the four segments included data from 12 15-sec units. This yielded a 2 × 4 (interview type by repeated measures) ANOVA across the four segments of the interview.

Coding

Two persons, David Steward and Joseph Driskill, served as coders. After piloting on an independent set of interview tapes, one-third of the tapes were coded by both persons. The remainder were coded by Joseph Driskill. Initially, each tape was reviewed in order to code a child on general behavioral style, defined for this study by rating on a five-point scale the intensity of seven characteristics of child temperament: activity level, distractibility, mood, intensity, task orientation, adaptability, and persistence. Then the videotapes were reviewed four more times in order to code in 15-sec units the following sets of behaviors for the child and the interviewer: (1) observed affect; (2) relational stance of the child toward the interviewer and of the interviewer toward the child; (3) the child's response style to task demands and the interviewer's performance of task and boundary management; and (4) the child's and the interviewer's behaviors with regard to proximity to one another and to the materials and with regard to posture. In all, 40 variables were coded. Many behaviors occurred too infrequently in the event samples to permit meaningful reliability to be calculated. Using a cutoff score of 85% agreement, adequate reliability was established on the 25 variables reported below.

RESULTS

Emotional Climate of the Interviews

The emotional climate of the interviews was dominantly neutral and remarkably stable for both the child and the interviewer (M's = 11.7 and 11.9). Children demonstrated more positive affect than did interviewers (M's = 1.1

and 0.3), while negative affect was rarely observed in either the child or the interviewer (M's = 0.4 and 0.3). The children were very responsive to the task (M = 10.43), initiating little verbal or behavioral distraction (M's = 0.44, 0.76). Interviewers provided encouragement to the children a little more than half the time (M = 7.4); disconfirmation was rare (M = 0.1).

Character and Pattern of the Interviews

In the first segment, the child in the drawing interview was seated in a chair with a lap board. Questions were presented verbally. The child in the computer-assisted interview was seated in front of the screen. He or she could see the interviewer's question prompts at the top of the screen and could see his or her own verbal responses being typed into the computer by the interviewer. In the remaining three segments, the graphic materials used in the drawing and computer-assisted interviews were identical. The child in the drawing interview was given the material on standard 8½ × 11-inch paper and recorded his or her judgments using a pencil. The child in the computer-assisted interview saw the same graphics on the computer screen and used the mouse to make a response.

The child looked at the interviewer approximately 75% of the time during the first segment, but a repeated-measures analysis demonstrated that looking at the interviewer dropped sharply after the first segment (M's = 9.2, 5.8, 6.0, and 5.6, respectively, $F[1, 22] = 10.853$, $p < .001$). Initial resistance on the part of the child lowered significantly over time ($F[3, 66] = 5.816$, $p = .001$). The child's interest in the task dropped across the time segments (M's = 11.7, 11.9, 11.6, and 11.2, respectively, $F[3, 66] = 2.911$, $p < .05$), although the child was still engaged 92% of the time in the final segment of the interview.

Children in both interviews looked at other objects in the room more during the first segment than during any of the remaining three segments ($F[1, 22] = 2.812$, $p < .05$). The distance between the interviewer and the child increased between segments 1 and 2 and again between segments 3 and 4 ($F[1, 22] = 6.541$, $p = .001$).

Differences between Drawing and Computer-assisted Interviews

The focus of the child's attention (the interviewer, the material, or the child's own self) was coded for each time unit. The child in the computer-assisted interview focused significantly more on the materials ($F[1, 22] = 89.980$, $p < .001$) and significantly less on the interviewer ($F[1, 22] = 38.251$, $p < .001$) than did the child in the drawing interview. There was a trend in both the first and the final segments for the child in the drawing interview to focus more attention on his or her own self than did the child in the computer-assisted interview ($F[1, 22] = 3.399, p < .10$).

There was no significant difference in the overall amount of time involved in the manipulation of materials. The child in the drawing interview began to manipulate materials in the second segment; the child in the computer-assisted interview began to touch the screen in the first segment and to manipulate the mouse in the third. This pattern was revealed by a significant repeated-measures effect ($F[3, 66] = 35.566, p < .001$) and an interview by repeated-measures interaction ($F[3, 66] = 3.804, p = .01$).

The child in the computer-assisted interview looked less frequently at the interviewer ($F = 19.231, p < .001$). The interviewer's behavior paralleled the child's, with a trend for the interviewer to look less often at the child in the computer-assisted interview ($F[1, 22] = 3.857, p < .10$). An interaction between type of interview and repeated measures demonstrated that the interviewer looked at the child less during the first and the third segments of the computer interview ($F[3, 66] = 3.588, p < .05$). In these segments, the interviewer joined the child in looking at the screen. The child in the computer-assisted interview became significantly less responsive to the interviewer than did the child in the drawing interview, especially during the third segment, when he or she was in charge of the mouse ($F[3, 66] = 3.063, p < .05$).

The child in the computer-assisted interview looked at the interview material more than the child in the drawing interview did ($F[1, 22] = 27.183, p < .001$). Repeated-measures analysis revealed that this was especially true in the first and fourth segments of the interviews ($F[3, 66] = 55.764, p < .001$). The child in the computer-assisted interview looked at other objects in the room less than the child in the drawing interview ($F[1, 22] = 8.662, p < .01$) and manipulated other objects in the room less ($F[1, 22] = 10.078, p < .01$). This difference was particularly striking in the first segment: whereas children in the computer-assisted interview looked at and touched the computer, children in the drawing interview were more likely to be focused on noninterview materials since they did not yet have graphic materials in hand ($F[3, 66] = 2.710, p = .05$).

Interviewers were coded on the animation they displayed in their relationship with the child. Given a coding option of "warm, animated toward the child," "open, receptive toward the child," or "cold, controlled, formal toward the child," interviewers were rated to be significantly more open toward the children in the drawing interviews ($F[1, 22] = 9.332, p < .01$) and significantly more warm toward the children in the computer-assisted interviews ($F[1, 22] = 5.598, p < .05$). The category "cold" was never observed.

A significant interaction between interview type and repeated measures showed that the interviewer was engaged more with the child in the first segment of the drawing interview than with the child in the computer-assisted interview ($F[3, 66] = 4.796$, $p < .01$). The engagement of the interviewer with the child dropped slightly over time with the child in the drawing interview and rose slightly with the child in the computer-assisted interview ($F[3, 66] = 2.300$, $p < .10$). The interviewer interrupted the flow of the interview significantly more in the first segment when working with the computer-assisted interview than when working with the drawing interview ($F[3, 66] = 2.737$, $p = .05$).

No differences were found in child's touch of interviewer, physical proximity to the interviewer, or movement toward or away from the interviewer. However, the interviewer touched the child in the computer-assisted interview more ($F[1, 22] = 5.944$, $p < .05$). This was true especially after the trackball was introduced in segments 3 and 4. The interviewer moved away from the child less in the computer-assisted interview ($F[1, 22] = 5.343$, $p < .05$). The differential movement away from the child may have been a function of the interviewer's need to present and withdraw the graphic materials for the child in the drawing interview and to record the child's responses.

DISCUSSION

The computer-assisted interview met several of the recommendations made by Ross and Ross (1984b): children controlled the pacing of the interview, they were more clearly in the expert role as they were responsible for handling the computer trackball, and they were less likely to be influenced by the interviewer since they were less closely connected interpersonally. Children seem to be captivated by the computer, by the opportunity to control the trackball, and by seeing their verbal responses being typed on the computer screen. One child leapt out of his chair as he saw his own name being spelled out on the screen: "Wow!" he said, "That's me!" An additional advantage was that the child was less likely to be distracted by other things in the room.

The computer-assisted interview may have changed the child-interviewer interaction. It may have given the child a greater sense of privacy, at the same time giving the interviewer a sense of the child's withdrawal from the interaction. Several writers caution that an investigator's reaction to a child's disclosure of abuse may be communicated to the child. The horror that a sensitive interviewer often feels, and does not mask, may cause the child later to falsely retract (Goldstein, 1987; Haugaard & Reppucci, 1988; Jones & McQuiston, 1988). The interruption of interpersonal communication offered by the computer-assisted interview may also serve to mute the potential misuse of authority by the adult, who may, in the urgency to uncover the truth, inappropriately employ personal power to pressure a child for an answer.

The relative privacy that young children experienced in the computer-assisted interview may have more pronounced effects on reporting when older children are interviewed. For older children and adolescents, social prohibitions against discussing sexual topics with strangers are more clearly understood (Goldman & Goldman, 1982, 1988). Saywitz et al. (1991) found that, unless asked directly about it, the 7-year-old girls in their study were less likely to reveal the genital touch of a physical examination than were the 5-year-old girls. The authors proposed either that information may have been deliberately edited out of the older girls' reports or that emotional blocking may have rendered some information temporarily unavailable.

Computerized interviewing is preferred in health care settings and is being used effectively to elicit sensitive information from adolescents. Using computers, Paperny, Aono, Lehman, Hammar, and Risser (1990) studied adolescents' reporting of high-risk health behaviors. They asked 3,327 adolescents in an outpatient clinic to document their preference for providing information about sensitive health-risk behaviors. Just 5% chose to report health-related information via a questionnaire, 6% chose a personal interview, and 89% preferred the computer-assisted interview. Only 1 in 40 adolescents refused to share the clinician's portion of the computer printout with the clinician. Millstein and Irwin (1983) found that 33 older adolescent girls readily reported sensitive information about their sexual behaviors on a computer terminal. A considerably larger number of participants denied having sexual intercourse in a face-to-face interview. When interviews with pregnant women were computer assisted, participants reported more risky behaviors such as smoking and drug use than when they were interviewed face to face (Lapham, Kring, & Skipper, 1991).

In our study, the computer-assisted interview was superior to the drawing interview on the rating of interviewer warmth. An emotionally supportive environment is superior to an intimidating one when children are being interviewed (Dent, 1977; Hill & Hill, 1987; Perry & Wrightsman, 1991), especially when difficult topics are being discussed (Ross & Ross, 1984b), and lessens children's suggestibility (Goodman et al., 1990). However, we would like to offer a counterintuitive interpretation of the relative "warmth" of the interviewers in the computer-assisted interview that comes from their informal comments. The clinical, therapeutic training of our interviewers allowed them to sense the distance between themselves and the children introduced by the computer, and they interpreted it as a signal to increase their positive interaction with the children.

Computer-assisted interviews promote the quality of data gathered in two ways. First, the computer helps less experienced interviewers sustain the interest and energy of the children they interview, and it helps keep the child cooperative and attentive to the interview materials. However, the computer does not replace the interviewer. Further research is needed to establish the prerequisite training and experience for interviewers conducting either face-to-face or computer-assisted interviews with young children.

Second, the computer helps the interviewer collect a complete set of data. In our study of children's reports of body touch, some data were lost. This occurred when our interviewers appropriately "followed" a child's lead during an interview but failed to return to complete our questions. One particularly vexing example was the failure to "double-check" key body touches that had not been spontaneously reported by a child during the initial free recall portion of the interview. This occurred in the doll and drawing interviews but not in the computer-assisted interview, for visual and auditory reminders were built into each section of the interview. While the computer-assisted interview format generally enabled interviewers to collect a more complete data set, we experienced two problems with the process: a computer "crash" during the pretesting phase due to a computer virus and an occasional printer malfunction. These are both technical problems that can be solved.

There are several research questions that might be asked with respect to computer-assisted investigative interviewing. Might the computer-assisted interview offer an advantage over a straight clinical interview for school-aged children? Is it necessary or useful for school-aged children to be left alone initially with the computer—as the studies conducted with adolescents and young adults have done—or can the same amount of information be elicited with the interviewer present? Finally, might the computer-assisted interview be useful for interviewing alleged perpetrators as well as alleged victims?

VIII. NONDISCLOSURE OF PAIN BY YOUNG CHILDREN FOLLOWING INVASIVE MEDICAL PROCEDURES

Julia Morgan and Margaret S. Steward

INTRODUCTION

At the initial, 1-, and 6-month interviews, children's pain ratings were positively correlated with the completeness of their spontaneous reports of body touch. In addition, the number of invasive medical procedures that the child experienced during the clinic visit was positively correlated with the accuracy of his or her reports of body touch. Clearly, most young children can accurately encode and vividly recall and describe painful and invasive procedures. However, there were 20 young children in the initial interview who did not report pain following invasive procedures rated by medical personnel as painful. This study examined the possible influence of three factors on the disclosure or nondisclosure of pain in subsequent interviews: differential pain thresholds, adult communications during the procedure, and behavioral indices of shame/embarrassment.

Child Distress as a Measure of Pain Threshold

One possible reason for disclosure or nondisclosure of necessary but painful medical procedures could be that the children experiencing similar procedures had different pain thresholds or tolerances for pain. Pain is unique to the individual and cannot be directly assessed by any physiological marker (McGrath, 1991; Ross & Ross, 1988). However, at least one way to estimate a child's experience of pain is to observe what the child does in the face of probably painful procedures. Fortunately, in this study, because we have videotapes of children during the clinic visit, it was possible to assess

Portions of this research were submitted by Julia Morgan in partial fulfillment of the requirements for a Ph.D. degree at the Professional School of Psychology, San Francisco.

behavioral responses to medical procedures. Jay (1988) has noted that children's behaviors such as crying, screaming, and physical resistance or flailing do not necessarily distinguish between anticipatory fear and actual pain and may encompass both these dimensions. That is quite acceptable from our perspective since in this study we are interested in the complex set of negative feelings that physical pain evokes.

We believe that there are two reasons why measuring the behavioral distress exhibited during a medical procedure will be an especially effective technique for estimating differential pain thresholds. First, during the preschool years, children have not yet learned to suppress their behavioral response to pain (Gunnar, Marvinney, Isensee, & Fisch, 1989). Second, the behavioral strategies of coping with unavoidable pain that children use at this developmental stage often rely on physical attempts to avoid or escape (Altshuler & Ruble, 1989). While cognitive or emotion-focused coping is difficult for most young children (Dahlquist et al., 1989), during the preschool years some children may begin to suppress the report of the magnitude of distress (Jacobsen et al., 1990; Jay et al., 1983; Katz et al., 1980). Given our interest in disclosure patterns of physically and sexually abused children, discrepancies between children's distress behaviors and subsequent self-reports of pain in this study may be instructive.

The Influence of Adult Behaviors on Subsequent Child Report

The influence of adults (family members and medical personnel) on the young child's experience of painful medical procedures has been explored in the research, with mixed findings. For example, although children generally prefer to have one or both parents present during the medical procedure (Gonzalez et al., 1989; Ross & Ross, 1984a), parents' behaviors and communications may not always promote adaptive coping (Blount et al., 1989; Blount, Sturges, & Powers, 1990; Broome & Endsley, 1989; Bush et al., 1989; Jacobsen et al., 1990; Jay, 1988; Jay et al., 1983). In general, parents' anxiety, criticism, and excessive reassurances tend to augment children's distress during medical procedures, while active assistance with coping strategies, distracting talk, and even humor serve to reduce distress. Because interactions with parents and other adults have been shown to influence children's distress during painful medical procedures, these adult behaviors might be directly or indirectly related to children's subsequent appraisals of their painful experience and to their ability or willingness to disclose pain.

Role of Shame/Embarrassment on Subsequent Child Report

According to Lewis (1990, 1991, 1992), the self-conscious emotions of shame and embarrassment are related to internalized standards, rules, and goals against which a child evaluates his or her actions. In the context of painful and distressing medical procedures, young children may experience shame related to any of several factors: the belief that a painful procedure or illness is a form of punishment for some transgression; failure to comply with parents' injunctions against overt expressions of distress (crying, screaming, etc.); direct criticism or negative evaluation of the child by a parent or another adult; and the child's own experience of physical exposure, powerlessness, or helplessness in a distressing or traumatic situation. Nathanson (1989) has suggested that the withholding of emotional expression represents a defense against feelings of shame. The potential role of shame or embarrassment remains unexplored in the literature on children's disclosure of painful medical experiences, but it may be that children's nondisclosure of pain following invasive medical procedures reflects feelings of shame and defenses against experiencing or acknowledging those feelings.

METHOD

Participants

There were 20 children in the initial interview who did not report pain following invasive medical procedures rated by medical personnel as being at least somewhat painful. Of these, 12 children (eight boys and four girls) in the "no reported pain" group who experienced procedures involving needles (spinal tap, bone marrow aspiration, venipuncture, shots, and blood sticks) were selected for study; the remainder experienced ear examinations with an otoscope and were not studied further. A control group of 12 children who did report pain was obtained from the original subject pool. Control children were matched for gender, age, and specific procedure. The participants ranged in age from 37 to 77 months. The mean age for the "no reported pain" group was 58 months, and the mean age for the "reported pain" group was 59 months.

Ten pairs of children were matched identically on procedures. For two pairs of children, there was a near match with parallel but not identical procedures. For one pair, a venipuncture was matched with a blood stick that required drawing four tubes of the child's blood. As in the venipuncture, this type of blood stick is a blood draw in which the child watches as several tubes of his or her blood are drawn. For the other pair, a bone marrow aspiration was matched with a spinal tap. Both the bone marrow aspiration and the spinal tap procedures involve needles in the back and the child being held so that he or she cannot observe the physician or the procedure.

The number of children who experienced each type of procedure is as follows: three pairs of children experienced a spinal tap or bone marrow aspiration, five pairs experie.1ced a venipuncture or blood stick that required drawing several tubes of blood, three pairs experienced shots, and one pair experienced blood sticks requiring a few drops of blood for a screen for anemia. No child from either group was undergoing a medical procedure that was the focus of this study for the first time.

Data were extracted from the original study to explore other factors that may have influenced a child's disclosure or nondisclosure of pain. The two groups of children did not differ significantly on mother's education, family income, the child's previous medical experience, and family life stress scores.

Measures

Three measures were used to code child and adult behaviors from the videotapes of each child's clinic visit and subsequent interview.

Child Distress

The Observational Scale of Behavioral Distress–Revised (OSBD-R; Jay & Elliott, 1986) was used to code child behaviors during the invasive medical procedures. The OSBD-R was designed to observe and code the distress behaviors of children undergoing bone marrow aspiration and spinal taps; it includes nonverbal as well as verbal behavioral manifestations of distress. Steward, Steward, Joye, and Reinhart (1991) have utilized this instrument for studying children's responses to other invasive medical procedures.

The OSBD-R has eight categories of child behaviors that are weighted to reflect the severity of distress. Child behaviors are recorded in continuous 15-sec intervals. The OSBD-R behavioral categories and their respective intensity weights are as follows: Information Seeking (1.5), Cry (2.5), Scream (4.0), Need for Physical Restraint (4.0), Verbal Resistance (2.5), Requests Emotional Support (2.0), Verbal Pain (3.0), and Flail (4.0). The category scores are added together to render a total distress score. Reliability and validity for the OSBD-R have been established in previous studies (Elliott et al., 1987; Jay & Elliott, 1986; Jay et al., 1983).

Adult Behaviors

The Child-Adult Medical Procedure Interaction Scale (CAMPIS; Blount et al., 1989) and the Child-Adult Medical Procedure Interaction Scale–Revised (CAMPIS-R; Blount et al., 1990) were designed to assess the relation between adult behaviors and coping by children during medical procedures. The CAMPIS includes 35 behavior codes, 16 for children's behaviors and 19 for adults'; however, in the present study, only the adult codes were utilized.

The behaviors of parents and staff are considered together as "adult" rather than being analyzed separately. In the CAMPIS-R, the adult codes obtained from the CAMPIS are clustered into three categories of adult behavior. They include adult vocalizations, which are determined to be either Coping Promoting, Distress Promoting, or Adult Neutral. The CAMPIS-R renders proportions for each of these categories of behavior. Blount et al. (1990) proposed the use of proportions because they are not dependent on the length of the sessions, the total number of vocalizations, or the rate of vocalizations. This was particularly important for this study because the different types of procedures involved varied in length. Reliability and validity for the CAMPIS and the CAMPIS-R have been established in previous studies (Blount et al., 1989; Blount et al., 1991; Blount et al., 1990).

Shame/Embarrassment

The shame/embarrassment behavioral indication procedure was based on a theoretically derived measure devised by Lewis, Sullivan, Stanger, and Weiss (1989) to identify the self-conscious emotion of embarrassment. The procedure identifies a sequence of three linked behaviors: (1) a smiling facial expression, followed by (2) gaze aversion and (3) the movement of the hands to touch the hair, clothing, the face, or other body parts. These behavioral criteria were used to code that part of the interview tape where the child was asked to report the body touch associated with his or her invasive medical procedure and pain. All three behaviors were required for a child to be scored as having shown embarrassment or shame.

Procedure

Phases of the Medical Procedure

For purposes of coding both the OSBD-R and the CAMPIS-R, all medical procedure sessions were divided into three phases. The first phase, the *anticipatory phase,* included 3 min before the child received a physical sensory cue of the procedure. Some of the children had less than 3 min in this phase. The onset of the second phase, the *procedural phase,* was determined by the physical sensory cue to the child that the procedure was about to occur. Since all the procedures involved the insertion of a needle, and since the area where the needle was to be inserted was always swabbed before insertion, the swabbing of the area was determined to be the sensory cue. This phase ended when the needle was withdrawn (or when the nurse stopped squeezing the child's finger for the blood stick). The procedural phase was quite short for children receiving shots. The duration of the third phase, the *postprocedural phase,* was the 1½ min following the second phase. Two children had less than 1½ min in this phase because they quickly left the room or someone turned off the video equipment.

Coding

The researcher and a psychology graduate student coded each child's medical procedure and subsequent interview. Interrater reliability of the coding judgments for the three measures was assessed for all data. The videotapes had been prepared for the original study by recording a signal every 15 sec on one of the two audio channels.

For the OSBD-R, each child studied was coded by noting the occurrence of any of the eight behaviors within each 15-sec interval. To obtain the OSBD-R scores, the frequencies of each behavior were multiplied by the intensity weights and then divided by the total number of 15-sec intervals within a phase. The weighted scores for the three phases were added together to render a total distress score for each child. Interrater reliability was calculated on all observations. The interrater agreement on the occurrence of behaviors was calculated using the formula for percentage agreement and was found to be quite high. The mean interrater reliability was 96%, with a range of 87%–98% across behaviors.

For the coding of the CAMPIS/CAMPIS-R, verbatim transcripts were constructed from the videotapes of each child's clinic visit. Because videotaping was done in several pediatric outpatient clinics in a university medical center setting, there were often medical students and several other health professionals present for procedures as well as the child's family members. All the adult vocalizations were coded. Transcripts were coded independently by the raters. The 19 CAMPIS adult codes were then transferred to the three adult behavior categories Distress Promoting, Coping Promoting, and Adult Neutral. Proportions for each of these categories were tabulated for each of the participants by dividing the total number of each of these behavioral categories by the total number of adult behaviors. Interrater reliabilities for the proportions of the three adult behavior categories were 95% for Distress Promoting, 96% for Coping Promoting, and 99% for Adult Neutral.

The interview tapes were viewed at the point when the child was asked to report the touch associated with the invasive medical procedure that he or she experienced and the resulting pain. It was determined that the three behaviors indicating shame or embarrassment would have to occur within 5 sec of the interviewer's inquiry about the invasive procedure experienced by the child. The most difficult behavior to discern on the videotapes was the child's facial expression because a fixed camera angle was used and sometimes the child's or an adult's movement blocked the view. Unless the raters

149

were sure that a smile occurred, it was not scored. Interrater reliability for the occurrence of shame or embarrassment was 100%.

RESULTS

A paired-comparisons t test revealed no significant differences in the amount of distress shown by the two groups of children as measured by the OSBD-R total weighted scores. Nor were significant differences found for the behavior of adults present with the two groups of children during the procedure as measured by Distress Promoting, Coping Promoting, or Adult Neutral behaviors.

A chi square analysis with Yates correction for continuity of the children's behavioral indications of shame or embarrassment revealed that none of the children who reported pain showed the three behaviors necessary to score shame while eight (67.7%) of the children who did not report pain showed all the shame behaviors ($\chi_c^2[1] = 9.187$, $p < .002$).

DISCUSSION

The nondisclosure of pain by children in this study cannot be attributed merely to an absence of pain since most of these children exhibited a significant amount of behavioral distress during the invasive procedures that had also previously been rated as painful by our medical staff. Adults present during the procedure did not differ in how they talked with the two groups of children according to the analysis of the proportions of Distress Promoting or Coping Promoting vocalizations. The small sample size may have precluded detection on the adult behavior variables of significant differences between the children who did not and those who did report pain. It is also possible that other aspects of adult influence were not tapped into by the measurement tools utilized in this study. Not all communication is verbal, for example, and it might be worth going back to the videotapes at a later date to determine whether the adults may have influenced children differentially in more subtle, nonverbal ways during the procedures. Parents' differential influence on their children may be mediated through personality variables that contribute to the quality of parent-child interaction. For example, Goodman and Quas (in press) employ attachment theory to suggest that anxious ambivalent parents may become preoccupied during a stressful event, resulting in their children experiencing higher stress, while children with avoidant parents may try to repress or deny their feelings when recounting features of a stressful event. Further research that joins personality assessments of parents with behavioral studies is needed to test this prediction.

The behavioral measure of shame/embarrassment was the only factor in this study that was found significantly to differentiate the two groups of children. None of the children who spontaneously reported their pain showed all three of the behaviors indicating shame or embarrassment. In fact, five of the children demonstrated none of the targeted behaviors, while the remaining seven demonstrated only one of the three behaviors employed to define shame. By contrast, all the children who did not report pain demonstrated at least one of the three behaviors, nine demonstrated two of the behaviors, and eight of twelve (68%) showed all three behaviors. It was the children in this latter group who could not or would not disclose their painful experience.

Unfortunately, this study did not yield any data suggesting *why* shame/embarrassment might differentially influence the disclosure or nondisclosure of pain. The nondisclosing children may have felt especially embarrassed by their behavior during a procedure and did not want to rehearse or reveal that experience. Many children from the larger study who did report pain did so with the caveat that, although a body touch had hurt, they had not cried. The sense of powerlessness and helplessness felt during a procedure may have left a child with a feeling of shame, much like victims of abuse (Nathanson, 1989). The prospect of exposing this helplessness to a stranger may have been more than a child could handle, and thus the denial of pain in the subsequent interview might be interpreted as a coping strategy on the part of a child—negating the experience.

A child's feelings of embarrassment or shame may also have interfered with access to information about his or her pain experience in the interview (Saywitz & Snyder, 1993). Informally, it was noted that the children who did not report pain were able to describe the persons present and the setting accurately, which suggests that they had at least a partial memory of the event. What they left out was the emotionally charged experience of their pain. The emotional blocking of the memory of part of the child's experience may reflect another form of coping, as suggested by Saywitz et al. (1991) and Terr (1991).

Ultimately, the key to understanding what differentiates nondisclosing from disclosing children may lie in factors relating to the child's socialization experiences within the family, including attachment history, communication patterns, and disciplinary practices. The child's gradual internalization of these experiences may affect the painful experience in ways that cannot be readily observed during the procedure itself, although it may in fact be the most significant influence on the child's experience and expression of pain (Lewis, 1992).

One child's experience was striking in both the intensity of his behavioral distress and his subsequent nondisclosure of pain. His mother exhibited a great deal of distress herself as she observed her child's distress during a bone

marrow aspiration. As her child was restrained and screamed his verbal protest and pain, she repeatedly cried out to the child, "We love you . . . you
just don't know how much we love you," throughout the procedure. It is
impossible to know how this child perceived his mother's proclamations. It
is possible that he was confused by the verbalizations of love intermingling
with his experience of pain. A young child's cognitive capacity for understanding the medical need for painful procedures is limited (Steward & Steward, 1981). The child at the preoperational level often perceives pain or illness as deserved punishment (Brewster, 1982). This child's experience was
also affected by his mother's obvious distress (Bush et al., 1989; Goodman &
Quas, in press). He may have felt responsible for her distress. How this child
internalized his pain experience is uncertain, but he is one of the children
who did not disclose pain, despite having the highest behavioral distress score
in the study.

This case underscores the need to relate interaction dynamics during
medical procedures to the overall history and quality of the parent-child relationship. It seems likely that how parents organize their caretaking behavior
around a distressing or traumatic event reflects important aspects of the
parent-child attachment history. The mother's behavior may in this case reflect a maladaptive, albeit unintentional, response that may in turn reflect a
pattern of role reversal in the parent-child history.

Finally, this study, as well as the larger study from which the data were
obtained, calls attention to the importance of children's self-report data. The
literature suggests that self-report measures are generally unreliable for children under the age of 7, and multiple measures of children's distress have
been proposed because of discrepancies between behavioral measures and
children's self-reports. However, while the question of reliability is germane
to the issue of accuracy in the details of an event or experience, the inclusion
of multiple measures is important in this case for a very different reason. The
finding of discrepancies between behavioral measures and children's self-
report in this case provided valuable clues that an internal process was at
work for these children. Thus, self-report data are important not only for
what the child tells us but also for what the child does not tell us. In this
case, rather than contradicting the child's report, the discrepancies led to the
important suggestion that, for some children, shame/embarrassment may be
a significant dynamic in the experience of invasive medical procedures. The
Panel on Research on Child Abuse and Neglect from the National Research
Council (1993) has identified the need for more research specifically on patterns of disclosure. We believe that one fruitful avenue is further research to
explore the factors that may differentiate children experiencing shame from
those who do not.

IX. RECOMMENDATIONS, LIMITATIONS, NEXT STEPS

In this chapter, we distill a set of seven recommendations for investigative interviewers who work with young children. We reflect on limitations that confront our work and identify a series of next steps in research.

RECOMMENDATIONS FOR INVESTIGATIVE INTERVIEWING OF YOUNG CHILDREN

We believe that there is no perfect interview protocol and that, even if one were to be created, a good interviewer should abandon the protocol in an instant to follow a child's narrative explanation. However, guidelines can be helpful, especially for interview protocols that are sensitive to the developmental needs of young children (Keary & Fitzpatrick, 1994; Ornstein et al., 1991). Several of our colleagues have offered perspectives and excellent suggestions (Berliner & Conte, 1990; Boat & Everson, 1993; Faller, 1990; Garbarino, Stott, et al., 1989; Goodman & Bottoms, 1993; Lamb, Sternberg, & Esplin, 1994; Perry & Wrightsman, 1991; Pynoos & Eth, 1986; Sas, 1991; Saywitz & Snyder, 1993; Steward, Bussey, Goodman, & Saywitz, 1993; White & Quinn, 1988; Yuille, 1988). Our research team has a set of seven recommendations for interviewing young children to offer frontline investigators, recommendations based on our experience with the 3–6-year-olds who participated in the current study.

1. Interview young children as soon as possible after an alleged event. The children in our study gave the most information and the most accurate information about their experiences during the initial interview.

2. Clarify the child's understanding of the purpose of the interview, asking, for example, "Who told you about our talk today?" or, "Do you know what we are going to talk about?" Some of the children in our study seemed to tire before we began because it took them so long to figure out the topic of discussion.

3. Employ open-ended questions to elicit a child's narrative first. Ask

direct questions to fill in the blanks, followed by another open-ended question. Seek corroboration from the child for every descriptive adjective he or she introduces. The children in our study answered both general and direct questions accurately and sometimes knew more than their first words would imply.

4. Elicit and attend to the child's appraisal of his or her experience of pain and distress. Note that the child's judgment may differ from that of the alleged perpetrator and from adult caretakers in the child's world. The children's assessment of pain was critically important in our study for predicting both the amount of information reported and the accuracy of children's reports of body touch and handling.

5. Have available and use judiciously the following: photographs to enhance the child's ability to identify other people, regular dolls to permit demonstration of actions, anatomically detailed body outlines or dolls to elicit children's unique names of body parts and to demonstrate location of body touch, and, finally, a pain scale and an emotion word list to assess the child's relative distress with respect to touch and handling. If anatomical cues are to be used, we strongly recommend familiarity with the guidelines of the American Professional Society on the Abuse of Children (Everson, Myers, & White, 1995). We discourage children's free access to a random assortment of toys and props.

6. Pretest a child and, if necessary, demonstrate and teach to acceptable criteria the use of materials that require choice or judgment (e.g., photographs) using neutral content (e.g., nonfamily members) before introducing critical material to the child (e.g., family members or close family friends).

7. Employ highly trained interviewers who are both skilled in communicating with young children and knowledgeable about the informational needs of law enforcement and child protection officials. When interviews are videotaped, it is relatively easy to spot poor interviewing techniques, inappropriate use of stimulus materials, or blatantly suggestive and coercive strategies. Peer review and responsible monitoring by law enforcement officials and the courts should result in poor interviewers being retrained or reassigned.

LIMITATIONS OF THE STUDY

The scope of this study was limited by the composition of the research team, the questions that focused our design decisions, and the children whom we interviewed. We share the limitations of all social science and developmental researchers that the application of group findings to an individual child is problematic. We share the limitations of other researchers seeking to balance professional ethics with the need to increase the ecological validity of our work for the legal system by conducting naturally occurring field studies of distressing events (Goodman et al., 1990; Merritt et al., 1994; Peters, 1991; Yuille & Wells, 1991). We consider it both a strength and a limitation that all the children in the study did not experience exactly the same events. Because child abuse takes many forms, we opted for a broader range of events, videotape and medical record documentation of those events, and the use of the child as his or her own control to test the efficacy of different interview strategies in enhancing the accuracy, completeness, and consistency of children's reports. It is possible that some of the children experienced events that were unique, more psychologically compelling, or, quite simply, more memorable than others. On the basis of our clinical experience in pediatric outpatient and inpatient settings, we chose to identify and assess those features common across all pediatric events that children find most distressing. While we feel comfortable generalizing from these findings to the design and conduct of investigative interviews, direct applications to the courtroom need to be made cautiously. Like our colleagues in autobiographical research, we did not badger the children, repeatedly question them after they had given a response, or challenge their reports by cross-examination (Brennan & Brennan, 1988; Fivush, 1993; Poole & White, 1991, 1995; Walker, 1993).

There are a number of interesting questions that could be explored that would yield information useful to investigative interviewers and to the court. Does the gender of the interviewer make a difference? Does a mix of different types of interview strategies yield more information? While we paired young children only with same-sex interviewers and with the same interviewer and interview protocol over time, one could design a study that systematically varied sex of child, sex of interviewer, and protocol. We did not include a control group or stagger the timing of children's interviews, yet there are legitimate questions to ask about how to minimize forgetting and memory distortion given the unpredictable temporal progression of abuse cases through the court system (Gray, 1993; McGough, 1994; Poole & White, 1995). Because the children in our study were followed for only 6 months, we cannot predict how accurate, complete, or consistent children's reports would be were a group to be followed longer (Usher & Neisser, 1993). Again, that information would be useful to the courts.

There continues to be considerable controversy over when and how to use anatomically detailed cues to elicit children's reports of genital touch (Ceci & Bruck, 1995; Everson, Myers, & White, 1995; Koocher et al., 1994). Our research protocols assessed only two uses of anatomically detailed cues by investigative interviewers: as a model to establish the child's body vocabulary with special interest in unique names for genitalia and as a demonstration aid to enhance spontaneous and doll-assisted direct questioning about genital touch (Everson & Boat, 1994; Jones & McQuiston, 1988; Kendall-Tackett & Watson, 1991; Sivan, 1987; White et al., 1987). We cannot speak to the issue of the reliability of children's responses when they have access to the dolls in free play as a comforter, an icebreaker, or a diagnostic screen (Kenyon-Jump, Burnette, & Robertson, 1991).

Our study may offer a low estimate of children's person identification skills in the real world because of the limitations that the research design and research budget put on our interviewers. The 1- and 6-month interviews were not typical forensic follow-up interviews since the interviewers did not build their questions on the findings of the initial interview but rather began each interview anew. In addition, our interviewers did not have available to them a team of investigative colleagues who might have pursued siblings or parents for corroboration or clarification, for example, to determine whether the father of the child who reported the doctor to be "taller than my daddy" is 5 feet, 7 inches or 6 feet, 4 inches tall. Nor did they call the children back the next day to fill in the gaps or resolve discrepancies in children's descriptive reports, for example, "You said there were two people, 'the big doctor and the lady who cut me,' and you told me what the doctor was wearing. Can you tell me more about the lady who cut you?"

Finally, it should be repeated that, although our children could not effectively refuse the experiences of body touch and handling by our medical staff, none of the staff approached the children for their own sexual pleasure or demanded that the children keep the experience a secret (Bussey, Lee, & Grimbeek, 1993).

NEXT STEPS IN RESEARCH

There has been a recent decision by the Appellate Court of New Jersey (*New Jersey v. Michaels,* 1994) to revisit a 115-count conviction of a teacher accused of child abuse in a day-care setting (*New Jersey v. Michaels,* 1993), a decision based in part on the "suggestive and coercive" pretrial questioning of child witnesses. This decision is a loud and clear announcement to those who work in the field of child abuse that the interviewer and the interview protocol are under extreme scrutiny. Continued research on interviewing is critical. It is also important to continue to build a research database that documents the reporting competencies of children who are participant eyewitnesses and to disseminate that information broadly because, as Goodman, Golding, and Haith (1984) and Leippe and Romancyzk (1987) documented, adults' conclusions about children's accuracy are linked to adults' judgments about the general credibility of child testimony. Reflecting on our own field research reported above, we believe that three issues merit further research: (1) the use of computer-assisted protocols in investigative interviews, (2) the refinement of measures of children's distress, and (3) the commitment to longitudinal research in natural settings where children may be highly stressed.

Computer-assisted Interviewing

In our study, the computer-assisted interview (1) focused the child's attention on the computer screen and therefore away from the interviewer, (2) presented a broad range of computer graphics, (3) allowed the child's verbal and nonverbal reports to be recorded, (4) gave the child some control through manipulation of the trackball in demonstrating touch, and (5) permitted the collection of data with as much quantity, texture, and accuracy as the other supported interviews, data that were more complete than those gathered in a traditional verbal interview. These results suggest that the computer-assisted interview might be useful for law enforcement and social welfare personnel who are assigned to conduct initial interviews with allegedly abused children on the front line. The computer's interruption of the personal interaction between child and interviewer may be a serendipitous finding—especially keeping in mind our interest in the analogue between these interviews and child abuse interviewing. In traditional interviews conducted with children who are alleged victims of abuse, the very presence of the interviewer—a stranger, usually a man, often in uniform, sometimes carrying a firearm or a stick—can be intimidating enough to silence the child.

There is a controversy in the field right now about the design of investigative interview protocols: some researchers advocate highly structured interviews (Raskin & Esplin, 1991; Skinner & Berry, 1993); other research teams recommend the incorporation of specific strategies, such as cognitive techniques (Geiselman, Saywitz, & Bornstein, 1993) and the use of graphic cues (Saywitz & Snyder, 1993); while others are satisfied with an *aide memoire* or a checklist (Jones & McQuiston, 1988). A computer-assisted interview could be programmed to serve a broad range of professionals and protocol "styles." Training of new investigative interviewers and in-service updating of experienced interviewers could also be presented via computer-assisted protocols (Boat & Everson, in press).

A police officer told us recently that, when he interviews a child who is an alleged victim of abuse, he does not need to ask a lot of questions, but he does need to ask *all the critical questions*. Even experienced investigators do not always use optimal or productive interviewing strategies (Geiselman et al., 1993). In our study, the computer-assisted interview was as effective as the other two enhanced interviews, and we found a clear advantage for the computer-assisted interview—very little data loss—because there were auditory and visual reminders programmed in the software to cue the interviewer that answers had not yet been recorded to certain critical questions. As researchers, we could grumble and pull the child with missing data out of a specific analysis, but the investigative interviewer with missing data would have had to set up another interview, further stressing both the interviewer and the child and further delaying the investigation and subsequent proceedings (Goodman et al., 1992; Tedesco & Schnell, 1987).

In our own state of California, there has been a recommendation by the California Child Victim Witness Judicial Advisory Committee (1988) to develop interagency protocols for interviewing child witnesses. According to the committee's final report, "These protocols should establish procedures to a) limit the number of interviewers, b) minimize the number of interviews, and c) ensure that comprehensive interviews are conducted by qualified interviewers" (p. 106). We anticipate that our experience with computer-assisted interviews in this research project may be useful as interagency protocols evolve, not only in California, but across the country (McGough, 1994; Myers, 1994). An important next step is to determine the potential use of computer-assisted interviewing with targeted populations such as allegedly abused school-aged children and adolescents, for the average age of the child abuse victim is 7–8 years (Gray, 1993; Putnam & Trickett, 1993). We are especially interested in the potential use of computer-assisted interviews with boys who have been victimized, as clinicians (Everstine & Everstine, 1989) and demographers (Finkelhor, 1993) continue to note their low disclosure rate. Finally, the success of several research teams (Lapham et al., 1991; Millstein & Irwin, 1983; Paperny et al., 1990) in eliciting information about high-risk behaviors from adolescents and young adults with computerized interviewing techniques suggests that research be conducted with alleged perpetrators to determine whether more detailed and complete confessions can be elicited thereby.

Refinement of Measures of a Child's Distress

The discrepancy that Mandler (1990) noted between recall and reporting—and particularly the potential of negative and self-evaluative emotions to widen that discrepancy—needs further attention. Research could be targeted toward self-report measures, physiological measures, and parents' judgments of children's distress.

Some of the conflicting results in the current literature relative to the role of stress in memory may be a result of the measurement of self-report, specifically the selection of instruments that children have been offered (Bruck, Ceci, Francoeur, & Barr, 1995; Goodman, Hirschman, et al., 1991; Merritt et al., 1994; Oates & Shrimpton, 1991). Although the stimuli from the Face Scale (Bieri et al., 1990) are not pleasing to look at, we urge other investigators to consider its use, given children's preference for using face scales (Wong & Baker, 1988). The features critical to the portrayal of negative emotion were originally drawn by children, and the instrument is psychometrically sophisticated. For the current study, we selected only four of the seven faces (faces 1, 3, 5, and 7) to use with very young children. We recommend the use of the full range of seven faces with children 6 years and older. There are other options to be found in the pediatric literature that offer a broader range of positive faces, but they all feature a crying child anchoring the extreme negative position (McGrath, 1987). Time and again in this study, even when choosing the extreme face, both boys and girls indicated that it hurt that much, "but I didn't cry" (even when they actually did). We are convinced that an extreme pain face option that includes tears will truncate some children's pain estimates.

There is an interesting but limited set of data on parents' judgments of children's distress (Goodman, Bottoms, et al., 1991; Ornstein et al., 1992; Peters, 1987) that suggests that parents' judgments should be incorporated into new models of distress and memory. In these studies, while the correlations between parents' judgments of children's distress and their children's later recall of the distressing events are significant, they are disappointingly few and low. It may be that, as researchers, we are asking parents the right questions but at the wrong time. We may not be maximizing the information that parents could provide by tapping their judgment of their child's distress only at the time of the distressing event—when their own emotions may be clouding their judgment (Blount et al., 1991; Bush et al., 1989).

In both laboratory studies and many natural settings, parents—unlike researchers—have access to their children before and after the distressing event. Howe et al. (1994) elicited parents' judgments of their children's distress twice: at the time of accidental injury and during the subsequent visit to a hospital emergency room for treatment. Unfortunately, they reported only the composite score of the parents' two estimates. This masked the significance of the memory performance of highly distressed children. New research by Goodman and Quas (in press) documents the usefulness of collecting parents' estimates of children's continuing distress after an event is over. We suggest gathering data from parents about four different time periods: the period prior to a stressful event, to record the child's anticipatory anxiety; the point immediately after the event, to document the child's unrehearsed response; the short term after the event, to document spontaneous poststimulus elaboration; and the long term after the event, to document rehearsal/review of the event. (See the rich descriptive detail recorded by Robertson, 1956, who spent 6 months documenting her daughter's coping strategies before and after a stressful 3-day hospitalization.) Our own (Steward, O'Connor, Acredolo, & Steward, 1996) pilot work with adolescent survivors of childhood cancer suggests that, although many parents believe that their children have forgotten stressful events, adolescents continue to remember vividly the distress of previous cancer treatment.

Finally, Peters (1987) suggested that physiological measures of children's distress may offer another line of investigation into the interaction of distress and memory, and we agree. There is strong support for the position that hormonal functions may mirror personal distress well (Chrousos & Gold, 1991; Gold, 1987). Gunnar et al. (1989) have chosen to work with cortisol, a steroid hormone secreted by the adrenal cortex. Working with a group of children coping with repeated necessary medical procedures, they have documented increases in cortisol as the children's overt behavioral manifestations of distress decrease from toddlerhood to the elementary school years. Their data suggest that, although older children may manifest fewer overt signs of distress, they may still be experiencing high rates of stress. One set of unanswered questions that merits research attention involves assessing children's conscious experience when they manifest high cortisol levels. Are they aware of changes in how they think and feel as cortisol rises and then falls to base rate—and do those thoughts and feelings give us clues to the variables that may influence cognitive and memory processes?

A second set of questions has to do with the differential influence of high cortisol in response to acute and chronically stressful conditions. Merritt et al. (1994) found high cortisol levels specifically related to 3–7-year-old children's experience of a very painful VCUG procedure, but there was no relation between the cortisol levels and either other measures of distress or the children's subsequent memory of the events. Yet chronic elevations of cortisol have been associated with neuronal loss in areas of the brain associated with memory storage (Sapolsky, Krey, & McEwen, 1985). Biochemical documentation of distress is very appealing, although, on the basis of our own preliminary work, we would caution that data collection and analysis are expensive; Putnam and Trickett (1993) estimate charges of $2,000 per subject. In addition, participants and their families must be highly cooperative if researchers are to complete the multiple assessments they need in order to develop an adequate base rate and rule out irrelevant perturbations.

Longitudinal Research in Natural Settings

Christianson (1992) noted the importance of field studies in identifying variables for further empirical investigation. Neisser (1988) asserted that a person is always nested in an environment that contributes to and extends the complexity of the phenomena to be studied. We believe that our study of children's visits to pediatric clinics expands the understanding of the effect of stress on young children's memory by following longitudinally children who experienced a very broad range of body touch and handling and displayed a wider range of emotional responses than could be found in a laboratory situation (Ceci & Bronfenbrenner, 1991). For example, it would be difficult to design prospectively in the laboratory a study of children who experience highly distressing events but fail to report them. In this study, we were able to identify a small but unique group of children who went "underground" with respect to their reports of a painful medical procedure. It should be noted, however, that it was possible to identify these children and their nearly matched control peers only after 2 years of videotaping and interviewing in the clinics and another 2 years of coding and analyzing the clinic and interview data. Yet the analysis of the experiences of this small group of children will add to the literature on self-evaluative emotions and should alert clinicians to be aware of the role and expression of shame as an important feature that might be observed during interviews with allegedly abused youngsters who fail to disclose abuse.

Nevertheless, the children from our study and those of Merritt et al. (1994) and Goodman, Quas, Batterman-Faunce, Riddlesberger, and Kuhn (1994) all need to be followed for longer periods of time because the careful documentation of children's experiences and multiple estimates of distress provides an invaluable database to use in evaluating both theoretical and practical issues related to long-term memory and forgetting. Janoff-Bulman (1992) documented the process of long-term reappraisal, especially of the causal role of the self, in adults following catastrophic experiences; but there are no parallel data for children. Williams (1993) offered retrospective judgments from adolescent and adult survivors, abused as children, that the cognitive variable of the perceived severity of the abuse accounted for the traumatic effect of the experience. Longitudinal follow-up of the children recently studied could identify developmental transformations of highly charged emotional events and further validate or possibly challenge adult survivors' reports.

Children experience stress not only in pediatric medical settings. Peterson et al. (1993) have shown that, even in the context of everyday injury, children are building a world of judgment—judgment that differs from that of their mothers—about how to cope cognitively and emotionally with the distress caused by their own bodily pain and about when to care for themselves and when to call for help. Researchers who have studied children following natural disasters such as floods (Durkin, Khan, Davidson, Zaman, & Stein, 1993) and hurricanes (Garrison, Weinrich, Hardin, Weinrich, & Wang, 1993) have identified dynamics useful in understanding children's responses to emotionally charged events. Paralleling laboratory methods even more closely, Kiser et al. (1993) reported the effect of anticipated stress by comparing measures of children's health and mental health taken before and after, not an actual disaster, but an anticipated and heavily publicized earthquake that never happened. Pynoos and his colleagues (Pynoos & Eth, 1986; Pynoos & Nader, 1989) have pioneered the study of interviewing extremely distressed children who have witnessed violence in the school or the home: the two settings in which children most often find themselves. But it has been difficult to compile results from such disparate settings. Recently, Fletcher (1994) proposed rating 26 dimensions that characterize stressful events so that researchers can profile and then contrast and compare findings from comparable cross-situational data sets. The ecological framing of research questions about memory and affect that places the child's experience within the context of the family and community holds great promise.

SUMMARY

In summary, we believe that our data speak descriptively and strongly to both the capacities and the limitations of young children, verifying that young children actively and accurately process their experiences and that the quality and quantity of their experiences affect their decisions about what to report. We join Leippe, Mannion, and Romancyzk (1993) in recommending that the courts issue pretrial instructions to jurors, contrary to current instructions, that urge them to guard against using their preconceptions to judge any witness, child or adult. We trust that the research findings reported in this *Monograph* will contribute to the development of more effective interviewing techniques to be used with young children. Better interviews may shorten investigation time, which may allow charges to be filed earlier and court proceedings to move ahead more rapidly, thereby lessening the secondary trauma for the individual child (Goodman et al., 1992; Jauders & Martone, 1992; Myers, 1994; Runyan et al., 1988). It is very difficult to interview young children well, and their reports are rarely seamlessly smooth. Yet it is worth the effort, for, as Flin, Bull, Boon, and Knox (1992) remind us, to elicit accurate and complete data from children never threatens the rights of an individual wrongly accused.

INITIAL VERBAL INTERVIEW

Introduction

Read the following instructions as appropriate:

1. "Hi! Remember when we talked before? I showed you some pictures and told you we were doing a Children's Memory Study. Now, I'm going to ask you a few more questions to see how much you can tell me about what you remember. When we're all done, I'll give you a snack and something to take home with you."

2. "What happened to you today?" *Or, if child fails to respond:* "What did you do today?"

3. *If child does not mention the physical examination, ask the following:* "What else happened to you today?" *Or, if child fails to respond:* "What else did you do today?"

4. *If child still does not mention the physical examination, ask the following:* "Did you visit the doctor's office today?"

Open-ended and Specific Verbal Prompts

Person[7]

1. *If not yet mentioned:* "Was anybody in the doctor's office with you?" *If child answers yes, inquire:* "Who?" *If child answers no, inquire:* "Who was in the doctor's office with you?"
    a) "Were there any other big people?"
    b) "Were there any other children?"

---

[7] Do not pursue information regarding family members beyond name.

2. "Tell me everything you can remember about ——— [person who performed procedure]."

    a) "Was the doctor a man or a lady?"

    b) "What was his/her name?"

    c) "What did he/she look like?"

    d) "What was he/she wearing?"

    e) "What color clothes was he/she wearing?" *If child indicates a color, ask which piece of clothing was that color:* "What was ——— [color]?"

    f) "What color was his/her hair?"

    g) "Was there anything special about the way he/she looked?"

Pain Ratings

1. *Ask child:* "Has anything ever happened to you that hurt a lot? What was it?" *If child fails to respond, say:* "How much does it hurt when you skin your knee? A lot, a little, or not at all?"

2. *Ask child:* "Has anything ever happened to you that hurt just a little? What was it?"

Action

Use the following series of questions to prompt the child's general recall of the interaction:

1. "You said that ——— was in the doctor's office. Tell me everything that you remember about what ——— did."

    a) "What was he/she there for?"

    b) "Did he/she say anything to you?"

    c) "Did he/she do anything to you?"

    d) "Did he/she touch you?"

        i) "Where were you touched?" *Mark area on anatomical drawing but do not allow the child to see the drawing. As each area is reported, ask:* "When the doctor touched you ———, did it hurt a lot, a little, or not at all?"

        ii) "What did he/she touch you with?"

        iii) "Why did he/she do that?"

    e) "Were you touched anywhere else?"

Direct Questions

1. "Did he/she hold you down?"

2. "Did your clothes get taken off?" *If the child answers yes, ask:* "How did your clothes get taken off?"

3. "Did anybody put anything inside your mouth?"

4. "Did anybody put anything inside your ear?"

5. "Did anybody put anything inside your body?"

6. "Were there any pictures being taken of you?" *If child says yes, differentiate between colposcope and videotape camera, then ask:* "Where was the camera?"

7. "Did anybody wrap anything around your arm?"

8. "Did anybody hit you with a hammer?"

9. "Did anybody put anything around your head?"

Environmental (Place)

1. "You said that you had ——— [insert procedure, e.g., blood draw]. Where did you go to have it done?"

    a) "Tell me everything you can remember about that place."

        i) "Where was the room?"

        ii) "What did the room look like?"

        iii) "What colors in the room do you remember?"

        iv) "Were there any smells in the room?"

        v) "Were there any sounds in the room?"

        vi) "What things were in the room?"

        vii) "Is there anything special that you remember about the room?"

Feelings Rating

1. "I would like you to help me know about the kinds of feelings you had in the doctor's office."

2. "How do you feel right now?" *Wait for child to answer.*

3. "Did you feel a lot ——— [specific feeling], a little ——— [specific feeling], or not at all ——— [specific feeling]?"

4. "When you were in the doctor's office, how ——— did you feel: a lot, a little, or not at all?" *Repeat for each of the following feelings: happy, sad, scared, angry, sleepy, safe, surprised, relaxed.*

Coping Strategies

1. *Ask the child:* "Did anything hurt you today in the doctor's office?" *If the child answers yes, ask:* "What did you do when it started to hurt?" *After the child responds, ask the following:*

    a) "Did you do anything to help it stop hurting?"

    b) "Did you pretend it wasn't happening to you?"

    c) "Did you try to think of something else?"

Preparation for Medical Procedure

Ask: "Did anyone talk to you about what was going to happen in the doctor's office today?" *Then ask each of the following questions:*
1. "What were you told?"
2. "Did they tell you what it would feel like?"
3. "Did it feel the way they said, or different?"
4. "Did anybody tell you something that helped you?"
5. "Did anybody tell you something that didn't help?"

FOLLOW-UP VERBAL INTERVIEW

Introduction

Introduce each of the follow-up interviews as follows:
1. *Initial introduction:* "Hi! Remember when we talked before? I showed you some pictures and told you we were doing a Children's Memory Study. Now, I'm going to ask you a few more questions to see how much you can tell me about what you remember. When we're all done, I'll give you a snack and something to take home with you."
2. "Do you remember when you came to the clinic and got a special certificate like this one? What happened to you that day?" *Or, if child fails to respond:* "What did you do that day?"
3. *If child does not mention the physical examination, ask the following:* "What else happened to you that day?"
4. *If child still does not mention the physical examination, ask the following:* "Did you visit the doctor's office that day?"

Open-ended and Specific Verbal Prompts

Continue with the open-ended and specific verbal prompts from the initial interview.

REFERENCES

Achenbach, T. M., McConaughy, S. H., & Howell, C. T. (1987). Child/adolescent behavioral ratings and emotional problems: Implications of cross-informant correlations for situational specificity. *Psychological Bulletin, 101,* 213–232.

Altshuler, J. L., & Ruble, D. N. (1989). Developmental changes in children's awareness of strategies for coping with uncontrollable stress. *Child Development, 60,* 1337–1349.

Baddeley, A. D. (1972). Selective attention and performance in dangerous environments. *British Journal of Psychology, 63,* 537–546.

Baker-Ward, L., Gordon, B. N., Ornstein, P. A., Larus, D. M., & Clubb, P. A. (1993). Young children's long-term retention of a pediatric examination. *Child Development, 64,* 1519–1533.

Banaji, M. R., & Crowder, R. G. (1989). The bankruptcy of everyday memory. *American Psychologist, 44,* 1185–1193.

Band, E. B., & Weisz, J. R. (1988). How to feel better when it feels bad: Children's perspectives on coping with everyday stress. *Developmental Psychology, 24,* 247–253.

Barnard, K. E., & Brazelton, T. B. (Eds.). (1990). *Touch: The foundation of experience.* Madison, CT: International Universities Press.

Bays, J. (1990). Are the genitalia of anatomical dolls distorted? *Child Abuse and Neglect, 14,* 171–175.

Bearison, D. J. (1990). *They never want to tell you.* Cambridge, MA: Harvard University Press.

Bearison, D. J., & Pacifici, C. (1989). Children's event knowledge of cancer treatment. *Journal of Applied and Developmental Psychology, 10,* 469–486.

Benedek, E., & Schetky, D. (1985). Allegations of sexual abuse in child custody and visitation disputes. In D. Schetky & E. Benedek (Eds.), *Emerging issues in child psychiatry and the law.* New York: Brunner/Mazel.

Bergmann, T., & Freud, A. (1965). *Children in the hospital.* New York: International Universities Press.

Berliner, L., & Conte, J. R. (1990). The process of victimization: The victims' perspective. *Child Abuse and Neglect, 14,* 29–40.

Berrick, J. D., & Gilbert, N. (1991). *With the best of intentions: The child sexual abuse prevention movement.* New York: Guilford.

Besharov, D. J. (1990). *Recognizing child abuse: A guide for the concerned.* New York: Free Press.

Beuf, A. H. (1979). *Biting off the bracelet: A study of children in hospitals.* Philadelphia: University of Pennsylvania Press.

Beyer, J. E. (1984). *The oucher: A user's manual and technical report.* Evanston, IL: Hospital Play Equipment Co.

Beyer, J. E., Berde, C. B., & Bournaki, M. C. (1991). Memories of pain in 3–7-year-old children. *Journal of Pain and Symptom Management, 6,* 174.

Beyer, J. E., & Wells, N. (1990). The assessment of pain in children. *Pediatric Clinics of North America: Acute Pain in Children, 36,* 837–854.

Bieri, D., Reeve, R. A., Champion, G. D., Addicoat, L., & Ziegler, J. B. (1990). The Faces Pain Scale for the self-assessment of the severity of pain experienced by children: Development, initial validation, and preliminary investigation for ratio scales properties. *Pain, 41,* 139–150.

Bjorklund, D. F. (1987). How age changes in knowledge base contribute to the development of children's memory: An interpretive review. *Developmental Review, 7,* 93–130.

Blount, R. L., Corbin, S. M., Sturges, J. W., Wolfe, V. V., Prater, J. M., & James, L. D. (1989). The relationship between adults' behavior and child coping and distress during BMA/LP procedures: A sequential analysis. *Behavior Therapy, 20,* 585–601.

Blount, R. L., Davis, N., Powers, S. W., & Roberts, M. C. (1991). The influence of environmental factors and coping style on children's coping and distress. *Clinical Psychology Review, 11,* 93–116.

Blount, R. L., Sturges, J. W., & Powers, S. W. (1990). Analysis of child and adult behavioral variations by phase of medical procedure. *Behavior Therapy, 21,* 33–48.

Boat, B., & Everson, M. (1986). *Using anatomical dolls: Guidelines for interviewing young children in sexual abuse investigations.* Chapel Hill: University of North Carolina, Department of Psychology.

Boat, B., & Everson, M. (1988). Use of anatomical dolls among professionals in sexual abuse evaluations. *Child Abuse and Neglect, 12,* 171–179.

Boat, B., & Everson, M. (1993). The use of anatomical dolls in sexual abuse evaluations: Current research and practice. In G. S. Goodman & B. L. Bottoms (Eds.), *Child victims, child witnesses: Understanding and improving testimony.* New York: Guilford.

Boat, B., & Everson, M. (1994). Exploration of anatomical dolls by nonreferred preschool-aged children: Comparison by age, gender, race and socioeconomic status. *Child Abuse and Neglect, 18,* 139–153.

Boat, B., & Everson, M. (in press). Concerning practices of interviewers when using anatomical dolls in child protective services investigations. *Child Maltreatment.*

Borke, H. (1971). Interpersonal perception of young children: Egocentrism or empathy? *Developmental Psychology, 5,* 263–269.

Bowlby, J., Robertson, J., & Rosenbluth, D. (1952). A two year old goes to the hospital. *Psychoanalytic Study of the Child, 7,* 82–94.

Brainerd, C. J. (1985). Model-based approaches to storage and retrieval development. In C. J. Brainerd & M. Pressley (Eds.), *Basic processes in memory development.* New York: Springer.

Brainerd, C., & Ornstein, P. A. (1991). Children's memory for witnessed events: The developmental backdrop. In J. Doris (Ed.), *The suggestibility of children's recollections.* Washington, DC: American Psychological Association.

Brennan, M., & Brennan, R. E. (1988). *Strange language.* Wagga Wagga, New South Wales: Riverina Literacy Centre.

Bretherton, I., & Beeghly, M. (1982). Talking about internal states: The acquisition of an explicit theory of mind. *Developmental Psychology, 18,* 906–921.

Brewster, A. B. (1982). Chronically ill hospitalized children's conceptions of their illness. *Pediatrics, 69,* 355–362.

Bronfenbrenner, U. (1979). *The ecology of human development.* Cambridge, MA: Harvard University Press.

Broome, M. E., & Endsley, R. C. (1989). Parent and child behavior during immunization. *Pain, 37,* 85–92.

Broome, M. E., & Hellier, A. P. (1987). School-age children's fears of medical experiences. *Issues in Comprehensive Pediatric Nursing, 10,* 77–86.

Brown, R. (1973). *The first language: The early stages.* Cambridge: Cambridge University Press.

Bruck, M., Ceci, S. J., Francoeur, E., & Barr, R. J. (1995). "I hardly cried when I got my shot!" Influencing children's reports about a visit to the pediatrician. *Child Development,* **66,** 193–208.

Bruck, M., Ceci, S. J., Francoeur, E., & Renick, A. (1995). Anatomically detailed dolls do not facilitate preschooler's reports of a pediatric examination involving genital touching. *Journal of Experimental Psychology: Applied,* **1,** 95–109.

Bulkley, J. (1989). The impact of new child witness research on sexual abuse prosecutions. In S. J. Ceci, D. F. Ross, & M. P. Toglia (Eds.), *Perspectives on children's testimony.* New York: Springer.

Bush, J. P., & Harkins, S. W. (Eds.). (1991). *Children in pain: Clinical and research issues from a developmental perspective.* New York: Springer.

Bush, J. P., Melamed, B. G., & Cockrell, C. S. (1989). Parenting children in a stressful medical situation. In T. W. Miller (Ed.), *Stressful life events.* Madison, CT: International Universities Press.

Bussey, K., Lee, K., & Grimbeek, E. J. (1993). Lies and secrets: Implications for children's reporting of sexual abuse. In G. S. Goodman & B. L. Bottoms (Eds.), *Child victims, child witnesses: Understanding and improving testimony.* New York: Guilford.

Bussey, K., Steward, M. S., Pipe, M. E., Peterson, C. C., & Lawrence, J. (1992). Current issues in developmental psychology and law. *Australian Journal of Educational and Developmental Psychology,* **9,** 2–11.

Caffey, J. (1946). Multiple fractures in the long bones of infants suffering from chronic subdural hematoma. *American Journal of Roentgenology,* **56,** 163–173.

California Child Victim Witness Judicial Advisory Committee. (1988). *Final report.* Sacramento: California Attorney-General's Office.

Cassel, W. S., & Bjorklund, D. F. (1995). Developmental patterns of eyewitness memory and suggestibility: An ecologically based short-term longitudinal study. *Law and Human Behavior,* **19,** 507–532.

Ceci, S. J. (1991). Some over-arching issues in the children's suggestibility debate. In J. Doris (Ed.), *The suggestibility of children's recollections.* Washington, DC: American Psychological Association.

Ceci, S. J., & Bronfenbrenner, U. (1991). On the demise of everyday memory: "The rumors of my death are much exaggerated" (Mark Twain). *American Psychologist,* **46,** 27–31.

Ceci, S. J., & Bruck, M. (1993). The suggestibility of the child witness: A historical review and synthesis. *Psychological Bulletin,* **113,** 403–440.

Ceci, S. J., & Bruck, M. (1995). *Jeopardy in the courtroom.* Washington, DC: American Psychological Association.

Ceci, S. J., Ross, D. F., & Toglia, M. P. (1987a). Age differences in suggestibility: Narrowing the uncertainties. In S. J. Ceci, M. P. Toglia, & D. F. Ross (Eds.), *Children's eyewitness memory.* New York: Springer.

Ceci, S. J., Ross, D. F., & Toglia, M. P. (1987b). Suggestibility of children's memory: Psycholegal implications. *Journal of Experimental Psychology: General,* **117,** 38–49.

Chance, J. E., & Goldstein, A. G. (1984). Face recognition memory: Implications for children's eyewitness testimony. *Journal of Social Issues,* **40,** 69–86.

Christianson, S. (1992). Emotional stress and eyewitness memory: A critical review. *Psychological Bulletin,* **112,** 284–309.

Chrousos, G. P., & Gold, P. W. (1991). *The concepts of stress and stress system disorders: Overview of behavioral and physical homeostasis.* Bethesda, MD: National Institutes of Health.

Clarke-Stewart, A., Thompson, L., & Lepore, S. (1989, March). Manipulating children's testimony through interrogation. In G. Goodman (Chair), *Can children provide accurate eyewitness testimony?* Symposium conducted at the meeting of the Society for Research in Child Development, Kansas City, MO.

Cohen, J., & Cohen, P. (1975). *Applied multiple regression/correlation analysis for the behavioral sciences.* Hillsdale, NJ: Erlbaum.

Cole, C. B., & Loftus, E. F. (1987). The memory of children. In S. J. Ceci, M. P. Toglia, & D. F. Ross (Eds.), *Children's eyewitness memory.* New York: Springer.

Cole, P. M. (1986). Children's spontaneous control of facial expression. *Child Development,* **57,** 1309–1321.

Conte, J., & Schuerman, J. (1987). Factors associated with an increased impact of child sexual abuse. *Child Abuse and Neglect,* **11,** 201–211.

Conte, J. R., Sorenson, E., Fogarty, L., & Dalla Rosa, J. (1991). Evaluating children's reports of sexual abuse: Results from a survey of professionals. *American Journal of Orthopsychiatry,* **61,** 428–437.

Coolbear, J. L. (1992). Credibility of young children in sexual abuse cases: Assessment strategies of legal and human service professionals. *Canadian Psychology,* **33,** 151–164.

Craig, K. D., McMahon, R., Morrison, J., & Zaskow, C. (1984). Developmental changes in pain expression during immunization injections. *Social Science in Medicine,* **19,** 1331–1337.

Daehler, M. W., & Greco, C. (1985). Memory in very young children. In M. Pressley & C. J. Brainerd (Eds.), *Cognitive learning and memory in children.* New York: Springer.

Dahlquist, L. M., Gil, K. M., Armstrong, F. D., DeLawyer, D. D., Greene, P., & Wuori, D. (1989). Preparing children for medical examinations: The importance of previous medical experience. *Health Psychology,* **5,** 249–259.

Davies, G. M. (1981). Face recall systems. In G. Davies, H. Ellis, & J. Sheperd (Eds.), *Perceiving and remembering faces.* London: Academic.

Davies, G. (1991). Research on children's testimony: Implications for interviewing practice. In C. R. Hollin & K. Howells (Eds.), *Clinical approaches to sex offenders and their victims.* New York: Wiley.

Davies, G. (1993). Children's memory for other people. In C. A. Nelson (Ed.), *Memory and affect in development* (Minnesota Symposium on Child Psychology, Vol. **26**). Hillsdale, NJ: Erlbaum.

Davies, G., Stevenson-Robb, Y., & Flin, R. (1988). Tales out of school: Children's memory for an unexpected incident. In M. M. Gruenberg, P. E. Morris, & R. N. Sykes (Eds.), *Practical aspects of memory: Current research and issues: Memory in everyday life* (Vol. 1). New York: Wiley.

Davies, G., Tarrant, A., & Flin, R. (1989). Close encounters of the witness kind: Children's memory for a simulated health inspection. *British Journal of Psychology,* **80,** 415–429.

DeJong, A., Hervada, A., & Emmett, G. (1983). Epidemiological variations in childhood sexual abuse. *Child Abuse and Neglect,* **7,** 155–162.

DeJong, A. R., & Rose, M. (1991). Legal proof of child sexual abuse in the absence of physical evidence. *Pediatrics,* **88,** 506–511.

DeLoache, J. (1987). Rapid change in the symbolic functioning of very young children. *Science,* **238,** 1556–1557.

DeLoache, J. (1989). Young children's understanding of the correspondence between scale model and a larger space. *Cognitive Development,* **4,** 121–129.

DeLoache, J. (1990). Young children's understanding of scale models. In R. Fivush & J. Hudson (Eds.), *Knowing and remembering in young children.* New York: Cambridge University Press.

DeLoache, J. (1991). Young children's understanding of models. In R. Fivush & J. Hudson (Eds.), *What young children remember and know.* New York: Cambridge University Press.

DeLoache, J. S., Kolstad, V., & Anderson, K. N. (1991). Physical similarity and young children's understanding of scale models. *Child Development,* **62,** 111–126.

DeLoache, J. S., & Marzolf, D. P. (1995). The use of dolls to interview young children: Issues of symbolic representation. *Journal of Experimental Child Psychology,* **60,** 1–19.

Dent, H. (1977). Stress as a factor influencing person recognition in identification parades. *Bulletin of the British Psychological Society,* **30,** 339–340.

Dent, H. (1982). The effects of interviewing strategies on the results of interviews with child witnesses. In A. Trankell (Ed.), *Reconstructing the past.* Deventer: Kluwer.

Dent, H., & Stephenson, G. M. (1979). An experimental study of the effectiveness of different techniques of questioning child witnesses. *British Journal of Social and Clinical Psychology,* **18,** 41–51.

Doris, J. (Ed.). (1991). *The suggestibility of children's recollections.* Washington, DC: American Psychological Association.

Dunning, D. (1989). Research on children's eyewitness testimony: Perspectives on its past and future. In S. J. Ceci, D. F. Ross, & M. P. Toglia (Eds.), *Perspectives on children's testimony.* New York: Springer.

Durkin, M. S., Khan, N., Davidson, L. L., Zaman, S., & Stein, Z. A. (1993). The effect of a natural disaster on child behavior: Evidence for posttraumatic stress. *American Journal of Public Health,* **83,** 1549–1553.

Easterbrook, J. A. (1959). The effect of emotion on cue utilization and the organization of behavior. *Psychological Review,* **66,** 183–201.

Eisenberg, A. R. (1985). Learning to describe past experiences in conversation. *Discourse Processes,* **8,** 177–204.

Eiser, C., Eiser, J. R., & Lang, J. (1989). Scripts in children's reports of medical events. *European Journal of the Psychology of Education,* **4,** 377–384.

Ekman, P., & Friesen, W. V. (1975). *Unmasking the face.* Englewood Cliffs, NJ: Prentice-Hall.

Eland, J. M. (1974). *Children's communication of pain.* Unpublished master's thesis, University of Iowa.

Eland, J. M., & Anderson, J. E. (1977). The experience of pain in children. In A. K. Jacox (Ed.), *Pain: A source book for nurses and other health professionals.* Boston: Little, Brown.

Elliott, C. H., Jay, S. M., & Woody, P. (1987). An observational scale for measuring children's distress during medical procedures. *Journal of Pediatric Psychology,* **12,** 543–551.

Emmerich, H. J., & Ackerman, B. P. (1978). Developmental differences in recall: Encoding or retrieval? *Journal of Experimental Child Psychology,* **25,** 514–525.

Engel, S. (1986). *Learning to reminisce: A developmental study of how young children talk about the past.* Unpublished doctoral dissertation, City University of New York.

Enos, W. F., Conrath, T. B., & Byer, J. C. (1986). Forensic evaluation of the sexually abused child. *Pediatrics,* **78,** 385–398.

Everson, M. D., & Boat, B. W. (1989). False allegations of sexual abuse by children and adolescents. *Journal of the American Academy of Child and Adolescent Psychiatry,* **28,** 230–235.

Everson, M. D., & Boat, B. W. (1994). Putting the anatomical doll controversy in perspective: An examination of major doll uses and related criticisms. *Child Abuse and Neglect,* **18,** 113–129.

Everson, M. D., Hunter, W. M., Runyon, D. K., Edelsohn, G. A., & Coulter, M. L. (1989). Maternal support following disclosure of incest. *American Journal of Orthopsychiatry,* **59,** 197–207.

Everson, M. D., Myers, J. E. B., & White, S. (1995). *Use of anatomical dolls in child sexual abuse assessment: Practice guidelines.* Chicago: American Professional Society on the Abuse of Children.

Everstine, D. S., & Everstine, L. (1989). *Sexual trauma in children and adolescents: Dynamics and treatment.* New York: Brunner/Mazel.

Fabes, R. A., Eisenberg, N., McCormick, S. E., & Wilson, M. S. (1988). Preschoolers' attribu-

171

tions of the situational determinants of others' naturally occurring emotions. *Developmental Psychology*, **24**, 376–385.

Fabes, R. A., Eisenberg, N., Nyman, M., & Michealieu, Q. (1991). Young children's appraisals of others' spontaneous emotional reactions. *Developmental Psychology*, **27**, 858–866.

Faller, K. C. (1990). *Understanding child sexual maltreatment.* Newbury Park, CA: Sage.

Finkelhor, D. (1979). *Sexually victimized children.* New York: Free Press.

Finkelhor, D. (1993). Epidemiological factors in the clinical identification of child sexual abuse. *Child Abuse and Neglect*, **17**, 67–70.

Finkelhor, D., & Baron, L. (1986). High-risk children. In D. Finkelhor et al. (Eds.), *Sourcebook on child sexual abuse.* Beverly Hills, CA: Sage.

Finkelhor, D., & Browne, A. (1985). The traumatic impact of child sexual abuse: A conceptualization. *American Journal of Orthopsychiatry*, **55**, 530–541.

Finkelhor, D., Williams, L. M., Burns, N., & Kalinowski, M. (1988, March). *Sexual abuse in day care: A national study.* Durham: Family Research Laboratory, University of New Hampshire.

Fisher, R. P., & Chandler, C. C. (1991). Independence between recalling interevent relations and specific events. *Journal of Experimental Psychology: Learning, Memory, and Cognition*, **17**, 722–733.

Fivush, R. (1993). Developmental perspectives on autobiographical recall. In G. S. Goodman & B. L. Bottoms (Eds.), *Child victims, child witnesses: Understanding and improving testimony.* New York: Guilford.

Fivush, R. (1994). Young children's event recall: Are memories constructed through discourse? *Consciousness and Cognition*, **3**, 356–373.

Fivush, R. (1995, April). The development of narrative remembering: Implications for the recovered memory debate. In P. A. Ornstein (Chair), *Remembering the distant past: Implications of research on children's memory for the recovered memory debate.* Symposium conducted at the meeting of the Society for Research in Child Development, Indianapolis.

Fivush, R., & Fromhoff, F. A. (1988). Style and structure in mother-child conversations about the past. *Discourse Processes*, **11**, 337–355.

Fivush, R., & Hamond, N. R. (1990). Autobiographical memory across the preschool years: Towards reconceptualizing childhood amnesia. In R. Fivush & J. A. Hudson (Eds.), *Knowing and remembering in young children.* New York: Cambridge University Press.

Fivush, R., Hamond, N. R., Harsch, N., Singer, N., & Wolf, A. (1991). Content and consistency in young children's autobiographical recall. *Discourse Processes*, **14**, 373–388.

Fivush, R., & Schwarzmueller, A. (1995). Say it once again: Effects of repeated questions on children's event recall. *Journal of Traumatic Stress*, **8**(4), 555–580.

Fivush, R., & Shukat, J. (1995). Content, consistency and coherence of early autobiographical memory. In M. S. Zaragoza, J. R. Graham, G. C. N. Hall, R. Hirschman, & Y. S. Ben-Porath (Eds.), *Memory and testimony in the child witness.* Thousand Oaks, CA: Sage.

Fletcher, K. E. (1994). *Dimensions of stressful events rating scale.* Unpublished manuscript, Department of Psychiatry, University of Massachusetts Medical Center, Worcester.

Flin, R., Bull, R., Boon, J., & Knox, A. (1992). Children in the witness box. In H. Dent & R. Flin (Eds.), *Children as witnesses.* Chichester: Wiley.

Foos, P. W., & Fisher, R. P. (1988). Using tests as learning opportunities. *Journal of Educational Psychology*, **80**, 179–183.

Forgas, J. P., Burnham, D. K., & Trimboli, C. (1988). Mood, memory and social judgments in children. *Journal of Personality and Social Psychology*, **54**, 697–703.

Freeman, K. R., & Estrada-Mullaney, T. (1988). *Using dolls to interview child victims: Legal concerns and interview procedures* (National Institute of Justice Reports, No. 107, Reports 1–6). Washington, DC: U.S. Department of Justice.

Freud, A. (1952). The role of bodily illness in the mental life of children. *Psychoanalytic Study of the Child*, **7**, 69–80.

Fridlund, A. J., Ekman, P., & Oster, H. (1987). Facial expressions of emotion. In A. W. Siegman & S. Feldstein (Eds.), *Nonverbal behavior and communication* (2d ed.). Hillsdale, NJ: Erlbaum.

Friedrich, W. N., Grambsch, P., Broughton, D., Kuiper, J., & Beilke, R. L. (1991). Normative sexual behavior in children. *Pediatrics*, **88**, 456–464.

Gaffney, A., & Dunne, E. A. (1986). Developmental aspects of children's definitions of pain. *Pain*, **26**, 105–117.

Garbarino, J., Stott, F. M., & the Faculty of the Erikson Institute. (1989). *What children can tell us*. San Francisco: Jossey-Bass.

Garrison, C. Z., Weinrich, M. W., Hardin, S. B., Weinrich, S., & Wang, L. (1993). Post-traumatic stress disorder in adolescents after a hurricane. *American Journal of Epidemiology*, **138**, 522–530.

Geiselman, R. E., Saywitz, K. J., & Bornstein, G. K. (1993). Effects of cognitive questioning techniques on children's recall performance. In G. S. Goodman & B. L. Bottoms (Eds.), *Child victims, child witnesses: Understanding and improving testimony*. New York: Guilford.

Gold, P. E. (1987). Sweet memories. *American Scientist*, **75**, 151–155.

Golden, D. B. (1983). Play therapy for hospitalized children. In C. E. Schaefer & K. J. O'Connor (Eds.), *Handbook of play therapy*. New York: Wiley.

Goldman, R., & Goldman, J. (1982). *Children's sexual thinking*. Boston: Routledge & Kegan Paul.

Goldman, R., & Goldman, J. (1988). *Show me yours*. New York: Penguin.

Goldstein, S. L. (1987). *The sexual exploitation of children*. New York: Elsevier.

Gonzales, J. C., Routh, D. K., Saab, P. G., Armstrong, F. D., Shifman, L., Guerra, E., & Fawcett, N. (1989). Effects of parent presence on children's reactions to injections: Behavioral, physiological and subjective aspects. *Journal of Pediatric Psychology*, **14**, 449–462.

Goodman, G. (1984). The child witness: Conclusions and future directions. *Journal of Social Issues*, **40**(2), 157–175.

Goodman, G., & Aman, C. (1990). Children's use of anatomically correct dolls to recount an event. *Child Development*, **61**, 1859–1871.

Goodman, G., Aman, C., & Hirschman, J. (1987). Child sexual and physical abuse: Children's testimony. In S. J. Ceci, M. P. Toglia, & D. F. Ross (Eds.), *Children's eyewitness memory*. New York: Springer.

Goodman, G. S., & Bottoms, B. L. (Eds.). (1993). *Child victims, child witnesses: Understanding and improving testimony*. New York: Guilford.

Goodman, G. S., Bottoms, B. L., Schwartz-Kenney, B. M., & Rudy, L. (1991). Children's testimony about a stressful event: Improving children's reports. *Journal of Narrative and Life History*, **1**, 69–99.

Goodman, G. S., Golding, J. M., & Haith, M. M. (1984). Jurors' reactions to child witnesses. *Journal of Social Issues*, **40**, 139–156.

Goodman, G. S., Hirschman, J., Hepps, D., & Rudy, L. (1991). Children's memories for stressful events. *Merrill-Palmer Quarterly*, **37**, 109–158.

Goodman, G., Levine, M., Melton, G., & Ogden, D. (1991). Child witnesses and the confrontation clause: The American Psychological Association brief in *Maryland v. Craig*. *Law and Human Behavior*, **15**, 13–30.

Goodman, G. S., & Quas, J. A. (in press). Trauma and memory: Individual differences in children's recounting of a stressful experience. In N. L. Stein, P. A. Ornstein, B. Tversky, & C. Brainerd (Eds.), *Memory for everyday and emotional events*. Hillsdale, NJ: Erlbaum.

Goodman, G. S., Quas, J. A., Batterman-Faunce, J. M., Riddlesberger, M. M., & Kuhn, J.

(1994). Predictors of accurate and inaccurate memories of traumatic events experienced in childhood. *Consciousness and Cognition*, **3**, 269–294.

Goodman, G. S., Quas, J. A., & Dunn, J. (1995, April). On the utility of anatomically detailed dolls when interviewing children. In G. S. Goodman & L. Baker-Ward (Chairs), *Children's memory for emotional and traumatic events*. Symposium conducted at the meeting of the Society for Research in Child Development, Indianapolis.

Goodman, G. S., & Reed, R. S. (1986). Age differences in eyewitness testimony. *Law and Human Behavior*, **10**, 317–322.

Goodman, G. S., & Rosenberg, M. S. (1987). The child witness to family violence: Clinical and legal considerations. In D. Sonkin (Ed.), *Domestic violence on trial*. New York: Springer.

Goodman, G., Rudy, L., Bottoms, B. L., & Aman, C. (1990). Children's concerns and memory: Issues of ecological validity in children's testimony. In R. Fivush & J. Hudson (Eds.), *Knowing and remembering in young children*. New York: Cambridge University Press.

Goodman, G. S., Taub, E. P., Jones, D. P. H., England, P., Port, L. K., Rudy, L., & Prado, L. (1992). Testifying in criminal court: Emotional effects on child sexual assault victims. *Monographs of the Society for Research in Child Development*, **57**(5, Serial No. 229).

Gordon, B. N., Schroeder, C. S., & Abrams, J. M. (1990). Children's knowledge of sexuality: A comparison of sexually abused and nonabused children. *American Journal of Orthopsychiatry*, **60**, 250–257.

Gordon, F. R., & Flavell, J. H. (1977). The development of intuitions about cognitive cuing. *Child Development*, **48**, 1027–1033.

Gray, E. (1993). *Unequal justice: The prosecution of child sexual abuse*. New York: Free Press.

Greenspan, S., Barenboim, C., & Chandler, M. (1976). Empathy and pseudo-empathy: The affective judgments of first- and third-graders. *Genetic Psychology*, **129**, 77–88.

Groth, A. N. (1984). *Anatomical drawings*. Newton Center, MA: Forensic Mental Health Associates.

Gunnar, M. R., Hertsgaard, L., Larson, M., & Rigatuso, J. (1991). Cortisol and behavioral responses to repeated stressors in the human newborn. *Developmental Psychobiology*, **24**, 487–505.

Gunnar, M., Marvinney, D., Isensee, J., & Fisch, R. O. (1989). Coping with uncertainty: New models of the relations between hormonal, behavioral and cognitive processes. In D. S. Palermo (Ed.), *Coping with uncertainty: Behavioral and developmental perspectives*. Hillsdale, NJ: Erlbaum.

Harbeck, C., & Peterson, L. (1992). Elephants dancing in my head: A developmental approach to children's concepts of specific pains. *Child Development*, **63**, 138–149.

Hashima, P. Y., Barton, K., & Steward, M. S. (1988). What does "touch" mean? An empirical study. *Perceptual and Motor Skills*, **67**, 683–690.

Haugaard, J. J., & Reppucci, N. D. (1988). *The sexual abuse of children*. San Francisco: Jossey-Bass.

Haugaard, J. J., Reppucci, N. D., Laird, J., & Nauful, T. (1991). Children's definitions of truth and their competency as witnesses in legal proceedings. *Law and Human Behavior*, **15**, 253–271.

Hill, P., & Hill, S. (1987). Videotaping children's testimony: An empirical view. *Michigan Law Review*, **85**, 809–833.

Howe, M. L. (1995, April). Early memory development and the emergence of autobiographical memory. In P. A. Ornstein (Chair), *Remembering the distant past: Implications of research on children's memory for the recovered memory debate*. Symposium conducted at the meeting of the Society for Research in Child Development, Indianapolis.

Howe, M. L., & Courage, M. L. (1993). On resolving the enigma of infantile amnesia. *Psychological Bulletin*, **113**, 305–326.

Howe, M. L., Courage, M. L., & Peterson, C. (1994). How can I remember when "I" wasn't there: Long-term retention of traumatic experiences and emergence of the cognitive self. *Consciousness and Cognition, 3,* 327–355.

Howe, M. L., Kelland, A., Bryant-Brown, L., & Clark, S. L. (1992). Measuring the development of children's amnesia and hypermnesia. In M. L. Howe, C. J. Brainerd, & V. F. Reyna (Eds.), *Development of long-term retention.* New York: Springer.

Howe, M. L., O'Sullivan, J. T., & Marche, T. A. (1992). Toward a theory of the development of long-term retention. In M. L. Howe, C. J. Brainerd, & V. F. Reyna (Eds.), *Development of long-term retention.* New York: Springer.

Hresko, W. P., Reid, D. K., & Hammill, D. D. (1981). *Test of Early Language Development (TELD).* East Aurora, NY: Slosson Educational.

Hudson, J. A. (1986). Memories are made of this: General event knowledge and the development of autobiographical memory. In K. Nelson (Ed.), *Event knowledge: Structure and function in development.* Hillsdale, NJ: Erlbaum.

Hudson, J. A. (1990). The emergence of autobiographical memory in mother-child conversations. In R. Fivush & J. A. Hudson (Eds.), *Knowing and remembering in young children.* New York: Cambridge University Press.

Hudson, J. A., & Fivush, R. (1987). *As time goes on: Sixth graders remember a kindergarten experience* (Emory Cognition Project Report, No. 13). Atlanta: Emory University.

Hudson, J. A., & Nelson, K. (1986). Repeated encounters of a similar kind: The effects of familiarity on children's autobiographical recall. *Cognitive Development, 1,* 253–271.

Hulse-Trotter, K., & Warren, A. R. (1990, April). *Do children believe in their own believability?* Poster presented at the meeting of the American Psychology and Law Society, Williamsburg, VA.

Idaho v. Wright, 110 S. Ct. 3139 (1990).

Izard, C. E. (1977). *Human emotions.* New York: Plenum.

Izard, C. E., Hembree, E. A., & Huebner, R. R. (1987). Infants' emotion expressions to acute pain: Developmental change and stability of individual differences. *Developmental Psychology, 23,* 105–113.

Jackson, E. B. (1942). Treatment of the young child in the hospital. *American Journal of Orthopsychiatry, 12,* 56–68.

Jacobsen, P. B., Manne, S. L., Gorfinkle, K., Schorr, O., Rapkin, B., & Redd, W. H. (1990). Analysis of child and parent behavior during painful medical procedures. *Health Psychology, 9,* 559–576.

Janoff-Bulman, R. (1992). *Shattered assumptions: Towards a new psychology of trauma.* New York: Free Press.

Jauders, P. K., & Martone, M. (1992). Interdisciplinary evaluations of alleged sexual abuse cases. *Pediatrics, 89,* 1164–1167.

Jay, S. M. (1988). Invasive medical procedures: Psychological intervention and assessment. In D. K. Routh (Ed.), *Handbook of pediatric psychology.* New York: Guilford.

Jay, S. M., & Elliott, C. H. (1986). *Observational Scale of Behavioral Distress–Revised.* Unpublished manuscript, University of Southern California School of Medicine, Los Angeles.

Jay, S. M., Elliott, C. H., Ozolins, M., Olson, R. A., & Pruitt, S. D. (1985). Behavioral management of children's distress during painful medical procedures. *Behavior Research and Therapy, 23,* 513–520.

Jay, S. M., Ozolins, M., Elliott, C. H., & Caldwell, S. (1983). Assessment of children's distress during painful medical procedures. *Health Psychology, 2,* 133–147.

Jessner, L., Blom, G. E., & Waldfogel, S. (1952). Emotional implications of tonsillectomy and adenoidectomy on children. *Psychoanalytic Study of the Child, 7,* 126–169.

Johnson, M. K., & Foley, M. A. (1984). Differentiating fact from fantasy: The reliability of children's memory. *Journal of Social Issues, 40,* 33–50.

Jones, D., & Krugman, R. (1986). Can a three-year-old child bear witness to her sexual assault and attempted murder? *Child Abuse and Neglect,* **10,** 253–258.

Jones, D., & McGraw, J. M. (1987). Reliable and fictitious accounts of sexual abuse in children. *Journal of Interpersonal Violence,* **2,** 27–45.

Jones, D., & McQuiston, M. (1988). *Interviewing the sexually abused child* (3d ed.). Oxford: Alden.

Jones, D. C., Swift, D. J., & Johnson, M. A. (1988). Nondeliberate memory for a novel event among preschoolers. *Developmental Psychology,* **24,** 641–645.

Jourard, S. (1966). Experimenter, subject distance and self disclosure. *British Journal of Social and Clinical Psychology,* **5,** 221–231.

Juniper, K. H., Addicoat, L., Champion, G. D., Cairns, D., & Ziegler, J. B. (1991). Subjective and behavioral responses to brief sharp physiological pain in 5 year old children. *Journal of Pain and Symptom Management,* **6,** 172.

Kail, R. (1989). *The development of memory in children.* San Francisco: Freeman.

Katz, E. R., Kellerman, J., & Siegel, S. E. (1980). Behavioral distress in children with cancer undergoing medical procedures: Developmental considerations. *Journal of Consulting and Clinical Psychology,* **48,** 356–365.

Katz, S., Schonfeld, D. J., Carter, A. S., Leventhal, J. M., & Cicchetti, D. G. (1995). The accuracy of children's reports with anatomically correct dolls. *Journal of Developmental and Behavioral Pediatrics,* **16,** 71–76.

Keary, K., & Fitzpatrick, C. (1994). Children's disclosure of sexual abuse during formal investigation. *Child Abuse and Neglect,* **18,** 543–548.

Kehinde v. Commonwealth, 338 S.E.2d 356 (1986).

Kempe, C. H., Silverman, F. N., Steele, B. F., Droegmueller, W., & Silver, H. R. (1962). The battered child syndrome. *Journal of the American Medical Association,* **181,** 17–24.

Kendall-Tackett, K. A. (1992). Professionals' standards of "normal" behavior with anatomical dolls and factors that influence these standards. *Child Abuse and Neglect,* **16,** 727–733.

Kendall-Tackett, K. A., & Watson, M. W. (1991). Factors that influence professionals' perceptions of behavioral indicators of child sexual abuse. *Journal of Interpersonal Violence,* **6,** 385–395.

Kenning, M., Merchant, A., & Tomkins, A. (1991). Research on the effects of witnessing parental violence: Clinical and legal policy implications. In M. Steinman (Ed.), *Woman battering: Policy responses.* Cincinnati: Anderson.

Kenyon-Jump, R., Burnette, M. M., & Robertson, M. (1991). Comparison of behaviors of suspected sexually abused and nonsexually abused preschool children using anatomical dolls. *Journal of Psychopathology and Behavioral Assessment,* **13,** 225–240.

Kessen, W. (1960). Research design in the study of developmental problems. In P. Mussen (Ed.), *Handbook of research methods in child development.* New York: Wiley.

King, M. A., & Yuille, J. C. (1987). Suggestibility and the child eyewitness. In S. J. Ceci, M. P. Toglia, & D. F. Ross (Eds.), *Children's eyewitness memory.* New York: Springer.

Kiser, L., Heston, J., Hickerson, S., Millsap, P., Nunn, W., & Pruitt, D. (1993). Anticipatory stress in children and adolescents. *American Journal of Psychiatry,* **150,** 87–92.

Kobasigawa, A. (1974). Utilization of retrieval cues by children in recall. *Child Development,* **45,** 127–133.

Koocher, G., Goodman, G. S., White, S., Friedrich, W. N., Sivan, A. B., & Reynolds, C. R. (1994, February). *Report of the anatomical doll task force to the American Psychological Association Council of Representatives.* Washington, DC: American Psychological Association.

Kuttner, L., Bowman, M., & Teasdale, J. M. (1989). Psychological treatment of distress, pain and anxiety for young children with cancer. *Journal of Developmental and Behavioral Pediatrics,* **9,** 374–381.

Kuttner, L., & Lepage, T. (1989). Faces scales for the assessment of pediatric pain: A critical review. *Canadian Journal of Behavioral Science, 21,* 198–209.

Lamb, M. E., Sternberg, K. J., & Esplin, P. W. (1994). Factors influencing the reliability and validity of statements made by young victims of sexual maltreatment. *Journal of Applied Developmental Psychology, 15,* 255–280.

Lapham, S. C., Kring, M. K., & Skipper, B. (1991). Prenatal behavioral risk screening by computer in a health maintenance organization–based prenatal care clinic. *American Journal of Obstetrics and Gynecology, 165,* 506–514.

LeBaron, S., & Zeltzer, L. (1984). Assessment of acute pain and anxiety in children and adolescents by self-reports, observer reports and behavioral checklist. *Journal of Consulting and Clinical Psychology, 52,* 729–738.

Leippe, M. R., Mannion, A. P., & Romancyzk, A. (1991). Eyewitness memory for a touching experience: Accuracy differences between child and adult witnesses. *Journal of Applied Psychology, 76,* 367–379.

Leippe, M. R., Mannion, A. P., & Romancyzk, A. (1993). Discernibility or discrimination? Understanding jurors' reactions to accurate and inaccurate child and adult eyewitnesses. In G. S. Goodman & B. L. Bottoms (Eds.), *Child victims, child witnesses: Understanding and improving testimony.* New York: Guilford.

Leippe, M. R., & Romancyzk, A. (1987). Children on the witness stand: A communication / persuasion analysis of jurors' reactions to child witnesses. In S. J. Ceci, M. P. Toglia, & D. F. Ross (Eds.), *Children's eyewitness memory.* New York: Springer.

Leventhal, J. M., Hamilton, J., Rekedal, S., Tebano-Micci, A., & Eyster, C. (1989). Anatomically correct dolls used in interviews of young children suspected of having been sexually abused. *Pediatrics, 84,* 900–906.

Levy, D. (1945). Psychic trauma of operations in children. *American Journal of Diseases of Childhood, 69,* 7–25.

Lewis, M. (1990). Social knowledge and social development. *Merrill-Palmer Quarterly, 36,* 93–116.

Lewis, M. (1991). Self-knowledge and social influence. In M. Lewis & S. Feinman (Eds.), *Social influences and socialization in infancy.* New York: Plenum.

Lewis, M. (1992). *Shame: The exposed self.* New York: Free Press.

Lewis, M., Sullivan, M. W., Stanger, C., & Weiss, M. (1989). Self development and self-conscious emotions. *Child Development, 60,* 146–156.

Lipovsky, J. A., Tidwell, R., Crisp, J., Kilpatrick, D. G., Saunders, B. E., & Dawson, V. L. (1992). Child witnesses in criminal court: Descriptive information from three southern states. *Law and Human Behavior, 16,* 635–650.

Loftus, E. F. (1979). *Eyewitness testimony.* Cambridge, MA: Harvard University Press.

Loftus, E. F. (1991). The glitter of everyday memory and the gold. *American Psychologist, 46,* 16–18.

Loftus, E. F., & Davies, G. M. (1984). Distortions in the memory of children. *Journal of Social Issues, 40,* 51–67.

Lollar, D. J., Smits, S. J., & Patterson, D. L. (1982). Assessment of pediatric pain: An empirical perspective. *Journal of Pediatric Psychology, 7,* 267–277.

Long, P. J., & Jackson, J. L. (1991). Children sexually abused by multiple perpetrators. *Journal of Interpersonal Violence, 6,* 147–159.

MacFarlane, K., & Krebs, S. (1986). Techniques for interviewing and evidence gathering. In K. MacFarlane & J. Waterman (Eds.), *Sexual abuse of young children.* New York: Guilford.

Malbourne, A. L., Ungerer, J. A., & Champion, G. D. (1991). Analysis of the judgements by nurses and parents of children's postoperative pain. *Journal of Pain and Symptom Management, 6,* 148.

177

Mandler, J. M. (1990). Recall and its verbal expression. In R. Fivush & J. A. Hudson (Eds.), *Knowing and remembering in young children*. New York: Cambridge University Press.

Manne, S. L., Jacobsen, P. B., & Redd, W. H. (1992). Assessment of acute pediatric pain: Do child self-report, parent ratings, and nurse ratings measure the same phenomenon? *Pain, 48,* 45–52.

Marin, B. V., Holmes, D. L., Guth, M., & Kovacs, P. (1979). The potential of children as eye witnesses. *Law and Human Behavior, 3,* 295–309.

Maryland v. Craig, 110 S. Ct. 3157 (1990).

Mason, M. A. (1991, Winter). A judicial dilemma: Expert witness testimony in child sex abuse cases? *Journal of Psychiatry and the Law,* 185–219.

Massie, R. K., Jr. (1985). The constant shadow: Reflections on the life of a chronically ill child. In N. Hobbs & J. M. Perrin (Eds.), *Issues in the care of children with chronic illness.* San Francisco: Jossey-Bass.

Masters, J. C., Barden, R. C., & Ford, M. E. (1979). Affective states, expressive behavior and learning in children. *Journal of Personality and Social Psychology, 37,* 380–390.

McCann, J. (1990). Use of the colposcope in childhood sexual abuse examinations. *Pediatric Clinics of North America, 37,* 863–880.

McCloskey, M., & Zaragoza, M. (1985). Misleading postevent information and memory for events: Arguments and evidence against the memory impairment hypothesis. *Journal of Experimental Psychology: General, 114,* 1–16.

McCubbin, H. I., Patterson, J. M., & Wilson, L. R. (1981). *Family Inventory of Life Events and Changes.* St. Paul: Family Social Science, University of Minnesota.

McGough, L. (1994). *Child witnesses: Fragile voices in the American legal system.* New Haven, CT: Yale University Press.

McGrath, P. A. (1987). An assessment of children's pain: A review of behavioral, physiological and direct scaling techniques. *Pain, 31,* 147–176.

McGrath, P. A. (1991). Versatile pain measures for children. *Journal of Pain and Symptom Management, 6,* 175.

McGrath, P. A., deVeber, L. L., & Hearn, M. T. (1985). Multidimensional pain assessment in children. In H. L. Fields, R. Dubner, & F. Cervero (Eds.), *Advancements in pain research and therapy* (Vol. 9). New York: Raven.

Mehrabian, A., & Wiener, M. (1967). Decoding of inconsistent communications. *Journal of Personality and Social Psychology, 6,* 109–114.

Melton, G. B. (1981). Children's competency to testify. *Law and Human Behavior, 5,* 73–85.

Melton, G. B. (Ed.). (1987). *Reforming the law: Impact of child development research.* New York: Guilford.

Melton, G. B., & Limber, S. (1989). Psychologists' involvement in cases of child maltreatment. *American Psychologist, 44,* 1225–1233.

Melton, G. B., Petrila, J., Poythress, N. G., & Slobogin, C. (1987). *Psychological evaluations for the courts.* New York: Guilford.

Melton, G. B., & Thompson, R. (1987). Getting out of the rut: Detours to less traveled paths in child-witness research. In S. J. Ceci, M. P. Toglia, & D. F. Ross (Eds.), *Children's eyewitness memory.* New York: Springer.

Melzack, R. (1975). The McGill Pain Questionnaire: Major properties and scoring methods. *Pain, 1,* 277–299.

Merritt, K. A., Ornstein, P. A., & Spiker, B. (1994). Children's memory for a salient medical procedure: Implications for testimony. *Pediatrics, 94,* 17–23.

Merskey, H. (1979). Pain terms: A list with definitions and notes on usage: Recommended by the International Association for the Study of Pain Subcommittee on Taxonomy. *Pain, 6,* 249–252.

Miller, P. J., Potts, R., Fung, H., Hoogstra, L., & Mintz, J. (1990). Narrative practices and the social construction of the self. *Journal of Child Language,* **15,** 293–315.

Millstein, S. G., & Irwin, C. E. (1983). Acceptability of computer-acquired sexual histories in adolescent girls. *Journal of Pediatrics,* **103,** 815–819.

Mischler, E. G. (1986). *Research interviewing: Context and narrative.* Cambridge, MA: Harvard University Press.

Monahan, J., & Walker, L. (1991). Judicial use of social science research. *Law and Human Behavior,* **15,** 571–584.

Mrazek, D. A., & Mrazek, P. B. (1981). Psychosexual development within the family. In P. B. Mrazek & C. H. Kempe (Eds.), *Sexually abused children and their families.* New York: Pergamon.

Myers, J. E. B. (1987). *Child witness law and practice.* New York: Wiley.

Myers, J. E. B. (1989). Allegations of child sexual abuse in custody and visitation litigation: Recommendations for improved fact finding and child protection. *Journal of Family Law* (University of Louisville School of Law), **28,** 1.

Myers, J. E. B. (1992). *Legal issues in child abuse and neglect.* Newbury Park, CA: Sage.

Myers, J. E. B. (Ed.). (1994, June). *Child Victim Witness Investigative Pilot Project: Research and evaluation final report.* Sacramento: California Attorney-General's Office.

Nasby, W., & Yondo, R. (1982). Selective encoding and retrieval of affectively valent information. *Journal of Personality and Social Psychology,* **43,** 1244–1255.

Nathanson, D. L. (1989). Understanding what is hidden: Shame in sexual abuse. *Psychiatric Clinics of North America,* **12,** 381–388.

National Research Council. (1993). *Understanding child abuse and neglect.* Washington, DC: National Academy Press.

Neisser, U. (1978). Memory: What are the important questions? In M. M. Gruneberg, P. E. Morris, & R. N. Sykes (Eds.), *Practical aspects of memory.* New York: Academic.

Neisser, U. (1988). New vistas in the study of memory. In U. Neisser & E. Winograd (Eds.), *Remembering reconsidered: Ecological and traditional approaches to the study of memory.* New York: Cambridge University Press.

Neisser, U. (1991). A case of misplaced nostalgia. *American Psychologist,* **46,** 34–36.

Nelson, K. (1988). The ontogeny of memory for real events. In U. Neisser & E. Winograd (Eds.), *Remembering reconsidered: Ecological and traditional approaches to the study of memory.* New York: Cambridge University Press.

Nelson, K. (1989). Remembering: A functional developmental perspective. In P. R. Solomon, G. R. Goethals, C. M. Kelley, & B. R. Stephens (Eds.), *Memory: Interdisciplinary approaches.* New York: Springer.

Nelson, K. (1993). Events, narratives, memory: What develops? In C. A. Nelson (Ed.), *Memory and affect in development* (Minnesota Symposium on Child Psychology, Vol. **26**). Hillsdale, NJ: Erlbaum.

Nelson, K., & Hudson, J. (1988). Scripts and memory: Functional relationships in development. In F. E. Weinert & M. Perlmutter (Eds.), *Memory development: Universal changes and individual differences.* Hillsdale, NJ: Erlbaum.

Nelson, K., & Ross, G. (1980). The generalities and specifics of long-term memory in infants and young children. In M. Perlmutter (Ed.), *Children's memory* (New Directions for Child Development, Vol. **10**). San Francisco: Jossey-Bass.

New Jersey v. Michaels, 625 A.2d 489 (N.J. Super. A.D.) (1993).

New Jersey v. Michaels, 1994 WL 278424 (N.J.).

Nurcombe, B. (1986). The child as witness: Competency and credibility. *Journal of the American Academy of Child Psychiatry,* **25,** 473–480.

Oates, K., & Shrimpton, S. (1991). Children's memories for stressful and non-stressful events. *Medical Science Law,* **31,** 4–10.

Odum, R., & Lemond, C. M. (1972). Developmental differences in the perception and production of facial expressions. *Child Development, 43,* 359–369.

Ornstein, P. A., Follmer, A., & Gordon, B. N. (1995, April). The influence of dolls and props on young children's recall of pediatric examinations. In M. Bruck & S. J. Ceci (Chairs), *The use of props in eliciting children's reports of past events: Theoretical and forensic perspectives.* Symposium conducted at the meeting of the Society for Research in Child Development, Indianapolis.

Ornstein, P. A., Gordon, B. N., & Larus, D. M. (1992). Children's memory for a personally experienced event: Implications for testimony. *Applied Cognitive Psychology, 6,* 49–60.

Ornstein, P. A., Larus, D. M., & Clubb, P. A. (1991). Understanding children's testimony: Implications of research on the development of memory. In R. Vasta (Ed.), *Annals of Child Development* (Vol. 8). London: Jessica Kingsley.

Paliwal, P., & Goss, A. E. (1981). Attributes of schematic faces in preschoolers' use of names of emotions. *Bulletin of the Psychonomic Society, 17,* 139–142.

Paperny, D. M., Aono, J. Y., Lehman, R. M., Hammar, S. L., & Risser, J. (1990). Computer-assisted detection and intervention in adolescent high-risk health behaviors. *Journal of Pediatrics, 116,* 456–462.

Paradise, J. E. (1990). The medical evaluation of the sexually abused child. *Pediatric Clinics of North America: Child Abuse, 37,* 839–862.

Parker, J. F., Haverfield, E., & Baker-Thomas, S. (1986). Eyewitness testimony of children. *Journal of Applied Social Psychology, 16,* 287-302.

Pearson, G. H. J. (1941). Effective operative procedures on the emotional life of the child. *American Journal of Diseases of Children, 62,* 716–729.

Pennsylvania v. Richie, 480 U.S. 39 (1987).

People v. Rich, 520 N.Y.S.2d 911 (1987).

Perlmutter, M., & Ricks, M. (1979). Recall in preschool children. *Journal of Experimental Child Psychology, 27,* 423–436.

Perry, N. W., & Wrightsman, L. S. (1991). *The child witness: Legal issues and dilemmas.* Newbury Park, CA: Sage.

Peters, D. P. (1987). The impact of naturally occurring stress on children's memory. In S. J. Ceci, M. P. Toglia, & D. F. Ross (Eds.), *Children's eyewitness memory.* New York: Springer.

Peters, D. P. (1991). The influence of stress and arousal in research on children's testimony. In J. Doris (Ed.), *The suggestibility of children's recollections.* Washington, DC: American Psychological Association.

Peterson, L., Harbeck, C., Farmer, J., & Zink, M. (1991). Developmental contributions to the assessment of children's pain: Conceptual and methodological implications. In J. P. Bush & S. W. Harkins (Eds.), *Children in pain: Clinical and research issues from a developmental perspective.* New York: Springer.

Peterson, L., Moreno, A., & Harbeck-Weber, C. (1993). "And then it started bleeding": Children's and mothers' perceptions and recollections of daily injury events. *Journal of Clinical Child Psychology, 22,* 345–354.

Peterson, L. J., & Mori, L. (1988). Preparation for hospitalization. In D. K. Routh (Ed.), *Handbook of pediatric psychology.* New York: Guilford.

Petrillo, M., & Sanger, S. (1980). *Emotional care of the hospitalized child* (2d ed.). Philadelphia: Lippincott.

Pillemer, D. B., & White, S. H. (1989). Childhood events recalled by children and adults. In H. W. Reese (Ed.), *Advances in child development and behavior.* New York: Academic.

Pipe, M.-E., Gee, S., & Wilson, C. (1993). Cues, props and context: Do they facilitate children's event reports? In G. S. Goodman & B. L. Bottoms (Eds.), *Child victims, child witnesses: Understanding and improving testimony.* New York: Guilford.

Plank, E. (1971). *Working with children in hospitals: A guide for the professional team* (2d ed.). Cleveland: Press of Case Western Reserve University.

Poole, D. A., & White, L. T. (1991). Effects of question repetition on the eyewitness testimony of children and adults. *Developmental Psychology, 27,* 975–986.

Poole, D. A., & White, L. T. (1995). Tell me again and again: Stability and change in the repeated testimonies of children and adults. In M. S. Zaragoza, J. R. Graham, G. C. N. Hall, R. Hirschman, & Y. S. Ben-Porath (Eds.), *Memory and testimony in the child witness.* Thousand Oaks, CA: Sage.

Price, D. W. W., & Goodman, G. S. (1990). Visiting the wizard: Children's memory for a recurring event. *Child Development, 61,* 664–680.

Putnam, F. W., & Trickett, P. K. (1993). Child sexual abuse: A model of chronic trauma. *Psychiatry, 56,* 82–95.

Pynoos, R. S., & Eth, S. (1986). Witness to violence: The child interview. *Journal of the American Academy of Child and Adolescent Psychiatry, 25,* 473–490.

Pynoos, R. S., & Nader, K. (1989). Children's memory and proximity to violence. *Journal of the American Academy of Child and Adolescent Psychiatry, 28,* 236–241.

Raskin, D. C., & Esplin, P. W. (1991). Assessment of children's statements of sexual abuse. In J. Doris (Ed.), *The suggestibility of children's recollections.* Washington, DC: American Psychological Association.

Ritter, K. (1978). The development of knowledge of an external retrieval cue strategy. *Child Development, 49,* 1227–1230.

Ritter, K., Kaprove, B. H., Fitch, J. P., & Flavell, J. H. (1973). The development of retrieval strategies in young children. *Cognitive Psychology, 5,* 310–321.

Robertson, D. M., Barbar, P., & Hull, D. (1982). Unusual injury? Recent injury in normal children and children with suspected non-accidental injury. *British Medical Journal, 285,* 1399–1401.

Robertson, J. (1956). A mother's observation on the tonsillectomy of her four-year-old daughter. *Psychoanalytic Study of the Child, 11,* 410–436.

Rogoff, B., & Mistry, J. (1990). The context of children's remembering. In R. Fivush & J. A. Hudson (Eds.), *Knowing and remembering in young children.* New York: Cambridge University Press.

Rose, S. A., & Blank, M. (1974). The potency of context in children's cognition: An illustration through conservation. *Child Development, 45,* 499–502.

Ross, D. M., & Ross, S. A. (1982). *A study of the pain experience in children: Final report* (Ref. No. 1 R01 HD 13672–01). Bethesda, MD: National Institute of Child Health and Human Development.

Ross, D. M., & Ross, S. A. (1984a). Childhood pain: The school-aged child's viewpoint. *Pain, 20,* 179–191.

Ross, D. M., & Ross, S. A. (1984b). The importance of type of question, psychological climate and subject set in interviewing children about pain. *Pain, 19,* 71–79.

Ross, D. M., & Ross, S. A. (1988). *Childhood pain: Current issues, research and management.* Baltimore: Urban & Schwarzberg.

Runyan, D. K., Everson, M. D., Edelsohn, G. A., Hunter, W. M., & Coulter, M. L. (1988). Impact of legal intervention on sexually abused children. *Journal of Pediatrics, 113,* 647–653.

Russell, D. (1984). *Sexual exploitation.* Beverly Hills, CA: Sage.

Saarni, C. (1984). An observational study of children's attempts to monitor their expressive behavior. *Child Development, 55,* 1504–1513.

Salmon, K., Bidrose, S., & Pipe, M. E. (in press). Providing props to facilitate children's event reports: A comparison of toys and real items. *Journal of Experimental Child Psychology.*

Sapolsky, R. M., Krey, L. C., & McEwen, B. S. (1985). Prolonged glucocorticoid exposure reduces hippocampal neuron number. *Journal of Neuroscience, 5,* 1221–1226.

Sas, L. D. (1991). *Reducing the system-induced trauma for child sexual abuse victims through court preparation, assessment and follow-up.* London, ON: Child Witness Project, London Family Court Clinic.

Sauzier, M. (1989). Disclosure of child sexual abuse. *Psychiatric Clinics of North America: Treatment of Victims of Sexual Abuse, 12,* 455–469.

Savedra, M. C., Holzemer, W. L., Tesler, M. D., & Wilke, D. J. (1993). Assessment of postoperative pain in children and adolescents using the Adolescent Pediatric Pain Tool. *Nursing Research, 42,* 5–9.

Savedra, M. C., & Tesler, M. D. (1989). Assessing children's and adolescents' pain. *Pediatrician, 16,* 24–29.

Saywitz, K. (1989). Children's conceptions of the legal system: "Court is a place to play basketball." In S. J. Ceci, D. F. Ross, & M. P. Toglia (Eds.), *Perspectives on children's testimony.* New York: Springer.

Saywitz, K. (1990). The child as witness: Experimental and clinical considerations. In A. LaGreca (Ed.), *Through the eyes of the child.* Boston: Allyn & Bacon.

Saywitz, K. J., Goodman, G. S., & Myers, J. E. B. (1990). Can children provide accurate eyewitness reports? *Violence Update, 1,* 9.

Saywitz, K. J., Goodman, G. S., Nicholas, E., & Moan, S. (1991). Children's memories of a physical examination involving genital touch: Implications for reports of child sexual abuse. *Journal of Consulting and Clinical Psychology, 59,* 682–691.

Saywitz, K. J., Jaenicke, C., & Camparo, L. (1990). Children's knowledge of legal terminology. *Law and Human Behavior, 14,* 523–535.

Saywitz, K. J., & Snyder, L. (1993). Improving children's testimony with preparation. In G. S. Goodman & B. L. Bottoms (Eds.), *Child victims, child witnesses: Understanding and improving testimony.* New York: Guilford.

Schmidt, C. R., & Schmidt, S. R. (1986). The use of themes as retrieval cues in children's memory for stories. *Journal of Experimental Child Psychology, 42,* 237–255.

Schneider, W., & Pressley, M. (1989). *Memory development between 2 and 20.* New York: Springer.

Schor, D. P., & Sivan, A. B. (1989). Interpreting children's labels for sex-related body parts of anatomically explicit dolls. *Child Abuse and Neglect, 13,* 523–531.

Secord, P., & Jourard, S. (1953). The appraisal of body cathexis: Body cathexis of the self. *Journal of Consulting Psychology, 17,* 343–347.

Seligman, M. E. P. (1975). *Learned helplessness: On depression, development and death.* San Francisco: Freeman.

Sheingold, K., & Tenney, Y. J. (1982). Memory for a salient childhood event. In U. Neisser (Ed.), *Memory observed.* San Francisco: Freeman.

Sivan, A. B. (1987). *Research on child sexual abuse: A pilot study of interactions of non-abused children with anatomically correct dolls.* Unpublished manuscript, Child Development Clinic, University Hospital School, University of Iowa, Iowa City.

Skinner, L. J., & Berry, K. K. (1993). Anatomically detailed dolls and the evaluation of child sexual abuse allegations. *Law and Human Behavior, 17,* 399–421.

Slackman, E. A., Hudson, J. A., & Fivush, R. (1986). Actions, actors, links, and goals: The structure of children's event representations. In K. Nelson (Ed.), *Event knowledge: Structure and function in development.* Hillsdale, NJ: Erlbaum.

Smith, B. S., Ratner, H. H., & Hobart, C. J. (1987). The role of cuing and organization in children's memory for events. *Journal of Experimental Child Psychology, 44,* 1–24.

Sorenson, T., & Snow, B. (1991). How children tell: The process of disclosure in child sexual abuse. *Child Welfare, 70,* 3–15.

Spencer, J., & Flin, R. (1990). *The evidence of children*. London: Blackstone.

State v. Eggert, 358 N.W.2d 156 (1984).

Stein, A., & Lewis, D. O. (1992). Discovering physical abuse: Insights from a follow-up study of delinquents. *Child Abuse and Neglect*, **16**, 523–531.

Stein, N. L., Trabasso, T., & Liwag, M. (1992). The representation and organization of emotional experience: Unfolding the emotional episode. In M. Lewis & J. Haviland (Eds.), *Handbook of emotion*. New York: Guilford.

Stein, N. L., Wade, E., & Liwag, M. (in press). A theoretical approach to understanding and remembering emotional events. In N. L. Stein, P. A. Ornstein, B. Tversky, & C. Brainerd (Eds.), *Memory for everyday and emotional events*. Hillsdale, NJ: Erlbaum.

Steward, M. S. (1988). Illness: A crisis for children. In J. Sandoval (Ed.), *Crisis counseling, intervention and prevention in the schools*. Hillsdale, NJ: Erlbaum.

Steward, M. S. (1993). Understanding children's memories of medical procedures: "He didn't touch me and it didn't hurt!" In C. A. Nelson (Ed.), *Memory and affect in development* (Minnesota Symposium on Child Psychology, Vol. **26**). Hillsdale, NJ: Erlbaum.

Steward, M. S., Bussey, K., Goodman, G. S., & Saywitz, K. (1993). Implications of developmental research for interviewing children. *Child Abuse and Neglect*, **17**, 25–37.

Steward, M. S., O'Connor, J., Acredolo, C., & Steward, D. S. (1996). The trauma and memory of cancer treatment in children. In M. H. Bornstein & J. L. Genevro (Eds.), *Child development and behavioral pediatrics*. Hillsdale, NJ: Erlbaum.

Steward, M. S., Schmitz, M., Steward, D. S., Joye, N., & Reinhart, M. (1995). Children's anticipation for and response to a colposcopic examination. *Child Abuse and Neglect*, **19**, 997–1005.

Steward, M. S., & Steward, D. S. (1981). Children's concepts of medical procedures. In R. Bibace & M. Walsh (Eds.), *The development of children's conceptions of health and related phenomena*. San Francisco: Jossey-Bass.

Steward, M. S., Steward, D. S., Joye, N., & Reinhart, M. (1991). Pain judgments by young children and medical staff. *Journal of Pain and Symptom Management*, **6**(3), 202.

Summit, R. (1983). The child sexual abuse accommodation syndrome. *Child Abuse and Neglect*, **7**, 177–193.

Tedesco, J. F., & Schnell, S. V. (1987). Children's reactions to sex abuse investigation and litigation. *Child Abuse and Neglect*, **11**, 267–272.

Terr, L. (1979). Children of Chowchilla: A study of psychic trauma. *Psychoanalytic Study of the Child*, **34**, 547–623.

Terr, L. (1983). Chowchilla revisited: The effects of psychic trauma four years after a school-bus kidnapping. *American Journal of Psychiatry*, **140**, 1543–1550.

Terr, L. (1990). *Too scared to cry*. New York: Harper & Row.

Terr, L. (1991). Childhood traumas: An outline and overview. *American Journal of Psychiatry*, **148**, 10–20.

Thoennes, N., & Tjaden, P. G. (1990). The extent, nature, and validity of sexual abuse allegations in custody/visitation disputes. *Child Abuse and Neglect*, **14**, 151–163.

Todd, C. M., & Perlmutter, M. (1980). Reality recalled by preschool children. In M. Perlmutter (Ed.), *Children's memory* (New Directions for Child Development, Vol. **10**). San Francisco: Jossey-Bass.

U.S. Attorney-General. (1984). *Task Force on Family Violence: Final report*. Washington, DC: Department of Justice.

Usher, J. A., & Neisser, U. (1993). Childhood amnesia and the beginnings of memory for four early life events. *Journal of Experimental Psychology: General*, **122**, 155–165.

Wagenaar, W. A., & Groeneweg, J. (1990). The memory of concentration camp survivors. *Applied Cognitive Psychology*, **4**, 77–87.

Walker, A. G. (1993). Questioning young children in court: A linguistic case study. *Law and Human Behavior*, **17**, 59–82.

Warner, K. (1990). Child witnesses—developments in Australia and New Zealand. In J. Spencer, G. Nicholson, R. Flin, & R. Bull (Eds.), *Children's evidence in legal proceedings*. Cambridge: Cambridge University Law Faculty.

Warren-Leubecker, A. (1991). Commentary: Development of event memories or event reports? In J. Doris (Ed.), *The suggestibility of children's recollections*. Washington, DC: American Psychological Association.

Waterman, J., & Lusk, R. (1986). Scope of the problem. In K. MacFarlane & J. Waterman (Eds.), *Sexual abuse of young children*. New York: Guilford.

Watt-Watson, J., Evernden, C., & Lawson, C. (1991). Parents' perceptions of children's acute pain experience. *Journal of Pain and Symptom Management, 6*, 149.

Weissman, H. N. (1991). Forensic psychological examination of the child witness in cases of alleged sexual abuse. *American Journal of Orthopsychiatry, 61*, 48–58.

Wellman, H. M. (1977). Tip of the tongue and feeling of knowing experience: A developmental study of memory monitoring. *Child Development, 48*, 13–21.

Wellman, H. M. (1978). Knowledge of the interaction of memory variables: A developmental study of metamemory. *Developmental Psychology, 14*, 24–29.

Whitcomb, D., Shapiro, E. R., & Stellwagen, L. D. (1985). *When the victim is a child: Issues for judges and prosecutors*. Washington, DC: U.S. Department of Justice, National Institute of Justice.

White, S. (1988). Should investigatory use of anatomical dolls be defined by the courts? *Journal of Interpersonal Violence, 3*, 471–475.

White, S., & Quinn, K. M. (1988). Investigatory independence in child sexual abuse evaluations: Conceptual considerations. *Bulletin of the American Academy of Psychiatry and Law, 16*, 269–278.

White, S., & Santilli, G. (1989). A review of clinical practices and research data on anatomical dolls. *Journal of Interpersonal Violence, 3*, 430–442.

White, S., Santilli, G., & Quinn, K. (1988). Child evaluators' roles in child sexual abuse assessments. In E. B. Nicholson & J. Bulkley (Eds.), *Sexual abuse allegations in custody and visitation cases: A resource book for judges and court personnel*. Washington, DC: American Bar Association.

White, S., Strom, G., & Santilli, G. (1986). *A clinical protocol of interviewing young children with sexually anatomically correct dolls*. Unpublished manuscript, Case Western Reserve University School of Medicine.

White, S., Strom, G., Santilli, G., & Halpin, B. M. (1986). Interviewing young sexual abuse victims with anatomically correct dolls. *Child Abuse and Neglect, 10*, 519–529.

White, S., Strom, G., Santilli, G., & Quinn, K. M. (1987). *Guidelines for interviewing preschoolers with sexually anatomically detailed dolls*. Unpublished manuscript, Case Western Reserve University School of Medicine.

Wilkinson, L. (1989). *SYSTAT: The system for statistics*. Evanston, IL: SYSTAT.

Williams, M. B. (1993). Assessing the traumatic impact of child sexual abuse: What makes it more severe? *Journal of Child Sexual Abuse, 2*, 41–59.

Wilson, J. C., & Pipe, M.-E. (1989). The effects of cues on young children's recall of real events. *New Zealand Journal of Psychology, 18*, 65–70.

Wong, D. L., & Baker, C. M. (1988). Pain in children: Comparison of assessment scales. *Pediatric Nursing, 14*, 9–17.

Worlock, P., Stower, M., & Barbar, P. (1986). Patterns of fractures in accidental and non-accidental injury in children: A comparative study. *British Medical Journal, 293*, 100–102.

Yarmey, A. D. (1984). Age as a factor in eyewitness memory. In G. L. Wells & E. F. Loftus (Eds.), *Eyewitness testimony*. New York: Cambridge University Press.

Yates, A. (1987). Should young children testify in cases of sexual abuse? *American Journal of Psychiatry, 144*, 476–479.

Yates, A., & Musty, T. (1988). Preschool children's erroneous allegations of sexual molestation. *American Journal of Psychiatry,* **145,** 989–992.

Yates, A., & Terr, L. (1988a). Debate forum: Anatomically correct dolls: Should they be used as a basis for expert testimony? *Journal of the American Academy of Child and Adolescent Psychiatry,* **27,** 254–257.

Yates, A., & Terr, L. (1988b). Debate forum: Issue continued: Anatomically correct dolls: Should they be used as a basis for expert testimony? *Journal of the American Academy of Child and Adolescent Psychiatry,* **27,** 387–388.

Yuille, J. C. (1988). The systematic assessment of children's testimony. *Canadian Psychology,* **29,** 247–262.

Yuille, J. C., & Tollstrup, P. A. (1992). A model of diverse effects of emotion on eyewitness memory. In S. A. Christianson (Ed.), *The handbook of emotion and memory: Research and theory.* Hillsdale, NJ: Erlbaum.

Yuille, J. C., & Wells, G. L. (1991). Concerns about the application of research findings: The issue of ecological validity. In J. Doris (Ed.), *The suggestibility of children's recollections.* Washington, DC: American Psychological Association.

Zaragoza, M. S. (1987). Memory, suggestibility, and eyewitness testimony in children and adults. In S. J. Ceci, M. P. Toglia, & D. F. Ross (Eds.), *Children's eyewitness memory.* New York: Springer.

Zaragoza, M. S. (1991). Preschool children's susceptibility to memory impairment. In J. Doris (Ed.), *The suggestibility of children's recollections.* Washington, DC: American Psychological Association.

Zimmerman, M. L., Wolbert, W. A., Burgess, A. W., & Hartman, C. R. (1987). Art and group work: Interventions for multiple victims of child molestation (Part II). *Archives of Psychiatric Nursing,* **1,** 40–46.

ACKNOWLEDGMENTS

This research was supported by grant 90CA1332 to Margaret Steward from the National Center on Child Abuse and Neglect, U.S. Department of Health and Human Services, and by a grant to Margaret Steward from Apple Computer, Inc., Community Affairs. During the 1989–1990 academic year, Margaret Steward and David Steward were hosted at the University of Nebraska as visiting faculty in the Department of Psychology and as affiliates at the Center for Children, Families and the Law. Colleagues from both the university and the center gave us wonderful support during our year with them. During 1990, Margaret Steward and David Steward were Rockefeller Scholars-in-Residence at the Villa Serbelloni in Bellagio, Italy. We greatly appreciate the generosity of the Rockefeller Foundation and the continuing support of our Bellagio colleagues from the "Class of 1990."

Portions of this research were presented at the twenty-sixth Minnesota Symposium on Child Psychology in October 1991, a lecture that was summarized in Steward (1993), and at the meeting of the American Psychological Association in San Francisco in August 1991 and the Australian Developmental Conference in Brisbane in July 1992, lectures that were summarized in Bussey, Steward, Pipe, Peterson, and Lawrence (1992). This *Monograph* represents the first presentation of the details of the procedures and of the coding and statistical analysis of the data.

A great number of very good people have worked with us on this study. First, we want to thank the children and families who participated in this study. Three persons served as interviewers on the research team: Dr. John Capel, Dr. Nicole Varzos, and Dr. Holly Ilfeld. All three are highly skilled clinicians, experienced in diagnostic and psychotherapeutic work with young children and their families. Young children can be a challenge to interview. Review of the videotapes confirms that our interviewers more than "earned their keep" by deftly balancing sensitivity to the children with the sometimes arbitrary demands of the research project. In addition to utilizing their skill in interaction with children and families, the interviewers were responsible for the maintenance of professional relationships with medical staff in seven pediatric clinics. Without their consistent attention to the interpersonal networks of children, families, and staff, this study would not have been possible.

Our coders, Laurie Nickel and Barbara Ashby, were creatively involved in the design of the coding system from the beginning and cheerfully worked through several evolutions before the final system was developed. We are grateful for their attention to detail, careful handling of the data, and respect for the children. Jonathan Matte designed the software program used in the computer-assisted interview. We appreciate his creativity in putting onto disk what had until then been only in our minds, his patience with us as we modified our requests of him, and his skill in producing a "state-of-the-art" program that did everything we asked of it.

Two program directors at the Early Childhood Laboratory on the University of California, Davis, campus deserve special recognition and our thanks: Kay Jean Stockman and Susan Weiss. The following students worked with us on various phases of the study, and we appreciate their labors: Stacy Glaser, Alison Kimmel, Martha Schmitz, Lyn Shelton, and Kaia Thompson. In addition, we want to thank several students who were themselves abused as young children and contributed their efforts on the research team but requested that we not name them.

The pioneers at the Sacramento County Multi-Disciplinary Interview Center have been tough, smart, and great collaborators, and we acknowledge their enormous contribution to our thinking and practice: Laura Coulthard, Paula Christian, Harriett Kekevian, Melinda Lake, Elizabeth Foster Ward, Helen Barber, and Kim Berardi.

We appreciate the access that our medical school colleagues gave us to their medical staff and patients in the pediatric specialty clinics. Thanks go to the following clinic directors: Dr. Charles Abildgaard, chief, Division of Hematology/Oncology; Dr. Robert Cannon, chief, Division of Pediatric Gastroenterology; Dr. Michael Choi, chief, Division of Pediatric Cardiology; Dr. Ruth McDonald, chief, Division of Pediatric Pulmonary Diseases; Dr. Mary Metcalf, medical director of the Pediatric Continuity Clinic; Dr. Michael Reinhart, chief of Ambulatory Pediatrics and medical director of the Child Protection Center; and Dr. Elizabeth Smithwick, medical director of the Juvenile Arthritis Clinic. Two University of California, Davis, faculty colleagues also deserve our gratitude. Dr. Curt Acredolo shares our love of numbers and worked closely with us on the development of the coding manual. He was an invaluable and enthusiastic statistical consultant. Dr. Jacqueline O'Connor patiently and deftly read and reread early drafts of the manuscript. The careful reviews of Dr. Robin Fivush and Dr. Peter Ornstein and a third, anonymous colleague were valuable in helping us communicate more clearly the research findings.

ACHIEVING REAL REFORM:
THE CASE FOR AMERICAN INTERVIEWING PROTOCOLS

Lucy S. McGough

This *Monograph* makes two significant contributions to our improved understanding of children as witnesses, an understanding that can fuel desperately needed reforms of the American legal system. The first contribution is the authors' finding that even very young children, their 3–6-year-old subjects, can be enabled to recall highly accurate memories of personally stressful events, despite a retrieval interval of 6 months. The second contribution lies in their search for an "enhanced" interviewing technique that will elicit greater completeness, without sacrificing accuracy, of the child's remembered account. Although each of these contributions will be eventually discussed, I will begin rather presumptuously with a concept that is not fully fleshed out in the *Monograph*'s introduction and that was, in fact, consciously avoided in the team's research design. I do so, not out of perverseness, but because I believe that at least a brief exploration of the effect on legal proceedings of a poorly conducted or highly suggestive interview is essential to an understanding of the current lamentable state of American justice in child sexual abuse cases. Perhaps more important, I confess that I am inclined more toward the social philosophy of Hamlet than Pollyanna: unless reformers can "catch the conscience of the King" by laying out the consequences of poor interviewing, we will never achieve better interviewing through the use of the paradigms employed by Steward and her colleagues.

The "Humpty-Dumpty Effect" of the Investigative Interview

English-speaking children delight in the rhyme and riddle of Humpty-Dumpty: "Humpty-Dumpty sat on a wall. / Humpty-Dumpty had a great fall. /

All the King's Horses and all the King's men / Couldn't put Humpty-Dumpty together again." The answer to this riddle is that Humpty was "an egg." The answer to the riddle of legal proceedings involving child witnesses is that, if the initial interview is improperly conducted, like Humpty-Dumpty, the child's account can never be put together again. Without exaggeration, the investigative interview is the single most important component of any trial involving a child witness. The skill of the interviewer is more important than the sophistication of the judge or jury assigned to decide the case, more important than any of the other players—the lawyers and their experts. A skilled interviewer can empower the child to capture his or her experiences while memory of them is most fresh and vibrant. When the child's memories are carefully and neutrally extracted, the needs of both the legal system and the child are well served. In contrast, when the interview is inartfully conducted, the "Humpty-Dumpty Effect" is set in motion.

Although pretrial interviews with an adult witness also always occur, ordinarily the quality of that interviewer-subject interaction is irrelevant.[1] However, the quality of the exchange between the interviewer and the child is crucial both to the empirical study of children's memory and to the child's role as a trial witness. In Wells's (1989) memorable metaphor, focusing exclusively on the abstract cognitive capabilities of a child and yet failing to consider the interactive process between the child and the interviewer is like studying the sound of one hand clapping. So, too, does a child's credibility as a trial witness hinge on the skill of the adult facilitator.

If the interviewer is merely inept, eliciting a benign but very vague and sketchy free recall account from the child, the case may well wash out of the system. The prosecutor or counsel in a civil case may decide that the child would be a poor witness because he or she appeared unconvincing in the interview. Although the empirical literature does not often talk about this consequence, in trials the issue is, not whether a child can give accurate, reliable evidence, but whether this particular child will be perceived by the fact finder as offering complete and accurate evidence. In the well-prepared case, the child's credibility quotient is assessed on the basis of the child's performance at the investigative interview. On the basis of the interviewer's notes or a videotape, counsel may well assume that the interview performance represents the child's optimal capability as a witness.[2]

---

[1] The methodology of the interview between adults becomes crucial when an alleged confession by a suspect is offered by the prosecution in a criminal trial. In such cases, the court must determine whether the confession is "voluntary," i.e., that it is not the product of police coercion, and hence is admissible (*Colorado v. Connelly*, 1986; *Miranda v. Arizona*, 1966).

[2] Busy lawyers in both criminal and civil practice often rely on witness statements taken by investigators or paralegals. Scheduling another interview with an unresponsive or equivocal child witness is a possibility, but it is an option fraught with difficulties. Opposing counsel

We do not know with any precision how many American sexual abuse cases involving children as principal witnesses are jettisoned on the basis of the poor quality of the initial interview—that is, never pursued to formal charges or dismissed before trial. The study of eight American jurisdictions by the National Council of Jewish Women found that, in over half the cases prosecutors review, charges are not brought or, if they are, are later dropped (Gray, 1993). In a recent comprehensive study of child abuse cases in Great Britain, the slippage rate was found to be substantial. Of 14,912 videotaped child witness interviews conducted by police investigators over an 18-month period, only 3,652 (24%) were submitted to prosecutors for charging review; of that number, only 1,199 (33%) went to trial (Davies, Wilson, Mitchell, & Milsom, 1995, pp. iii, 17). In an analysis of a representative sample of 40 cases, it was found that only 18% failed to go to trial owing to a guilty plea from the defendant. Thus, one of every three interviews prompted a prosecutorial decision to avoid trial, either because the interview was deemed to have "no evidential value" (30%) or because it would be "inadmissible in court" (3%) (Davies et al., 1995, p. 23). Although the British and American trial processes are not identical, there is no procedural distinction that would suggest that American prosecutors are any more eager to try flawed cases or that American forensic interviewers are more sophisticated.

Indeed, from reported legal decisions (McGough, 1994) and empirical research (Warren, Woodall, Hunt, & Perry, 1996), we now have good reason to suspect that American interviewers have yet to adapt their practice to scientifically proved methods for enhancing a child's accuracy and completeness of recall. Furthermore, we know that questioning techniques are greater sources of distortion than any underlying deficits in children's cognitive capabilities (Aldridge, 1992; Ceci & Bruck, 1993). Like any other evidence, the reliability of the child's elicited account is the principal requirement for its consideration by the fact finder. Is the child's account an accurate recapitulation of his or her own memory or, instead, the product of someone else's will or biases?[3] We do not ordinarily ask such questions about an adult witness

---

will predictably claim that the new interview caused the child to succumb to pressure to come up with fabricated, albeit more convincing, "facts." Additional evaluative interviews can also impose substantial stress on the child and his or her family.

[3] Although not the subject of this Commentary, there is an additional reliability issue that arises when the interviewer offers only memory-based testimony about disclosures a child made during a pretrial interview. All too often today, interviewers are permitted to offer their remembered versions of the interview, usually based on their notes of the exchange. Obviously, the law must also be concerned about whether the interviewer has accurately remembered and reported what was said or demonstrated by the child. Videotaping the child's interviews permitted Steward and her colleagues to assess the accuracy and consistency of the child's allegations over time. Likewise, this technology provides the trial fact finder with a superior record of what was said, a better record than any possible recall of the interaction by either the interviewer or the child (McGough, 1995).

because we assume that most adults freely and autonomously can remember an important personal experience. However, in contrast, as age decreases, children recall less information spontaneously and must be assisted to recall all that they know. Although, as Steward et al. note, there is lively theoretical debate about whether this is due to lack of encoding or to storage or retrieval failures in the child, there is universal agreement among empiricists that children need an adult facilitator in order to provide a comprehensive as well as comprehensible account of their experiences.

From empirical research, we now know a great deal about the potential risks in the interviewing process, and that information has now filtered down to the practicing bar (McGough, 1995; Murray, 1995; Myers, 1987; Perry & Wrightsman, 1991). In both criminal prosecutions and civil cases, particularly those involving allegations of child sexual abuse, the possible contamination of the child's account by the interviewer will be the focus of the strategy elected by any well-prepared lawyer and expert witnesses. The interviewer should expect cross-examination about the use of leading questions, the use of other suggestive questions and props, the application of pressure on the child to acquiesce to some statement of events, interviewer bias, and the lack of exploration of alternative hypotheses during the interview. If counsel can demonstrate distortion of the child's recall, then the court has the authority to exclude the interview as evidence (Federal Rules of Evidence, Rule 403, and similar state rules). At a minimum, the cross-examination about the potential distortions of the child's account might cause the court to give the child's pretrial allegations diminished weight (Federal Rules of Evidence, Rule 104[D], and similar state rules).

Some American courts would go further and refuse to hear any testimony from the child at trial if the pretrial interview is so distorted that the child can no longer discriminate between the details of his or her own experience and those that may have been altered by the interviewer. As Steward et al. note, in *State v. Michaels* (1993, 1994), the New Jersey appellate courts ruled that the investigative interviews were so suggestively conducted that they had spoiled any possibility that the children could later accurately remember what, if anything, had happened to them at their day-care center. Consequently, finding "irreparable taint," the court held that the children could not give trial testimony in any reprosecution of the accused teacher. *Michaels* may be a shocking case because the court employed the extreme sanction of the suppression of potential evidence, but its judgment is perfectly compatible with the known risks from empirical research concerning the creation in the child of an altered "subjective reality" (Feher 1988, p. 233) or a false memory (Ceci & Bruck, 1995; Loftus & Ketcham, 1994). So long as research continues to demonstrate that the young child has a weakened ability to "source-monitor" (Johnson & Raye 1981; Poole & Lindsay, 1995)—to separate out his or her own remembered real experiences from imaginings or pseudofacts contributed by others, including the interviewer—the lingering and perhaps irreversible effects of interviewer distortion will and should continue to be a matter of grave concern to our courts. *Michaels* is a most significant case, with influence far beyond New Jersey. Already, its ripple effect is being felt in meetings of the bar and the bench, and it has been the subject of extensive commentary in both psychological and legal journals (Dugas, 1995; Myers, 1994b; Sales, 1995).

Even if the child is permitted to give testimony at trial, the fact finder may become so concerned about the potential for pretrial interviewing contamination that it mistrusts the child's account and acquits the accused because the proof is not convincing. As the foreman of the McMartin jury observed in attempting to explain the acquittal verdict in that most infamous child sexual abuse case, *People v. Buckey* (1984), "We felt there was evidence of molestation in some cases, but that by and large we really don't know if the children's remarks were true or if they were being led by adults. There's some truth in there somewhere, but we couldn't find it" (Schindehette et al., 1990).

The Humpty-Dumpty Effect of a poor investigative interview can also curdle the admissibility or persuasiveness of other evidence in a legal proceeding. In *B v. B* (1994), a custody and visitation case, the mother offered powerful testimony about the bizarre and highly sexualized behaviors of her 4- and 3-year-old sons. In her view, their games and vocabulary at home in the interim between their first complaint and trial could be explained only by their exposure to sexual abuse at the hands of her former husband during visitation. The court ultimately rejected this portion of the mother's testimony, finding, instead, that the children's behaviors were provoked by a highly suggestive series of investigative interviews.

In sum, the Humpty-Dumpty Effect means that various types of potential evidence pivot on the investigative interview. If the investigative interview is unreliable because it is improperly conducted, any disclosures resulting from the interview may be lost as evidence, the child may not be permitted to give evidence, and the child's caretakers may not be permitted to give an account of their experiences with the child once the interviews began. All the King's Horses and all the King's men (and women) can't put Humpty-Dumpty together again.

Aside from cases won or lost, without accurate, undistorted evidence of the child's experiences, a just result becomes impossible to attain. As Miller and Allen (in press) have observed, "A wrongful acquittal leaves behind a child twice abused, first by an adult and next by a trial that failed to redeem his or her courage in coming forward. A wrongful conviction snares an innocent defendant in a net of blame for one of the most odious of crimes." But, even in a civil custody case, the stakes are formidably high. An alleged abusing parent can be prevented by emergency orders from seeing his or her children for months or even years, and the harm cannot be undone, no matter what the court decides. The accusing parent rarely becomes persuaded that he or she overreacted or misinterpreted the child's reports, and suspicion and hostility continue to enmesh the parents and the child's extended family. And what of the child? Children who have testified as victims in sexual abuse trials have been found to be still distressed 2½ years later (Tedesco & Schnell, 1987). Even when there is substantial evidence that the child's beliefs were altered by the overreaching interviewer, the child may persist in those beliefs. Ten years later, despite the acquittals, the McMartin Pre-School children still believed that they had been sexually abused and exposed to satanic rituals.

Although the trial or appellate court or the lawyers are easy targets for blame when poor interviewing clouds the child's account, it is the interviewer who has crippled the child in such cases. And the ultimate responsibility lies with policy makers who have failed to give the interviewer the information, training, and monitoring necessary to achieve a skillfully conducted interview. Do we have it within our grasp to improve the quality of investigative interviews with children? The answer is clearly yes in view of the accumulated empirical data in hand, including confirmation contributed by the Steward et al. *Monograph.*

The Potential Accuracy of Children's Accounts

The *Monograph* replicates the finding of other researchers that young children, the authors' 3–6-year-olds, can faithfully recall body touch experiences. The subjects' spontaneous descriptions of body touch were highly accurate, with no age differences, although the youngest children freely reported less information. Again, replicating prior research, all children were less accurate when interviewed with direct questions about actions, and the youngest children were less accurate than the oldest. Steward and her colleagues refine extant research about the accuracy of the place of body touch: reports of genital touch and head and mouth touch remained accurate and stable, despite a 6-month delay between the occurrence and the final interview. They also refine our understanding of the role of pain in young children's memory, finding that the child's self-rating of intense pain and emotional distress was directly correlated with accuracy and completeness of report.

This bright picture of the capabilities of very young children's memory is in sharp contrast to the views of early twentieth-century empiricists (Ceci & Bruck, 1993), which, in turn, reinforced the law's skepticism of children as witnesses.[4] As one social scientist has wryly observed, "What one generation

---

[4] Traditionally, children were excluded as trial witnesses because of their presumed incompetence, especially their lack of an appreciation of the theological significance of the witness oath. In this century, even when children were permitted to demonstrate competency, the test usually consisted of an inquiry regarding wholly irrelevant mental tasks such

of lawyers prefer to understand as 'common sense' often depends upon the theory and findings of the previous generation of [scientific] investigators" (Yarmey, 1979, p. 227).

The introduction portion of the Steward et al. *Monograph* is especially helpful in summarizing the explosion of empirical research about children's capabilities that has occurred within the past 25 years. The child witness reform movement in American law has been clearly fueled by that body of research (McGough, 1994). Three principal legal reforms have resulted: altering the courtroom environment to reduce the trauma of a child's giving in-court testimony; streamlining the criminal investigation process; and lowering the barriers to the receipt of out-of-court statements—"hearsay"—by child eyewitnesses (Myers, 1987; Whitcomb, Shapiro, & Stellwagen, 1992). The research of Steward and her colleagues confirms that blunderbuss legal rules requiring a special showing of competency or corroboration for any account of sexual abuse when the witness is a child have been appropriately discarded by American law. Nevertheless, in her 1993 study of eight American jurisdictions, Gray found that these legal innovations had accomplished little change in the workaday world, that prosecutors were proceeding in much the same ways as before. Unfortunately, we have spent our time and energy wallpapering the trial process rather than repairing the crack in the pretrial foundation: the investigative interview.

If children, even preschoolers, can be effective witnesses, the task for the next decade is to work for systemic reforms that will optimize their recovery of important details of their experience.

Institutionalizing Interviewing Protocols

As discussed in the first part of this Commentary, the major child witness issue today is not the competence of children's memory but, instead, whether the particular child's account has been contaminated by delay or through his or her interactions with others. Ironically, as courts and legislators become educated to potential reliability risks of memory fade and heightened suggestibility, we may face a counterrevolution or "backlash" (Myers, 1994a) that

---

as arithmetic or spelling or recall of the names of former teachers (McGough, 1994). Furthermore, juries were routinely instructed that children's evidence should be received with caution because, e.g., they "are susceptible of impressions that are ofttimes of erroneous character, and it is with great difficulty that they can ofttimes repeat, accurately, the things which they see or hear" (*State v. Morasco*, 1912, p. 571). States also developed requirements that any testimony given by a child must be confirmed or "corroborated" by other persuasive evidence in the case, owing to children's "disposition to weave romances and to treat imagination for verity" (Wigmore, 1904, secs. 509, 640) or other similar suppositions about children's cognitive processes.

would return the American legal system to old notions that children are not worthy of belief. It is difficult for a trial judge to review a biasing, suggestive, or otherwise poorly conducted interview in a particular case without worrying that all child abuse investigative interviews are similarly flawed. Legislators, who perhaps too quickly embraced sweeping reforms, may too quickly call for a retreat.

Although some communities and states have sought to improve the quality of investigative interviews (Myers, 1994b, pp. 878–884), there as yet is no national consensus on or commitment to this key reform. Presumably even John Myers, an eminent legal scholar and one of the coauthors of this *Monograph,* would agree that the "considerable reduc[tion]" of the overzealousness of child sexual abuse investigations of the 1980s is faint praise for a country that prides itself on child witness reform. Specially trained child victim/witness interviewers have long been the norm in the civil law system, in Israel, and in the Scandinavian countries (Spencer, Nicholson, Flin, & Bull, 1989). In Great Britain, the *Memorandum of Good Practice* (1992), which resulted from the collaboration of empiricists, clinicians, and lawyers, has been adopted by the Home Office. The *Memorandum,* which describes general protocols for conducting an investigative interview with a child witness, has quickly become the gold standard within the police, social work, and legal communities. Similar interprofessional ventures have resulted in reform in Canada, Australia, and Scotland (Davies, Lloyd-Bostock, McMurran, & Wilson, 1996).

There are two barriers to the creation of a similar national agenda for interviewing reform in this country: the informational barrier and the political barrier. Of the two, the availability of scientific information may well be the easier barrier to surmount. The books and articles written about child witness interviewing can now fill a small room, and this *Monograph's* lengthy reference list collects the major works. General guidelines, from interview preparation to exit reassurance to the child, have already been prepared (McGough & Warren, 1994). We have in hand the "stepwise interview" (Raskin & Esplin, 1992; Steller & Boychuk, 1992), the "structured interview" (Yuille, 1988), the "enhanced cognitive interview" (Geiselman, 1988), and the "phased approach interview" (*Memorandum of Good Practice,* 1992). Although the labels vary and perhaps lead to a mistaken impression of dissonance, the core recommendations are stunningly similar. Indeed, the essential features of the child victim/witness interview have achieved "convergent validity" (Davies et al., 1996, p. xiv). The seven explicit recommendations of the Steward research team are perfectly consistent with this existing body of knowledge.

It is beyond the scope of this Commentary (and my expertise) to write a definitive set of American protocols; however, sketching the extent of scientific agreement in the context of the recommendations made by Steward and her colleagues may help prove the feasibility of such an undertaking. In chronological order, reflecting the stages of interviewer-child interaction, here are the points of apparent consensus.

First, the current literature emphasizes the importance of interview preparation. Knowledge of the structure of a child's family, the basics of the child's allegations, and the child's developmental competence increases the interviewer's ability to appreciate the relevance of statements made by the child during the interview and maximizes the interviewer's ability to work at the child's pace and level of comprehension.[5] The identification of an easily and quickly administered language assessment test proposed by the Steward team could be an important addition to standard interview preparation.

Second, there is universal agreement about the timing of the interview, that it should be accomplished as soon as possible after an alleged event (or its first report) (Steward et al.'s recommendation 1). All research on children's long-term memory confirms the presence of memory fade for at least peripheral details if not the core memory; however, the loss of detail may mean the loss of significant investigative leads that may confirm the child's account.

Third, all researchers agree that there should be a settling-in period during which the child is helped to understand the reason for the interview (Steward et al.'s recommendation 2). Whether this period is called *rapport building* or not, understanding the task at hand as well as the ground rules of the interview can facilitate the child's performance. Unfortunately, *rapport building,* the usual term for this phase, connotes a sort of warm, fuzzy, even smarmy atmosphere of comfort for the child. In actuality, this introductory stage can accomplish more than simply allaying the child's anxiety and establishing trust. It can offer the child a transition from the everyday world of casual interaction to that of forensic remembering, a performance that requires a higher concentration from the child than ordinary recall. Instructions like "Tell me only what you really remember," "If you don't know, it's OK to say that you don't remember," and the encouragement "Think very hard about what happened" should be explicitly given. The child should also explicitly be reassured that, in this encounter, it is perfectly all right to correct the interviewer if he or she makes a mistake in repeating or misinterpreting

---

[5] We might intuit that the best way to achieve an objective interview is to appoint a neutral professional who is totally unaware of the child's experiences. Knowing the substance of the allegations in advance could, of course, create bias in the interviewer (Davies & Flin, 1988). However, ignorance of the child's previous reports creates other, more serious problems of miscommunication and misinterpretation and, in the real world of referrals for investigative interviewing, is impossible to attain. Most interviewers will know at least the gravamen of the child's complaint. The solution to this apparent impasse is for the interviewer to construct and explore viable alternative hypotheses other than an accusation of abuse in conducting the interview (see, generally, Ceci & Bruck, 1995).

something the child reported.[6] These expectations can be made more meaningful through a demonstration.

Forensic remembering appears to be a learned skill. Researchers have found that retrieval is enhanced by showing children how to exercise recall with the recollection of a neutral, recent memory like describing what they did when brushing their teeth that morning (Memon, Cronin, Eaves, & Bull, 1996) or describing their last birthday party (Lamb, Sternberg, & Esplin, 1995). The practice session contributes to children's understanding of the interviewer's expectations as well as increasing their comfort. Modeling the expectations of the investigative exchange during the preliminary or rapport stage increases children's later production of freely recalled information (Sternberg et al., 1996). Thus, "Tell me all about the people you live with" is an open-ended question inviting more information than the forced-choice or "yes/no" type of closed questions typically used during the rapport-building portion of the interview.

Fourth, all researchers agree that open-ended questions should be used first to elicit a child's narrative (Steward et al.'s recommendation 3). Similarly, open-ended, nonleading, follow-up questions for clarification are in order for any facts that are offered by the child during the narrative. At this point, some differences among professionals emerge about when to begin direct questions about issues that have not been brought up voluntarily by the child, especially when to employ closed questions. Proponents of the "enhanced cognitive interview" have demonstrated that the use of context reinstatement and mnemonic strategies has resulted in substantial increases in correct information recalled by the subject (Geiselman, 1988). The true significance of a detail, whether trivial or important, may not have been appreciated by the child and thus not produced in his or her narrative, nor will the interviewer know what details lie in the child's memory. The cognitive interview, which was developed for use with adult witnesses, has been adapted for use with children (Geiselman & Padilla, 1988). Preliminary results with children indicate that, in comparison with a standard interview, older, grade school children were able to retrieve substantially more accurate facts about their experience without an increase in the amount of incorrect information reported (Geiselman, Saywitz, & Bornstein, 1992; McCauley & Fisher, 1996; Milne, Bull, Kohnken, & Memon, 1994). Closed questions should be used only as a last resort, although surveys demonstrate that even seasoned inter-

[6] A child comes to a forensic interview with misleading script memory of how he or she is to behave in an encounter with a questioning adult. Even young children are highly socialized to accommodate to authoritative adults (e.g., Clarke-Stewart, Thompson, & Lepore, 1989; King & Yuille, 1987). Unless redirected, a child might otherwise believe that the adult knows the correct answers and is quizzing the child to see whether he or she also knows them; that he or she should come up with some answer, even if unsure; and that it is rude to correct an adult.

viewers tend to use them too early and too often (Davies et al., 1995; George & Clifford, 1996; Warren et al., 1996). Increasing the motivation for both child and interviewer to achieve a more complete recollection is clearly a important feature that should be incorporated into interview protocols.

Steward and her colleagues also recommend that the interviewer elicit information from the child about his or her experience of pain and distress. Using the materials for self-rating that they suggest, the pain scale and the emotion word list, seems like a valuable addition to existing protocols.

The use of cues is perhaps the most controversial part of this *Monograph* (Steward et al.'s recommendations 5 and 6). The research reported here compares the effectiveness of four parallel interview procedures: a traditional verbal interview, two enhanced interviews with cues (one with anatomically detailed dolls and other play equipment, the other with body outline drawings), and a computer-assisted interview. The studies that Steward et al. conducted indicate no clear-cut finding, except that real props associated with both the child's particular experience and general use were distractors, creating confusion and inaccurate recall. Although the use of anatomical cues increased more spontaneous and complete recall, the drawings elicited erroneous reports of genital touch, and the anatomically detailed dolls elicited erroneous reports of anal touch. In the end, Steward and her colleagues include the caveat that stimulus materials "be used conservatively, that is, to clarify spontaneous narrative, to stimulate memories of people and actions, and to slow down the pacing of the interview" (p. 130). There appears to be a consensus that no diagnosis of child sexual abuse can be derived from doll-play behavior (Fisher & Whiting, in press; Lamb, 1994; cf. APA, 1991). While most researchers would join in a limited endorsement of the use of dolls to clarify information volunteered by the child, many would recommend against the use of anatomically detailed dolls to stimulate recall.

An interviewing protocol must address the role of dolls and other props in view of the prevalence of their continued use by investigative interviewers (Fisher & Whiting, in press, note that 92% of mental health professionals report the use of anatomically detailed dolls in child sexual abuse evaluations). It should alert professionals to the potential misuse of cuing materials, encourage special training, and counsel caution until empirical research is more definitive.[7]

---

[7] As the *Memorandum of Good Practice* (1992, p. 24) advises: "'Props' include dolls, drawings, dolls' houses and small figures which can serve as potentially very useful communication aids in interviews carried out for the purposes of this Memorandum. Young children and those with communication difficulties, may be able to provide clearer accounts when such props are used, compared with purely verbal approaches. . . . All props should be used with caution and without leading questions. The need for their use should be carefully considered before the interview. Particular care is necessary when genitalled dolls are used, where it is important that the interviewer is skilled and trained in their use and misuse. A combination

Finally, current guidelines all agree about the importance of the closing phase of the interview, in which the important parts of the child's account, in the child's own words, are reviewed for correction with the child. The child should also be given the opportunity to add to that account or further explain any information he or she may have given. The child or the child's caretaker should be provided with a name and telephone number in case the child later desires to discuss his or her experiences further. The closing phase is also an opportunity to permit the child to ask questions of the interviewer. The interviewer bears the responsibility for informing the child (or the caretaker of a very young child) about subsequent pretrial and trial procedures that will probably require the child's cooperation and participation.

Beyond the interview, as Steward and her colleagues recommend (their recommendation 7), training based on the standardized materials is essential to improving the quality of the all-important investigative interview. Just as thorough, accurate recall is a learned skill for the child, so too is a thorough, accurate interview a learned skill for the professional. All surveys of the current state of interviewer skill suggest that there is room for great improvement. Research suggests that interviewing skills can be learned and honed in an experiential setting and that any training program must include a component for subsequent continuing review (Aldridge, 1992).

In sum, standardized training materials, pulling together the best of current research, can and should be developed for all interviewers of child witnesses in the United States. Although it is tempting for conscientious empiricists to believe that, with only one or two more studies, the perfect, detailed protocol can be developed, such perfection is illusory. There will always be new, relevant empirical findings that can be incorporated to improve a current interviewing model, and, for that matter, the need for revision of any set of guidelines should be anticipated and endorsed at the outset. With nearly 5 years' experience, the authors of the British *Memorandum of Good Practice* are already contemplating potential revisions (Bull & Davies, 1996).

The second barrier to the development and dissemination of interviewing protocols, the political barrier, is more formidable. There is a booming cottage industry of private entrepreneurial groups offering child sexual abuse workshops and interviewing training, some offering invariant "rules" for interviewing and shaky scientific methodology. Some professionals in that enterprise may resist any move toward consensus guidelines or government endorsement of competing training programs. Nevertheless, as has been the

---

of leading questioning style and the use of genitalled dolls can be particularly error prone, and is unlikely to produce evidence which could be used in criminal proceedings. In the main, genitalled dolls should only be used as an adjunct to the interview to establish the meaning of terms used by the child *once the child has finished his or her free narrative account, and the general substance of his or her evidence is reasonably clear.*"

experience in other countries, the government's imprimatur and delivery system are crucial to the universal implementation of any professional protocols and training initiative.

For efficiency, protocols should be developed at the federal level for use throughout the country. Proper interviewing techniques to optimize the accuracy and comprehensiveness of a child's account do not differ from state to state, any more than they differ from country to country. Of course, in a federal system like ours, the processing of criminal cases is within the authority of the various states. However, the Department of Justice, by authority delegated by Congress, certainly possesses the power to shape state criminal procedure by extracting compliance with its regulations in order for a state to be eligible to receive federal crime control funds. There is ample precedent for the Department of Justice to intervene in this issue.[8] Similarly, and again by delegated congressional authority, the Department of Health and Human Services possesses the power to shape states' child welfare policy and practices.[9] The National Institute of Child Health and Human Development is yet another government entity that might logically take the lead in establishing a national agenda for the development of interviewing protocols, of interagency cooperative interviewing compacts, and of professional training. There are also numerous private organizations, many of which have developed interviewing materials, whose expertise ought to be tapped.[10]

Paradoxically, with so many government agencies committed to the protection of children and the integrity of the judicial system, no one agency has yet to assume leadership in and responsibility for the critical reform of investigative interviewing. The time is now ripe for the development of a national consensus. Without a national and state dedication of the resources needed to encourage interagency cooperation, to agree on interviewing protocols, and to train and monitor interviewer skills, the hard-won gains of the 1980s may be merely cosmetic surgery—a gambit of political showmanship, manifesting no genuine commitment to children. In the United States, the missing capstone of the child witness reform movement is the improvement of the interviewing process, the foundation for all the pretrial decision making and, ultimately, the trial itself.

[8] As but one example, the Juvenile Justice and Delinquency Prevention Act has required states to eliminate the pretrial use of jails for the detention of accused juvenile delinquents.

[9] The Department of Health and Human Services has conditioned the continued receipt of federal funds on various requirements, including the enactment of child abuse reporting statutes and expedited child support collection remedies.

[10] Among those private, national professional organizations that have developed interview materials are the American Prosecutors Research Institute, the National Center for Prosecution of Child Abuse; the American Professional Society on the Abuse of Children; and the National Legal Resource Center for Child Advocacy and Protection, the American Bar Association.

References

Aldridge, J. (1992). The further training of professionals dealing with child witnesses. In H. Dent & R. Flin (Eds.), *Children as witnesses*. New York: Wiley.

American Psychological Association (APA). (1991, 8 February). *Statement on the use of anatomically detailed dolls in forensic evaluations*. Washington, DC: APA Council of Representatives.

B v. B, 2 FLR 713 [1994] (Family Division Court, Great Britain).

Bull, R., & Davies, G. (1996). The effect of child witness research on legislation in Great Britain. In B. Bottoms & G. Goodman (Eds.), *International perspectives on child abuse and children's testimony*. Thousand Oaks, CA: Sage.

Ceci, S. J., & Bruck, M. (1993). The suggestibility of the child witness: A historical review and synthesis. *Psychological Bulletin*, **113**, 403–439.

Ceci, S. J., & Bruck, M. (1995). *Jeopardy in the courtroom: A scientific analysis of children's testimony*. Washington, DC: American Psychological Association.

Clarke-Stewart, A., Thompson, W., & Lepore, S. (1989, May). *Manipulating children's interpretations through interrogation*. Paper presented at the meeting of the Society for Research in Child Development, Kansas City, MO.

Colorado v. Connelly, 479 U.S. 157 (1986).

Davies, G. D., & Flin, R. (1988). The accuracy and suggestibility of child witnesses. In F. G. Davies & J. Drinkwater (Eds.), *The child witness: Do the courts abuse children?* Leicester: BPS.

Davies, G. D., Lloyd-Bostock, S., McMurran, M., & Wilson, C. (1996). *Psychology, law, and criminal justice: International developments in research and practice*. New York: Walter de Gruyter.

Davies, G. D., Wilson, C., Mitchell, R., & Milsom, J. (1995). *Videotaping children's evidence: An evaluation*. London: Home Office.

Dugas, C. M. (1995). Note, *State of New Jersey v. Michaels:* The due process implications raised in interviewing child witnesses. *Louisiana Law Review*, **55**, 1205–1234.

Feher, T. L. (1988). The alleged molestation victim, the rules of evidence, and the Constitution: Should children really be seen and not heard? *American Journal of Criminal Law*, **14**, 227–255.

Fisher, C. B., & Whiting, K. A. (in press). How valid are child sexual abuse validations? In S. J. Ceci & H. Hembrooke (Eds.), *What can (and should) an expert witness tell the court?* Washington, DC: American Psychological Association.

Geiselman, R. E. (1988). Improving memory through mental reinstatement of context. In Davies, G. M., & Thomson, D. M. (Eds.), *Memory in context: Context in memory*. Chichester: Wiley.

Geiselman, R. E., Bornstein, G., & Saywitz, K. J. (1992, May). Effects of cognitive questioning techniques on children's recall performance. In *New approach to interviewing children: A test of its effectiveness: Research in brief*. Washington, DC: National Institute of Justice, U.S. Department of Justice.

Geiselman, R. E., & Padilla, J. (1988). Interviewing child witnesses with the cognitive interview. *Journal of Police Science and Administration*, **16**, 236–242.

George, G. C., & Clifford, B. R. (1996). The cognitive interview—does it work? In G. Davies, S. Lloyd-Bostock, M. McMurran, & C. Wilson (Eds.), *Psychology, law, and criminal justice: International developments in research and practice*. New York: Walter de Gruyter.

Gray, E. (1993). *Unequal justice: The prosecution of child sexual abuse*. New York: Free Press.

Johnson, M. K., & Raye, C. L. (1981). Reality monitoring. *Psychological Review*, **88**, 67–85.

King, M. A., & Yuille, J. (1987). Suggestibility and the child witness. In S. J. Ceci, M. P. Toglia, & D. F. Ross (Eds.), *Children's eyewitness memory*. New York: Springer.

Lamb, M. E. (1994). The investigation of child sexual abuse: An international, interdisciplinary consensus statement. *Family Law Quarterly, 28*, 151–162.

Lamb, M. E., Sternberg, K. J., & Esplin, P. W. (1995). Making children into competent witnesses: Reactions to the Amicus Brief *In re Michaels. Psychology, Public Policy, and Law, 2*, 438–449.

Loftus, E. F., & Ketcham, K. (1994). *The myth of repressed memory: False memories and allegations of sexual abuse.* New York: St. Martin's.

McCauley, M. R., & Fisher, R. P. (1996). Enhancing children's eyewitness testimony with the cognitive interview. In G. Davies, S. Lloyd-Bostock, M. McMurran, & C. Wilson (Eds.), *Psychology, law, and criminal justice: International developments in research and practice.* New York: Walter de Gruyter.

McGough, L. S. (1994). *Child witnesses: Fragile voices in the American legal system.* New Haven, CT: Yale University Press.

McGough, L. S. (1995). For the record: Videotaping investigative interviews. *Psychology, Public Policy, and Law, 2*, 370–386.

McGough, L. S., & Warren, A. R. (1994). The all-important investigative interview. *Juvenile and Family Court Journal*, 13–29.

Memon, A., Cronin, O., Eaves, R., & Bull, R. (1996). An empirical test of the mnemonic components of the cognitive interview. In G. Davies, S. Lloyd-Bostock, M. McMurran, & C. Wilson (Eds.), *Psychology, law, and criminal justice: International developments in research and practice.* New York: Walter de Gruyter.

Memorandum of good practice. (1992). London: Home Office.

Miller, J. S., & Allen, R. J. (in press). The expert as educator. In S. J. Ceci & H. Hembrooke (Eds.), *What can (and should) an expert witness tell the court?* Washington, DC: American Psychological Association.

Milne, R., Bull, R., Kohnken, G., & Memon, A. (1994). *The cognitive interview and suggestibility.* Paper presented at the Fourth European Conference of Law and Psychology, Barcelona.

Miranda v. Arizona, 384 U.S. 436 (1966).

Murray, J. M. K. (1995). Comment: Repression, memory, and suggestibility: A call for limitations on the admissibility of repressed memory testimony in sexual abuse trials. *University of Colorado Law Review, 66*, 477–522.

Myers, J. E. B. (1987). *Child witness law and practice.* New York: Wiley.

Myers, J. E. B. (Ed.). (1994a). *The backlash: Child protection under fire.* Thousand Oaks, CA: Sage.

Myers, J. E. B. (1994b). Taint hearings for child witnesses? A step in the wrong direction. *Baylor Law Review, 46*, 873–946.

People v. Buckey, No. A-750900 (Ca. Crim. Dist. Ct. 1984).

Perry, N. W., & Wrightsman, L. S. 1991. *The child witness: Legal issues and dilemmas.* Newbury Park, CA: Sage.

Poole, D., & Lindsay, D. S. 1995. Interviewing preschoolers: Effects of nonsuggestive techniques, parental coaching, and leading questions on reports of nonexperienced events. *Journal of Experimental Child Psychology, 60*, 129–154.

Raskin, R. C., & Esplin, P. W. (1992). Statement validity assessment: Interview procedures and content analysis of children's statements of sexual abuse. *Behavior Assessment, 13*, 265–291.

Sales, B. (Ed.). (1995). Suggestibility of child witnesses—the social science of Amicus Brief *State of New Jersey v. Margaret Kelly Michaels* (Special Issue). *Psychology, Public Policy, and Law, 2*(June).

Schindehette, S., Keely, J., Bacon, D., Wohlfert, L., Micheli, R., & Tamarkin, C. (1990, 5 February). After the verdict, solace for none. *People*, 70–80.

Spencer, J. R., Nicholson, G., Flin, R. H., & Bull, R. (1989). *Children's evidence in legal proceedings: An international perspective.* Cambridge: J. R. Spencer.

State v. Michaels, 625 A.2d 489 (N.J. App. 1993), *aff'd,* 642 A.2d 1372 (N.J. Sup. 1994).

State v. Morasco, 128 Pac. 571 (Utah 1912).

Steller, M., & Boychuk, T. (1992). Children as witnesses in sexual abuse cases: Investigative interview and assessment techniques. In H. Dent & R. Flin (Eds.), *Children as witnesses.* Chichester: Wiley.

Sternberg, K. J., Lamb, M. E., Hershkovitz, I., Yudilevitch, L., Orbach, Y., Larson, C., Esplin, P. W., & Hovav, M. (1996, March). *Effects of introductory style on children's abilities to describe experiences of sexual abuse.* Paper presented at the meeting of the American Psychology and Law Society, Hilton Head, SC.

Tedesco, J. F., & Schnell, S. V. (1987). Children's reactions to sex abuse investigations and litigation. *Child Abuse and Neglect,* 11, 267–272.

Warren, A. R., Woodall, C. E., Hunt, J. S., & Perry, N. W. (1996). "It sounds good in theory, but . . .": Do investigative interviewers follow guidelines based on memory research? *Child Maltreatment,* 1(3).

Wells, G. S. (1989, June). *Presentation.* Cornell Conference on the Suggestibility of Children's Recollections, Ithaca, NY.

Whitcomb, D., Shapiro, E. R., & Stellwagen, L. D. (1992). *When the victim is a child: Issues for judges and prosecutors* (2d ed.). Washington, DC: National Institute of Justice. (Original work published 1985)

Wigmore, J. H. (1904). *Wigmore on evidence* (Vol. 1). Boston: Little, Brown.

Yarmey, D. (1979). *The psychology of eyewitness testimony.* New York: Free Press.

Yuille, J. C. (1988). The systematic assessment of children's testimony. *Canadian Psychology,* 29, 247–262.

ISSUES IN THE SCIENTIFIC VALIDATION OF INTERVIEWS WITH YOUNG CHILDREN

Maggie Bruck and Stephen J. Ceci

In the past decade, there has been a flurry of studies on the accuracy, consistency, and completeness of young children's reports. To a large degree, many of these studies have been couched in terms of forensic issues, as they address aspects of interviewing that are relevant to the child who is suspected of being a participant in or witness to a crime. In many, if not most, cases, the intended focus of such studies is the child who is suspected of having been sexually abused.

An apt metaphoric summary of this literature is that the reliability of children's reports can be viewed as either a half-filled or a half-emptied glass, depending on one's perspective and the target of generalization. The results of many past studies have highlighted the accuracy of children's reports— showing that they are quite accurate over a long period of time (e.g., Fivush, 1993; Ornstein, 1995; Peterson, 1996). However, as was found in the present study, there is also a fair amount of forgetting and inconsistency in young children's reports over time, much of it occurring within the first month of an actual experience. Nonetheless, this and other studies demonstrate that, under certain conditions, young children can provide reliable, consistent reports of past events, thus giving rise to the "half-filled glass" view of the accuracy of children's reports.

At the same time, there is another group of studies that have focused on the inherent weaknesses of children's reports, especially when they are subjected to a variety of suggestive interviewing techniques. The findings from this camp (also known as the half-empty glass position) reveal that, when children are repeatedly interviewed by biased interviewers who use suggestive interviewing techniques and fail to test alternative hypotheses, their reports can quickly become inaccurate (for a review, see Ceci & Bruck, 1995). At times, children may even fabricate whole events that never occurred (e.g., Leichtman & Ceci, 1995); at times, they can be led to confuse suggestions with actual events to the point that they later insist that the suggested events actually occurred (Bruck, Ceci, Francoeur, & Barr, 1995). According to some researchers, when children undergo repeated suggestive interviewing over long periods of time, it becomes impossible for professionals to differentiate true from false reports (Bruck, Ceci, & Hembrooke, in press).

As these studies are becoming part of the conventional literature on children's reporting, some researchers are now turning their attention to even more practical matters, namely, the construction of scientifically valid interviewing techniques that would yield complete, accurate, and consistent reports and at the same time would reduce, if not eliminate, the baleful effects of suggestive interviewing procedures. The major problem in constructing such interviews is that, when young children are asked open-ended questions (e.g., "What happened?"), they generally provide very little information, but what they *do* provide tends to be highly accurate. In order to obtain more complete information, direct, more closed-ended, and more prompted techniques may be required. Under these circumstances, children do provide more information, but more of the information they provide is inaccurate.

Therefore, the search has begun for techniques that allow for accurate as well as complete reporting. Some researchers focus on verbal techniques, such as the "cognitive interview" (Saywitz, Geiselman, & Bornstein, 1992), the "step-wise interview" (Yuille, Hunter, Joffe, & Zaparniuk, 1993), or the "structured interview" (Memon, Wark, Koehnken, & Bull, in press). Other researchers, including Steward et al., have chosen to focus on the effectiveness of certain nonverbal enhancement techniques that could be used as supplements to verbal questioning with young children. In the present study, the specific focus was on anatomical dolls, anatomical drawings (with and without computer assistance), medical props, and photo arrays. In what follows, we comment on various aspects of these authors' formidable effort to validate these enhancement techniques and to compare them with more traditional verbal techniques. In light of the many concerns, criticisms, and qualifications that follow, it is important that we state at the outset our belief that this work is highly commendable for its extensiveness, care, and quality. These authors deserve the gratitude of all who labor in this field not only for the results they reported but, more important, for the great care they took to report these results in a fair-minded, nonpolemical manner. We state these positive features of Steward et al.'s research at the outset so that they will not be lost amid the critique that follows.

Before commenting on the specific findings of the study, we examine an overarching issue of our Commentary: the rationale and design of evaluations of interview protocols to be used in sexual abuse settings.

Cost-Benefit Analysis

The scientific validation of an interview procedure is not straightforward. On the one hand, it requires interviewing children about an event they have experienced in order to determine which of several techniques produces the "best retrieval of information" under pristine (i.e., nonsuggestive) conditions. This method allows one to evaluate the potential "benefits" of various techniques.

Much more is desired of a technique's validation, however, than the determination of its potential benefits under ideal conditions; an evaluation of its potential risks is also desired. That is, one must systematically estimate rates of "false positive" responses made by children who have *not* been exposed to an event but who are questioned using the same interviewing procedures as children who have been exposed to an event. Furthermore, such data must be gathered under conditions that mimic those that inhere in actual forensic investigations. For example, in actual frontline investigations, the interviewer frequently does not know whether the child was abused or exactly what he or she witnessed; as a result, interviewers must guess or, if they are skilled, entertain a variety of hypotheses. Importantly, frontline interviewers must deploy their techniques within a tapestry of forces that are absent from the present study. The tapestry may include a galaxy of pressures on the child to conform to the wishes of a threatening perpetrator or to those of an appealing parent who "lobbies" the child repeatedly prior to the first official interview and then periodically in between interviews.

Steward and her colleagues at times seem unaware of these preexisting conditions, as shown in the following quote, "The verbal interview . . . was designed to provide an opportunity to determine the efficacy of the strictly verbal interviews commonly used by the staff of law enforcement and social welfare agencies" (p. 36). However, reviews of existing transcripts and studies of cases workers' methods show that the verbal interview used in the present study was atypical in its use of open-ended questions and direct nonleading questions (e.g., Lamb et al., in press; McGough & Warren, 1994).

At other times, however, Steward et al. seem deliberately to elect to eliminate or ignore many of the features of forensic and therapeutic interviews with young children. For example, they decided to conduct the subsequent 6-month interview, not as a follow-up to the 1-month interview, but as a new interview that did not build on the child's prior answers. In our experience, this seldom happens in actual forensic investigations, and, further, it would probably not be an effective strategy under ideal conditions. In the real world, when children are reinterviewed, the later interviewers frequently have access to and build on the child's answers in the earlier interview, seeking both to confirm and to elaborate the child's responses. It is under such conditions that a technique's risks can be determined.

At other times, Steward and her colleagues elect to ignore features of real-life interviews on ethical grounds, which makes it a perfectly reasonable decision. In their words: "Our intention was to design a straightforward interview that would elicit cooperative responses from young children but not lead them into saying things about their experiences with their doctors that were not true. . . . The prototype . . . included a set of nine yes/no questions. . . . Our research team decided, as an ethical point, to refrain from including knowingly false allegations about the medical staff in the set of direct yes/no questions since, even if the "misleading questions" were accurately denied, they might remain in children's minds and later undermine the ongoing relationship between the children and their doctors" (pp. 34–35).

Readers who are familiar with our own research (e.g., Bruck, Ceci, Francoeur, & Renick, 1995; Ceci & Bruck, 1995) will not be surprised by our opposite stance on this issue. We have chosen to include in our studies procedures to measure the risks of various interviewing techniques that are commonly used in investigative and therapeutic arenas. We feel that, if these techniques are to be recommended for widespread use by professionals, then there is a need to evaluate not only their benefits but their risks, too, and to do so under conditions that begin to incorporate the myriad contaminating factors that characterize real-world sex abuse investigations. We reasoned that any harm that might be associated with using potentially risky procedures in a strictly controlled experimental environment was insubstantial. After all, these procedures are routinely used by parents and teachers, albeit in a casual and nonsystematic manner. We have also assured ourselves that our procedures are safe on a number of grounds. First, after following up on the subjects in the many studies that we have carried out (in both medical and nonmedical settings), we have determined that our procedures do not appear to have had any observable negative effects either in the short term or in the long term. Second, whenever we are concerned about the consequences of an inaccurate report, the children in our studies are debriefed by highly trained research assistants.

So we find Steward et al.'s "ethical" argument regrettable because it prevented them from providing the missing data that are so critical in evaluating the utility of the very procedures they recommend. Of course, because in the present study some children did not undergo all procedures, they were on occasion asked about events that did not happen. But this was not a systematic effort and, as we show below, may have led to an overestimate of the utility of some, although not all, of the results.

To conclude, the authors of this study have made a very promising start at collecting valuable validity data on so-called enhancement techniques, but they elected to stop short of evaluating the risks of using these techniques under actual field conditions. This is unfortunate because one requires the same type of systematic data for the risks as well as for the benefits of proposed interviewing techniques in order to evaluate their forensic effectiveness under conditions that approximate field investigations. The same techniques that lead to the best retrieval of events that actually occurred (i.e., "hits") could also lead to a high rate of retrieval of events that never occurred (i.e., false positives). Ultimately, the final decision about the acceptable level of trade-off between hits and false positives must be made by policy makers, but they need adequate data on both risks and benefits to arrive at this decision.

Ecological Validity

The issue of ecological validity must also be considered when planning and evaluating studies of interviewing methods. When all is said and done, it is important to determine to what degree the results of a validation study can generalize to the real conditions of child interviewing. Steward and her colleagues state: "We anticipate that the findings gleaned from observing and following young children through an experience that offers an ecologically valid analogue to critical features of sexual and physical abuse will have implications for the process of investigative interviewing and will focus attention on the product, children's testimony" (p. 118).

Although this study does inform us about the accuracy and completeness of children's reporting of touch during a medical procedure, it is not at all clear that this setting or the features of the study are an ecologically valid analogue to critical features of sexual and physical abuse. Steward and her colleagues seem to use the concept of ecological validity as a catchall for sample generalizability and procedure generalizability.

Sample generalizability is something we leave to demographers who study the characteristics of abused children, their age, race, socioeconomic status, etc.; they can comment on whether the modal abuse investigation involves samples similar to the ones studied here. The claim of ecological validity of procedure is, however, open to question. The basic issue that must be raised is whether the data from these interviews with children who have undergone societally sanctioned medical acts can be useful for the construction of interviews for children who have been sexually abused or who are suspected of having been sexually abused. The analogue might not be as straightforward as the authors had hoped. First, societally endorsed medical procedures lack critical aspects of the ecology of abuse: there is no dynamic within the family inhibiting the child from or propelling him or her toward disclosing, no familiar perpetrator, no betrayal by a trusted caregiver. One also wonders whether these enhanced techniques would provide useful information if used with children who have sustained violent/traumatic attack by a caregiver and who are having a difficult time disclosing? A related issue is whether the target interviews would actually produce reliable information and would be deemed safe if used with children who have not been sexually abused.

The Enhanced Interviews

The authors have used a number of nonverbal techniques to enhance the reports of their subjects. We focus on a few of these. From the results of this and other studies (e.g., Gee & Pipe, 1995; Salmon, Bidrose, & Pipe, 1995), it is clear that providing children with props does not increase, but rather decreases, accuracy of reporting. We focus, however, not on this aspect of the study but rather on three other techniques that the authors believe hold promise for obtaining accurate testimony from young children: the use of anatomically detailed dolls, line drawings of anatomical figures, and photo arrays to assist with the identification of person and place.

We begin with the dolls because so much has been written on their use and misuse that even readers who pride themselves as being up-to-date on the scientific literature may be having a hard time reconciling contradictory claims. Following this discussion, we delve into the use of drawing- and photograph-assisted interviews.

Anatomical Dolls

In general, Steward and her colleagues feel that, if the dolls are used "properly," then children may be able to provide more details of past touching than would be the case without the dolls. This seems to be true, not only for genital and buttocks touching, but also for reports of touching to the ear and belly button. The authors state that the risk of commission errors (children alleging touching when none occurred) was quite low—nowhere near the rate of 50% that we obtained in our studies of 3- and 4-year-olds (Bruck, Ceci, Francoeur, & Renick, 1995, and Bruck et al., in press, respectively). Of course, as the authors point out, we used leading and also misleading questions in our interviews rather than open-ended or direct yes/no questions, as they did in the present study. How can we reconcile these seemingly incompatible claims about the usefulness of dolls?

If all doll-centered interviews were conducted with the same degree of control and structure as those in the present study, and if all child witnesses could be shielded from suggestions by adults who have access to them prior to and during the interview, then Steward et al.'s findings would demonstrate that one could have great confidence in the effectiveness of anatomical dolls. As they repeatedly note, the use of the dolls led to disclosures that were not forthcoming when only verbal techniques were used. This is a potentially useful and important finding.

But we do have the following concerns. The type of control that they were able to exert on their interviewers may prove to be impossible in a world where even trained interviewers often are not aware that they are using leading and misleading questions (for descriptions of studies where interviewers are "blind" to their biases, see Ceci & Bruck, 1995) and in a world where children are often confronted by partisan parents outside the context of the interview and subsequently interviewed by interviewers who may have a priori beliefs about their abuse and who might use the dolls in a more aggressive manner than that used in the present study. As we have shown (Bruck, Ceci, Francoeur, & Renick, 1995; Bruck et al., in press), when interviewers ask mildly leading questions (which could be inadvertent in real-life interviews) or focus much of the interview on the dolls, young children will make many false claims about touching.

Therefore, it is one thing to assert that dolls do not introduce contamination into young children's responses when the important people in their lives (parents, interviewers) have not seeded misleading responses; it is quite another matter to say that the dolls can be used without risk of inducing commission errors if the adults who have access to the children have introduced misleading suggestions. It is an empirical question, of course, whether a particular child has been the recipient of misleading suggestions prior to being exposed to anatomical dolls, but, if children have been, then, on the basis of the total body of research available, we believe that the present conclusions about the safety and productivity of dolls are not warranted.

It is also the case that, when children are repeatedly interviewed, the use of dolls may not be as safe as the results suggest. In fact, Steward et al. do acknowledge the risks associated with doll use even under the pristine conditions of their structured interviewing format, and for this they are to be commended. For example, depending on which of their many analyses one seizes on, commission errors with doll use ranged anywhere from 7% to 36%; the ratio of accurate to inaccurate disclosures ranged from very high (98%) to as low as a 37% error rate for newly reported information during the second interview; and over the course of a single month those children in the doll condition who had access to medical props showed sizable decrements in accurate reporting in contrast to their peers who used only verbal descriptions. Thus, these data do raise concerns about the use of dolls in repeated interviews.

Drawing-assisted Interviews

Steward et al.'s use of line drawings as an investigative technique seems promising, but more work is required, a conclusion we are sure these authors would endorse. A recently completed study carried out by Dr. Jane Rawls (1996) in New Zealand provides a different perspective on the usefulness of line drawings, especially when they are paired with closed-ended questions (similar to the double-check procedure used in Steward et al.'s study). In the

Rawls study, 5-year-old children played a dress-up game with a male research assistant. Four interviews were conducted over the next 1–2 weeks. A body-parts diagram (i.e., a line drawing) was introduced into the second interview. Rawls found that, over the course of the four interviews, children became increasingly inaccurate: many of the children first made errors in the second interview when they were asked closed-ended questions about the body-parts diagram. Although many of the errors seemed benign, over a quarter of the total sample reported inappropriate adult-child touching. These results suggest that using body-parts diagrams could result in a number of false positive errors especially when children are repeatedly asked closed-ended questions.

There is, in fact, some hint of a similar pattern in the Steward et al. study. At the initial interview, 18% of children who were given the enhanced interviews (this included dolls, props, and drawings) inaccurately reported that their anus had been touched. This figure increased to 30% at the 1-month follow-up and to 36% at the 6-month follow-up (see their Tables 12, 21, and 31). Thus, some of these procedures may not be as "safe" as they first seem.

In line with the concerns about anatomical doll–based interviewing noted above, we worry about the use of line drawings in the context of cases where a child has been previously exposed to repeated suggestive and misleading interviews by parents, teachers, and social workers. Perhaps these techniques pose little risk the first time they are introduced *if the child has no history of prior taint.* But we cannot be certain of even this because Steward et al.'s data give one pause. Consider the following result: direct doll/drawing-assisted questioning helped four additional children accurately disclose that they were touched genitally and two additional children accurately disclose that they were touched anally. Against this yield of six disclosures one must balance the following: one additional child who was untouched claimed that he had been touched genitally and four that they had been touched anally. Thus, the enhanced techniques helped six previously silent children disclose, but at the same time they prompted five other children to make false disclosures. As we have argued elsewhere in this Commentary, we fear that these commission errors could be expected to increase in a climate more typical of actual sex abuse investigations, one where adults make frequent misleading suggestions.

Photo Displays

Finally, it appears that the authors have some faith in the potential importance of using photo displays. This is of particular importance because children often have a great deal of difficulty describing the physical appearance of strangers (e.g., Davies, Tarrant, & Flin, 1989; Goodman, Rudy, Bottoms, & Aman, 1990). Therefore, the use of pictures as cues seems to be an ideal technique. Although children can do well in selecting a target from an array of photographs (as shown in the present study), a major problem that was not dealt with here is that children are particularly prone to making false identifications when provided with so-called target-absent lineups, that is, when the perpetrator is not included in the lineup (King & Yuille, 1987; Parker & Carranza, 1989). In fact, when confronted with target-absent lineups, one commonly observes rates of false identification among preschoolers that exceed 50% and that can run as high as 70% (see Peters, 1991). Furthermore, even when children are provided with direct training on the task and told that the "target person" may not be present in a lineup, their performance is still not very good (e.g., Goodman, Bottoms, Schwartz-Kenney, & Rudy, 1991; Schwartz-Kenney, Bottoms, & Goodman, 1996).

The present study, therefore, fails to evaluate the risk of using photographic displays with young children. A full evaluation is imperative if the results of this study are to be applicable to the world of forensic investigations. After all, in most situations, when photo displays are created, the investigator does not know who the perpetrator is, and, as a result, target-absent lineups are probably quite common. On the basis of existing research, our expectation is that, if the target-absent condition had been included in the present study as a control, the children's performance would have been much poorer, leading to less faith in the picture-identification task.

Conclusions

To conclude, there is no perfect interview protocol—each will have a different combination of risks and benefits, and various partisans in the juvenile and criminal justice systems will tend to favor one combination over another. What we have to do is make interviewers aware of the risks and benefits of each technique or combination of techniques so that they can challenge cherished beliefs, test alternative hypotheses, and adopt the most scientifically valid practices. We owe a debt of gratitude to Steward and her associates in this latter regard, for in their extensive and careful program of research they have provided important new information about the benefits of using a host of nonverbal techniques. They have shown how full the glass can be. The goal of the next wave of such research will need to focus on how empty the glass can get as conditions resemble those of actual forensic investigations: the focus will need to be on the assessment of the risks of these techniques as well on as their benefits. We can only hope that this work proceeds with the same moderate and nonpolemical voice that Steward and her colleagues have shown here.

References

Bruck, M., Ceci, S. J., Francoeur, E., & Barr, R. J. (1995). "I hardly cried when I got my shot!" Influencing children's reports about a visit to their pediatrician. *Child Development,* **66,** 193–208.

Bruck, M., Ceci, S. J., Francoeur, E., & Renick, A. (1995). Anatomically detailed dolls do not facilitate preschoolers' reports of a pediatric examination involving genital touch. *Journal of Experimental Psychology: Applied,* **1,** 95–109.

Bruck, M., Ceci, S. J., & Hembrooke, H. (in press). Children's reports of pleasant and unpleasant events. In D. Read & S. Lindsay (Eds.), *Recollections of trauma: Scientific research and clinical practice.* New York: Plenum.

Ceci, S. J., & Bruck, M. (1995). *Jeopardy in the courtroom: A scientific analysis of children's testimony.* Washington, DC: APA Books.

Davies, G., Tarrant, A., & Flin, R. (1989). Close encounters of the witness kind: Children's memory for a simulated health inspection. *British Journal of Psychology,* **80,** 415–429.

Fivush, R. (1993). Developmental perspectives on autobiographical recall. In G. S. Goodman & B. Bottoms (Eds.), *Child victims and child witnesses: Understanding and improving testimony.* New York: Guilford.

Gee, S., & Pipe, M. E. (1995). Helping children to remember: The influence of object cues on children's accounts of a real event. *Developmental Psychology,* **31,** 746–758.

Goodman, G., Bottoms, B., Schwartz-Kenney, B., & Rudy, L. (1991). Children's testimony about a stressful event: Improving children's reports. *Journal of Narrative and Life History,* **1,** 69–99.

Goodman, G., Rudy, L., Bottoms, B., & Aman, C. (1990). Children's concerns and memory: Issues of ecological validity in the study of children's eyewitness testimony. In R. Fivush & J. Hudson (Eds.), *Knowing and remembering in young children.* New York: Cambridge University Press.

King, M., & Yuille, J. (1987). Suggestibility and the child witness. In S. J. Ceci, D. Ross, & M. Toglia (Eds.), *Children's eyewitness memory.* New York: Springer.

Lamb, M. E., Hershkowitz, I., Sternberg, K. J., Esplin, P. W., Hovav, M., Manor, T., & Yudilevitch, L. (in press). Effects of investigative utterance types on Israeli children's responses. *International Journal of Behavioral Development.*

Leichtman, M. D., & Ceci, S. J. (1995). The effects of stereotypes and suggestions on preschoolers' reports. *Developmental Psychology,* **31,** 568–578.

McGough, L. S., & Warren, A. R. (1994). The all-important investigative interview. *Juvenile and Family Court Journal,* **45,** 13–29.

Memon, A., Wark, L., Koehnken, G., & Bull, R. (in press). Isolating the effects of the cognitive interview. *British Journal of Psychology.*

Ornstein, P. (1995). Children's long-term retention of salient personal experiences. *Journal of Traumatic Stress,* **8,** 581–605.

Parker, J. F., & Carranza, L. (1989). Eyewitness testimony of children in target-present and target-absent lineups. *Law and Human Behavior,* **13,** 133–149.

Peters, D. P. (1991). The influence of stress and arousal on the child witness. In J. L. Doris (Ed.), *The suggestibility of children's recollections.* Washington, DC: American Psychological Association.

Peterson, C. (1996). The preschool child witness: Errors in accounts of traumatic injury. *Canadian Journal of Behavioural Science,* **28,** 36–42.

Rawls, J. (1996). How question form and body-parts diagrams can affect the content of young children's disclosures. In D. Read & S. Lindsay (Eds.), *Recollections of trauma: Scientific research and clinical practice.* New York: Plenum.

Salmon, K., Bidrose, S., & Pipe, M. E. (1995). Providing props to facilitate children's events reports: A comparison of toys and real items. *Journal of Experimental Psychology, 60,* 174–194.

Saywitz, K., Geiselman, R. E., & Bornstein, G. K. (1992). Effects of cognitive interviewing and practice on children's recall performance. *Journal of Applied Psychology, 77,* 744–756.

Schwartz-Kenney, B., Bottoms, B., & Goodman, G. S. (1996). Improving children's person identification. *Child Maltreatment, 1,* 121–133.

Yuille, J., Hunter, R., Joffe, R., & Zaparniuk, J. (1993). Interviewing children in sexual abuse cases. In G. S. Goodman & B. Bottoms (Eds.), *Child victims, child witnesses: Understanding and improving testimony.* New York: Guilford.

TO INTERVIEW A CHILD:
IMPLICATIONS OF RESEARCH ON CHILDREN'S MEMORY

Peter A. Ornstein

In recent years, the distinction between "basic" and "applied" research on memory and cognition has become quite blurred, and nowhere is this more evident than in the area of eyewitness testimony. Indeed, there is an emerging consensus that well-designed eyewitness memory studies can have relevance for basic cognitive and developmental theory and that fundamental research can have implications for the management of children who are called upon to provide evidence in legal proceedings (Ceci & Bruck, 1995; Morrison & Ornstein, in press). Consistent with this perspective, the *Monograph* by Margaret Steward and her colleagues reflects the authors' very strong commitment to the building of bridges between two worlds, that of the basic research laboratory and that concerned with the interviewing of child victims and witnesses. Moreover, the study that they report certainly does have the potential to influence our thinking about how young children should be interviewed in the context of the legal system.

In reflecting upon Steward et al.'s interesting exploration of memory for touch—and aspects of the situation in which touch is experienced—it may be useful to consider some of the ways in which research on children's remembering can be applied to the difficult task of assessing what child witnesses can remember about salient and often difficult experiences. First, by increasing our basic understanding of children's memory, studies of long-term retention can generate important baseline information concerning what we would expect children of different ages to be able to remember over extended periods of time. By examining a range of personally experienced events that differ in terms of prior knowledge (and hence understanding), stressfulness, etc., we may be able to place young children's reports of abuse in a broader perspective. For example, we can learn about the degree to which children of different ages have similar or contrasting initial impressions of an event that they have experienced. Given that subsequent memory depends on initial encoding and memory storage, differences in early recall can have profound implications for interpreting later problems in responding to the questions of interviewers. Moreover, studies of the development of memory can document the extent to which children of different ages respond to questions of varying degrees of structure as well as how they respond characteristically to questions about events that did not happen. Further, research on children's long-term retention can inform us about the degree to which children's reports of an earlier event can be influenced by repeated questioning and other experiences that may serve to reinstate or distort the episode.

This increased understanding of children's abilities to remember should also influence the ways in which we think about the interview process (see Gordon, Schroeder, Ornstein, & Baker-Ward, 1995). For example, information about age differences in the rate of decay will permit better understanding of appropriate times for the effective interviewing of child victims. Similarly, what we know about children's differential responses to repeated and suggestive questions and to intervening experiences can provide guidelines for interviewers who must try to determine whether individual children's responses reflect their memory of some target event, or the questions of previous interviewers, or general knowledge, or even fantasy. Further, evidence of developmental differences in the extent to which an interview must be structured in order to elicit recall would have strong implications for the types of questions that should be posed as well as the props and supports that might be employed profitably with children of different ages. Because younger children are known to differ from older children on many of these dimensions—that is, in terms of initial encoding, rate of decay, susceptibility to suggestive questions, reliance on specific types of questions, etc.—systematic studies of children's remembering over extended periods of time should have considerable relevance for influencing the ways in which we question child witnesses (see, e.g., Ceci & Bruck, 1995; Doris, 1991; Ornstein, Larus, & Clubb, 1991).

Given this orientation toward the linkage between research on memory and the construction of interview protocols, how shall we view the work presented by Steward and her colleagues? Over the course of the last 10 years, a number of researchers (e.g., Goodman, Aman, & Hirschman, 1987; Ornstein, Gordon, & Larus, 1992; Peters, 1987) have focused on children's memory for different types of medical experiences because these events have been viewed as being partially analogous to various abusive situations. Steward et al.'s research on touch is certainly consistent with this body of work, but it also represents a significant extension of the range of medical experiences that have been studied and a very interesting examination of the effects of several covariates thought to influence both the encoding and the delayed reporting of information. Capitalizing admirably on a range of naturally occurring hospital-based medical experiences as "stimuli" to be remembered, Steward and her colleagues have used medical records and videotapes to verify the children's reports of their experiences, and, for a substantial subsample, they have been able to present information about the accuracy, completeness, and consistency of these reports out to a delay of 6 months. Moreover, all this has been done in the context of a serious investigation of alternative interview protocols, a focus that is especially welcome given that young children typically provide relatively little information in response to open-ended verbal probes (Ornstein et al., 1991).

From my perspective, Steward et al.'s study is at one and the same time a basic exploration of children's memory and an applied investigation of strategies for interviewing. As I see it, these researchers make a very useful contribution to our thinking about the assessment of children's long-term retention of salient personal experiences. Nonetheless, as I reflect on the issues that they raise, it seems important to place their work in a broader developmental context (see Ornstein, 1991). Indeed, a developmental analysis prompts us to ask about factors that influence both the course of remembering, on the one hand, and the assessment of what is being remembered, on the other. In this discussion, I will consider two central issues that have implications for understanding children's long-term retention and its assessment in the context of an interview: the nature of the event that is being remembered and the ways in which memory is probed.

What Is Being Remembered?

Consider first the nature of the to-be-remembered event. All events are not created equal! Indeed, recent work indicates that both the nature of the event that is being remembered and the conditions prevailing as it is experienced make a real difference in terms of initial encoding in memory and the course of retention (Baker-Ward, Ornstein, & Principe, in press; Ornstein, Shapiro, Clubb, Follmer, & Baker-Ward, in press). Thus, the internal structure of the event can readily affect remembering, with the retention of integrated or cohesive experiences being superior to that of events composed of seemingly unrelated component features (see Bauer, 1992). Similarly, children's understanding of that which is being experienced, determined in part by prior knowledge that supports "going beyond the information given," facilitates remembering but, under some conditions, can lead to distortion. Further, the stress experienced as an event unfolds can facilitate remembering if it results in focused attention and can interfere with memory if encoding is disrupted (Ornstein et al., 1991).

These issues become relevant to any consideration of the retention functions that are implicit in the Steward et al. *Monograph* because it turns out that there is considerable uncertainty concerning just what the children were asked to remember. Although the authors have been truly inventive in examining touch in a number of medical situations, they pool over contrasting clinic experiences that may differ in many ways. For example, the various clinic visits (i.e., the "to-be-remembered stimuli") may vary markedly in terms of their internal structure and the children's understanding of their experiences. To illustrate, consider some of the problems associated with the definition of a "touch." From my perspective, even the same touch to the same bodily location may have different meanings in different clinical settings. Indeed, at the extreme, it seems likely that a genital examination may mean different things when it is carried out in a well-child checkup and in a sexual abuse clinic. Yet it is the experience as it is understood and interpreted that becomes the stimulus that is remembered by the individual child. These difficulties, moreover, would seem to be exacerbated when we consider different types of touches that are encountered in the various clinics. Thus, when looked at in context, the events that are being remembered by the children and analyzed by the authors may be quite different, with the possibility of markedly discrepant retention functions being averaged together.

One clear determinant of children's understanding is their prior experience with the events that are to be remembered. In general, prior experience leads to enhanced knowledge, which, in turn, facilitates interpretation, encoding, and remembering (Ornstein et al., in press). Indeed, children whose understanding of a given event varies may remember it quite differently. But knowledge is a double-edged sword that can also lead to errors, particularly as details fade over time and subjects quite unconsciously fill in the gaps on the basis of knowledge and expectation (Ornstein et al., 1996). In the context of the Steward et al. investigation, it would seem that some of the children were quite familiar with the clinic settings in which the events to be remembered took place. To the extent that the subjects could be viewed as "experts" in the various clinic routines, it may in fact be quite difficult to differentiate between their reports of the details of a specific clinic visit and their general knowledge about what typically takes place during such a visit. Such a determination requires the inclusion of a substantial number of questions about activities that were consistent with expectations but not included in the specific events that are being remembered, a matter that takes us directly to questions of memory assessment.

Questioning Children

Let us now consider the diagnostic difficulties that confront both the memory researcher and the clinical/legal interviewer. At the outset, it needs to be acknowledged that any assessment (or diagnosis) of young children's memory depends to a considerable extent on the types of questions that are posed by the interviewer. For example, as suggested above, in contrast to older children, younger children provide relatively little information in response to open-ended questions and must accordingly be probed with more specific types of questions (Baker-Ward, Gordon, Ornstein, Larus, & Clubb, 1993; Ornstein et al., 1991). Accordingly, quite different impressions of young children's memory are derived from considerations of their responses to open-ended probes taken alone or in combination with more specific (e.g., yes/no) questions. Indeed, the performance of young preschoolers looks dramatically different if we include responses to more specific types of questions, with younger children appearing more "competent" when these probes are included.

But the use of specific questions carries with it a liability in that high rates of "correct" responding (.50, in the case of yes/no questions) can be obtained on the basis of random guessing. Therefore, in order to understand young children's reports of their past experiences, it becomes essential to ask about activities that had not been included in the events that are being remembered. That is, accurate diagnoses of their abilities to remember require assessments of the extent to which they can say "yes" to things that happened and "no" to things that did not take place. Given this orientation, the question then arises as to whether the children interviewed by Steward and her colleagues were questioned adequately about nonexperienced actions. As I understand it, these researchers included in their protocol a set of nine yes/no questions about particular pediatric procedures, about half of which were expected to have been experienced by the individual children. In this way, they were able to ask about some—but not very many—procedures that not been experienced.

From one perspective, the authors have taken an admirable stand in their refusal to include probes about knowingly false allegations about the medical staff because they were concerned that these probes might "later undermine the ongoing relationship between the children and their doctors" (p. 35). But it can be argued that this decision led to a failure to include an adequate number of questions about "absent features" and thus to a weakening of the conclusions about children's remembering that can be derived from their data. As I see it, this is a rather important matter in that the inclusion of substantial numbers of questions about activities not included in the event being remembered is conceptually equivalent to asking a clinical or legal interviewer to evaluate seriously hypotheses that are inconsistent with the one that is being pursued (and perhaps believed).

More generally, issues concerning the ways in which children's memory can effectively be probed are at the core of Steward et al.'s *Monograph,* as their major aim was to examine alternative interview protocols involving different types of supports for remembering. But, in this regard, it becomes essential to consider the degree to which such scaffolding might introduce complexities of its own by confusing the children and otherwise interfering with an adequate assessment of performance. At one level, there is the question of whether young children have sufficient cognitive maturity to make effective use of props such as dolls. Indeed, a considerable amount of evidence suggests that 3-year-olds might have difficulties in viewing a doll simultaneously as a toy and as a representation of the self (DeLoache, 1990; Gordon et al., 1993).

At another level, there is the question of whether the evocative properties of dolls and props can essentially lead a child away from a "memory interview" and into a situation that is dominated by play and confabulations and thus to what amount to false reports. Of course, Steward and her colleagues are aware of this potential problem, and they address it to some extent in their *Monograph*. But, on the weight of two recent reports that indicate problems that arise when realistic dolls and props are used in assessments of young children's memory, I wish to underscore the seriousness of the resulting interpretive dilemma. One study dealt with the use of dolls within interviews about an aversive radiological procedure involving urinary catheterization (Goodman, Dunn, & Quas, 1995), and the other concerned the use of dolls alone and dolls in combination with realistic medical props in a procedure in which children were free to act out the details of a visit to the doctor (Ornstein, Follmer, & Gordon, 1995). Facilitation resulted from the use of dolls in the Goodman et al. study and of dolls plus props in the Ornstein et al. study, but there was also a notable increase in problematic reports.

Some General Strategies for Interviewing

From my perspective, the issues discussed here about the nature of to-be-remembered events and the assessment of memory that were prompted by a consideration of Steward et al.'s interesting *Monograph* have very direct implications for interviewing children in legal settings. Consider the following "rules of thumb" about making diagnostic decisions about children's reports:

1. Some events are more easily remembered than others, and additional research is needed to specify precisely the retention profiles associated with various types of experiences. Nonetheless, we know that a critical determinant of remembering is a child's understanding and interpretation of an event as it unfolds. Simply put, events that are not well understood should not be remembered effectively, and high levels of recall for these experiences, particularly at extended delays, should raise an interviewer's suspicions about the accuracy of a child's report. Unexpectedly high levels of recall may reflect accurate remembering, but they may also stem from a range of intervening

experiences, including repetitions of the to-be-remembered event, other interviews, and/or "preparation" for the assessment.

2. Related, of course, is the general question of whether children's delayed reports reflect remembering or whether they may be driven by prior knowledge and expectation. Interviewers must understand that remembering involves constructive, knowledge-driven processes, especially in assessment contexts that include "evocative" stimuli. In general, interviewers need to be aware that, over longer periods of time, details may fade and children (and adults, for that matter) may unconsciously fill in the gaps on the basis of expectation and their beliefs about what they thought must have happened.

3. Assessments of memory require evidence that a child can differentiate between what was and what was not experienced at a particular point in time. Similarly, effective interviewing requires that interviewers recognize the importance of making an active effort to test alternative hypotheses about the events in question.

These rules of thumb clearly do not constitute an interview protocol, but they do reflect a perspective on interviewing that is consistent with the implications of research on children's memory, and they represent a starting point for the development of such guidelines for interviewing. Of course, these guidelines would need to be evaluated in the context of comprehensive studies such as that reported by Steward and her colleagues.

References

Baker-Ward, L., Gordon, B. N., Ornstein, P. A., Larus, D. M., & Clubb, P. A. (1993). Young children's long-term retention of a pediatric examination. *Child Development, 64,* 1519–1533.

Baker-Ward, L., Ornstein, P. A., & Principe, G. F. (in press). Revealing the representation: Evidence from children's reports of events. In P. van den Broek, P. Bauer, & T. Bourg (Eds.), *Developmental spans in event comprehension and representation: Bridging fictional and actual events.* Hillsdale, NJ: Erlbaum.

Bauer, P. (1992). Holding it all together: How enabling relations facilitate young children's event recall. *Cognitive Development, 7,* 1–28.

Ceci, S. J., & Bruck, M. (1995). *Jeopardy in the courtroom: A scientific analysis of children's testimony.* Washington, DC: American Psychological Association.

DeLoache, J. (1990). Young children's understanding of models. In R. Fivush & J. Hudson (Eds.), *Knowing and remembering in young children.* New York: Cambridge University Press.

Doris, J. (1991). *The suggestibility of children's recollections.* Washington, DC: American Psychological Association.

Goodman, G. S., Aman, C., & Hirschman, J. (1987). Child sexual and physical abuse: Children's testimony. In S. J. Ceci, M. P. Toglia, & D. F. Ross (Eds.), *Children's eyewitness testimony.* New York: Springer.

Goodman, G. S., Dunn, J., & Quas, J. A. (1995, April). Children's memory for a stressful event: Developmental, individual differences, and interviewing considerations. In G. S. Goodman & L. Baker-Ward (Chairs), *Children's memory for emotional and traumatic experi-*

ences. Symposium conducted at the meeting of the Society for Research in Child Development, Indianapolis.

Gordon, B. N., Ornstein, P. A., Nida, R. E., Follmer, A., Crenshaw, M. C., & Albert, G. (1993). Does the use of dolls facilitate children's memory of visits to the doctor? *Applied Cognitive Psychology, 7,* 459–474.

Gordon, B. N., Schroeder, C. S., Ornstein, P. A., & Baker-Ward, L. E. (1995). Clinical implications of research on memory development. In T. Ney (Ed.), *True and false allegations of child sexual abuse: Assessment and management.* New York: Brunner/Mazel.

Morrison, F. J., & Ornstein, P. A. (in press). Cognitive development. In R. B. Cairns, G. H. Elder Jr., & E. J. Costello (Eds.), *Developmental science.* New York: Cambridge University Press.

Ornstein, P. A. (1991). Commentary: Putting interviewing in context. In J. Doris (Ed.), *The suggestibility of children's recollections.* Washington, DC: American Psychological Association.

Ornstein, P. A., Follmer, A., & Gordon, B. N. (1995, April). The influence of dolls and props on young children's recall of pediatric examinations. In M. Bruck & S. J. Ceci (Chairs), *The use of props in eliciting children's reports of past events: Theoretical and forensic perspectives.* Symposium conducted at the meeting of the Society for Research in Child Development, Indianapolis.

Ornstein, P. A., Gordon, B. N., & Larus, D. H. (1992). Children's memory for a personally experienced event: Implications for testimony. *Applied Cognitive Psychology, 6,* 49–60.

Ornstein, P. A., Larus, D. M., & Clubb, P. A. (1991). Understanding children's testimony: Implications of research on the development of memory. In R. Vasta (Ed.), *Annals of Child Development* (Vol. **8**). London: Jessica Kingsley.

Ornstein, P. A., Merritt, K. A., Baker-Ward, L., Gordon, B. N., Principe, G., & Furtado, E. (1996, July). *Children's knowledge, expectation, and long-term retention.* Paper presented at the International Conference on Memory, University of Padova.

Ornstein, P. A., Shapiro, L. R., Clubb, P. A., Follmer, A., & Baker-Ward, L. (in press). The influence of prior knowledge on children's memory for salient medical experiences. In N. Stein, P. A. Ornstein, B. Tversky, & C. J. Brainerd (Eds.), *Memory for everyday and emotional events.* Hillsdale, NJ: Erlbaum.

Peters, D. P. (1987). The impact of naturally occurring stress on children's memory. In S. J. Ceci, M. P. Toglia, & D. P. Ross (Eds.), *Children's eyewitness memory.* New York: Springer.

COMMUNICATING SCIENTIFIC FINDINGS

Margaret S. Steward

Lucy S. McGough, Maggie Bruck and Stephen J. Ceci, and Peter A. Ornstein identify the problem to be solved as the reliability of children's reports, a concern we share. My colleagues and I appreciate the commentators' commitment of time and energy to reviewing our clinical research study and welcome this opportunity to engage in discussion with them.

Different Research Teams Ask Different Questions

In their Commentary, Bruck and Ceci employ the metaphor of the half-empty/half-full glass to characterize research on the reliability of children's reports. We believe that that metaphor is insufficient. We challenge the underlying assumption that there is only one glass and, by analogy, only one research question and therefore limited decisions for design and methods of conducting research. The half-empty/half-full metaphor masks the fact that there are many glasses, many research questions, and that there is great need for multiple designs and methodologies. The focus of our research has been the construction and use of a set of experimental interviews in order to study how to maximize children's ability to report salient experiences of body touch and handling. In contrast, Bruck and Ceci have focused their research on "the inherent weaknesses of children's reports, especially when they are subjected to a variety of suggestive interviewing techniques" (p. 204). As the physicians, teachers, and therapists of abused children, we fully acknowledge Bruck and Ceci's point that there currently are children in the legal pipeline who have been so poorly interviewed that it will be impossible for anyone to unravel their reports or to understand their original experiences of abuse.

For these children, to use McGough's provocative metaphor, Humpty-Dumpty-has already fallen off the wall. However, we do not believe that the status quo should be seen as either normative or inevitable—that is precisely why we initiated this research on interviewing!

Can a Medical Visit Inform Child-Abuse Investigation?

Bruck and Ceci raise the issue of ecological validity and challenge what they term the "procedure generalizability" (p. 208) of our study. We remind the reader of the reasons we give in our discussion for the choice of a medical visit to serve as an analogue for abuse. First, child abuse is not a single phenomenon. Second, while adults may cognitively understand medical procedures as "societally sanctioned acts," that sanction does not protect children from the experience of direct, often unwanted, and painful body touch during medical procedures (cf. Bearison, 1990; Peterson, 1996). Third, while it is unethical to create abusive experiences experimentally in order to study them directly, our clinical and research evidence suggests that all the issues that Bruck and Ceci believe to be absent in the medical visit analogue—family dynamics inhibiting disclosure, familiar perpetrator, and betrayal by a trusted caregiver—are potentially present. Something for which we cannot establish an analogue is the reason the adult touched the child's body; no staff member interacted with a child for purposes of sexual gratification. We believe that our results, focusing on the quality, quantity, and location of body touch that children experience during a medical visit, carry an ecological validity that informs work with abused children. For example, contrasting children's failure to report benign touch to their highly accurate and consistent informational and emotional reporting of painful touch offers a model for understanding children's reports of different kinds of abusive experiences; likewise, the example of children who demonstrated shame and withheld information following painful experiences may encourage investigative interviewers to continue to probe if they are faced with behavioral manifestations of shameful silence from allegedly abused children.

How Should Specific Results Be Read and Used?

While we share Bruck and Ceci's concern about the cost/benefit of investigative interviewers' use of anatomically detailed dolls and drawings, we do not want the reader to throw the anatomical baby out with the bathwater! Let me restate our findings that, in the initial interview, no child with access to the dolls made a spontaneous commission error reporting genital touch and no child with access to the drawings made a spontaneous erroneous report of anal touch. Unfortunately, Bruck and Ceci's review of our findings with regard to the efficacy of dolls and drawings is confusing. They mistakenly discuss the errors elicited by direct questions about anal touch under the heading of *drawings,* although direct questions about anal touch were pursued only with children who had access to dolls. They also confound from the second interview the results of accuracy of body touch in the doll interview with accuracy of reports of "touch with." In contrast to children who did not have medical props, the accuracy of reports of "touch with" dropped for children with medical props, but the accuracy of reports of body touch did not. I cannot comment on their assertion that the ratio of accurate to inaccurate disclosure errors ranged from 98% to 37% because they do not specify which interview conditions, which sessions, which body touches (total or specific), and which responses (accurate assertion and/or accurate denial; errors of omission and/or commission) they selected to construct those statistics.

In each of the three interview sessions, there is an increase in commission errors in the reporting of genital and anal touch that can be specifically attributed to the interviewer's shift in strategy from giving a child access to dolls or drawings to asking a doll/drawing-assisted direct question. It is that strategy shift from doll access to doll-assisted direct question that is revealed in the statistics highlighted by Bruck and Ceci when commission errors raised from 7% to 36% for reports of anal touch at 6 months. We trust that information should be helpful to an investigative interviewer, who, when working with an individual child, could decide whether to increase the chance of eliciting an erroneous response by shifting from access to anatomically detailed materials to a doll/drawing-assisted direct question. In the study, we recommended that children have access to anatomically detailed materials, but we did not recommend the use of doll/drawing-assisted direct questions—the condition that gave rise to the most extreme commission error rates in every interview session.

Given our recommendations, the more interesting set of statistics from our data is, I believe, the fact that the reporting rate of genital touch for children in the enhanced interviews who have access to anatomical cues is more than double the rate of children in the verbal interview across all three interviews, that is, 62% versus 27% in the initial interview, 69% versus 18% after a 1-month delay, and 72% versus 33% after a 6-month delay. A parallel and very important finding is that, while children in the verbal interview never disclosed anal touch, some children with access to dolls disclosed anal touch at every interview. We never suggest that it is "safe" to use dolls; omission and commission error data are presented so that an interviewer can make an informed decision about the cost/benefit of the use of anatomically detailed materials. At our Multi-Disciplinary Interview Center (MDIC) in Sacramento County, which has become a model for the State of California (Myers, 1994), the child interview specialists use drawings and dolls sparsely, dic-

225

tated by the need to clarify names of body parts, sexual acts, and/or experiences that children report. The anatomical materials are brought out *only after* the child's narrative introduces the material—and *only if* the child's verbalization is not clear to the adult listener (at the MDIC, *adult listener* includes the child interview specialist, staff from law enforcement and/or social service agencies, and an attorney from the district attorney's office).

We noted in our discussion, as did Bruck and Ceci, that the target-absent foil is missing from our design. Although we were not aware of the work with "target-absent" photo lineups when we initiated the study, we agree that a "none of the above" alternative is important and support Davies's (1993) recommendation to include a "Mr. Nobody" rather than presenting a target-absent lineup. This strategy is compatible with our concern to facilitate a child's ability to report what he or she knows rather than to trick a child into responding to a question that has no right answer. However, the critique of the absence of target-absent foils may be a moot point. Bruck and Ceci assert that, "in most situations, when photo displays are created, the investigator does not know who the perpetrator is" (p. 212). This may be true for the investigative interviewing of adults. However, it has been our experience at the MDIC that, in the majority of child-abuse cases, the alleged perpetrator is known to the child and to several, if not all, of the adults in the child's world, including the investigator. As we discussed in our study, one use of the photo array could be to help a child communicate his or her knowledge to the interviewer, and a second use could be to help the interviewer clarify to the child exactly which of the many persons in the child's life the interviewer is inquiring about. Like the anatomical cues, the photo array should be employed only if necessary and should be tailored to the communication task at hand.

Did the Children Share a Common Experience?

As a developmental researcher who has devoted much of his career to studying children's memory of events, Ornstein would, we believe, agree that *event* is a devilishly complex concept in field or clinical research. Who gets to identify and operationalize the events to be studied and on which inquiry is based—the researcher, the parent (cf. Price & Goodman, 1990), the parent and the child (cf. Peterson, Moreno, & Harbeck-Weber, 1993), or the child (cf. Peterson, 1990)? Even establishing when events begin and end is not easy. Parents and their children often extend the event that we have arbitrarily defined well beyond our purview and our control. In our new study (Steward, O'Connor, Acredolo, & Steward, 1996), some parents, who had to travel long distances to our medical center to obtain cancer treatment for their children, have described extensive anticipatory conversations with their children about how the treatment would go, while others reported that they studiously filled the time with distracting talk about everything but the inevitable medical treatment. Thus, for some children and their parents, the *event* would extend beyond the clinic visit in both temporal directions to include coming to the clinic and going home again.

In his Commentary, Ornstein stated that "there is considerable uncertainty concerning just what the children were asked to remember" (p. 218). To the contrary, it is quite clear what the child was asked to remember, for there is both a video and a medical record of each child's visit, and the accuracy, completeness, and consistency of each child's responses were compared with his or her own experience. We agree with Ornstein's concern that one should attend to the differential meaning that similar events may hold for children. We believe that the meaning that children assign to events may hold a key to understanding the dynamics that would in turn help explain the discrepancy that we and others have found between remembering and reporting. Further, we believe that, even for these young children, a visit to the doctor was a meaningful experience with integrity—they never confused it with a picnic or a trip to the zoo! In this study, in addition to exploring child and family variables that might contribute to differential reporting, we chose to identify—on the basis of our own work with children in medical settings— specific components of a medical visit that would catch their attention: the relative amount of pain and invasiveness of medical procedures, the number and location of body touches. By opting to study several components of the medical visit as variables, we investigated whether and how children's reports of their experiences would vary significantly along the breadth or range of the variables.

Ornstein continues his critique about events by asking "whether the children interviewed by Steward and her colleagues were questioned adequately about nonexperienced actions" (p. 219), but he never states his own estimate of how many are enough. We are not sure that there is an absolute number of nonevent questions that should be asked during an initial interview. There is no doubt that nonevent questions can be helpful in testing whether the child understands his or her role in the interview, in testing whether the child understands a particular set of questions, and in revealing response bias— that is, when the child gives the same response to every question, regardless of veracity. We agree that nonevent questions are also useful in exploring alternative explanations for allegedly abusive phenomena. In our study, our pediatric team members created a generic list of events that might occur during a child's pediatric visit. Approximately half the direct questions we asked were about experiences that a child might have had with a medical staff member but that did not actually occur during the particular visit we were studying. It should be noted that too many nonevent questions may actually increase the risk of tainting an investigative interview. For example, too many irrelevant questions may tire a child, distract him or her from the event the interviewer wants to focus on, and even raise the question in the child's mind of whether the interviewer is really asking for a playful, rather than a truthful, response. While investigative interviewers often frame their inquiries about nonevents as yes/no questions, Ornstein notes that this question format carries a high base rate of error (50%), and Lamb et al. (in press) have demonstrated that yes/no questions actually limit the length and richness of a child's responses.

Do Ethical Commitments Compromise Our Study?

The issue of ethical decisions in research with young children was raised directly by Bruck and Ceci and indirectly by Ornstein. Fisher (1993) noted that current guidelines are not sufficient for grappling with the ethical dilemmas faced by developmental researchers and that the scientific and the ethical dimensions of research with high-risk children and youths often appear to have mutually exclusive goals. Ethics, especially within the context of child-abuse studies, deserves a broader forum and fuller discussion than I can provide in this Reply. Suffice it to say here that the decisions that our research team made about how we would conduct this study, the strategies that we would introduce experimentally, and even the questions we would ask were made in full cognizance, not ignorance, of the state of the fate of allegedly abused children in the social service and court systems. It is our view that children need not be subject to harassing or misleading questions in order to determine the effectiveness of a good interview. Although we agree that adults can confuse children this way, we do not believe that it is necessary to do so in order to elicit their testimony. In fact, avoiding the secondary abuse of children in this manner is at the heart of what we believe a good interview to be. Our results speak to the effectiveness of an interview conducted within our ethical principles.

Specifically, we strongly disagree with Bruck and Ceci about the ease with which young children can be debriefed if they have been deceptively interviewed. The panel from the Nation Research Council (1993) studying research on child abuse and neglect stated that "dehoaxing is sometimes harmful and desensitizing is sometimes impossible." They state further that "deception in research has profound implications, since it may carry over into relationships of the subjects with their family members as well as with clinicians, social workers, law enforcement personnel . . ." (p. 331). In their Commentary, Bruck and Ceci report results from their own research studies that document when children are repeatedly interviewed by biased interviewers who use suggestive interviewing techniques: "Children may even fabricate whole events that never occurred (e.g., Leichtman & Ceci, 1995); at times, they can be led to confuse suggestions with actual events to the point that they later insist that the suggested events actually occurred (Bruck, Ceci, Francoeur, & Barr, 1995)'' (p. 205). That is precisely why we stand by our decision, made more than a decade ago, to refrain from including knowingly false allegations about the medical staff. We would make the same decision again tomorrow.

The Importance of the Initial Interview

McGough provides a compelling argument for focusing research attention on the initial interview and calls for the creation of a national protocol. She is cognizant of all the problems and disagreements in the field, but she is also aware of a central core of consensus that is available from the current research arena. Her report of efforts to create interview protocols in Israel, the Scandinavian countries, and Great Britain is inspiring, and her call for a national consensus on the creation of a definitive set of American protocols is intriguing. Response to McGough's recommendation for the creation of an American version of Great Britain's *Memorandum of Good Practice* (1992) would require a major commitment of time and federal dollars and collaboration across disciplines and experience. Her call may be timely since there is evidence that developmental researchers are interested in collecting and making more generally available the interview guidelines and protocols currently in use around the country (D. A. Poole, personal communication, May 1996). Surely, this is an important first step, although, as McGough notes, unfortunately, many of the protocols that have been developed (e.g., the Cognitive Interview) were designed for older children and are ineffective or inappropriate when they are utilized in interviews with very young children. Our MDIC child interview specialists, who consult with staff from other interview centers across the state, have noted two practical issues that deserve the attention of those who would draft a national gold standard. First, they have found that there is a troublesome gap, especially for new interviewers, between "guidelines" and the actual give-and-take between child and interviewer when conducting an interview; second, the format of most protocols is not very user friendly, if one keeps in mind the task of interviewing an active young child.

The Need for Training in Investigative Interviewing with Children

With the introduction of highly trained child interview specialists, one of the issues that we have faced is the change in the role that frontline law enforcement agents and social agency staff members play. Many of these individuals were drafted into their positions with little or no training in child

interviewing, and most have never received effective supervision of their interviewing strategies. It takes time, patience, and goodwill for them to understand the necessity for and to respect the role of a highly trained child interview specialist. One afternoon recently, I joined a near-retirement sheriff
from a neighboring county in the observation room as an interview was being
conducted with a tired, scared, balky youngster. The sheriff reached over to
greet me and whispered, "God, I miss interviewing 'my own' kids!" At the
conclusion of a very difficult but extremely effective interview, he slapped my
knee and said, "God, I'm glad I didn't have to do that one!" We also face
a high burnout rate and subsequent frequent turnover of staff in law enforcement and social service agencies who work with child-abuse cases. The task
is similar to one we face in medical education: new staff/students must be
educated and brought on board in the midst of delivering excellent clinical
care.

Whether or not we develop a national gold standard protocol for interviewing, the focus of our energy should be on training, supervising, and consulting with staff across the broad spectrum of agencies who are responsible
for conducting initial interviews with children and with judges who can assure
children the opportunity to report their experiences in court. We believe that
the research findings offer a compelling argument in support of three things:
training, training, and training! First, it is important to train interviewers to
conduct excellent, clean initial interviews. Our goal is not that investigative
interviewers conduct a "perfect" interview or that they rigidly follow a static
protocol—but rather that they conduct an interview that maximizes the
child's ability to report his or her experiences. Lamb and his colleagues
(Lamb et al., in press; Sternberg et al., in press) report that, although open-
ended "invitations" to children to report their experiences result in significantly longer and more detailed responses, investigators in both Israel and
the United States rarely issue them. These findings are echoed by Warren,
Woodall, Hunt, and Perry (1996), who found that the majority of sexual
abuse interviewers whom they studied failed to incorporate the wisdom already documented by memory researchers; for example, they failed to begin
their abuse-related questioning with general, open-ended questions, relying
instead on specific yes/no questions throughout the interview, and they frequently introduced new material not previously disclosed by the children.

Second, to maintain high interview standards, and to keep the protocols
dynamic, it is critical to develop both regularly scheduled peer review and
in-service training that provides consultation with experts in the fields of law
enforcement and child development who can offer both a translation of new
research and a review and critique of actual interviews. We want investigative
interviewers to be aware of their own biases, monitor their language carefully,
and not "read" children's thoughts or feelings for them. At the MDIC, the
staff have developed a protocol to use in peer review of videotapes of their

own investigative interviews with children. The practice of peer review and my monthly consultation with staff and review of videotaped and live interviews have been an integral part of the center's operating procedures since its inception 6 years ago. Warren et al. (1996) and Wood, McClure, and Birch (1996) have generated some specific, practical suggestions for in-service training that would improve interviewing in child protection agencies.

Finally, we believe that it is critically important to increase judicial training. Much of the confusion that children experience in our court system is a result of trying to get adults, not children, to tell the truth. McGough noted that judges must often rule on the admissibility of evidence collected in pretrial interviews, where specific attention to the quality of the interview is critical. Furthermore, the judge is the only person in the courtroom who can demand that a confusing, multipronged question to a child be restated, that a reference to a person be clarified, that harassing, repetitive questioning cease when a child has already answered the question.

In the interim between completing the final draft of the *Monograph* and writing this Reply, I had the opportunity to join a research team whose goal was to identify the oldest, tallest trees in the Tongass National Forest in Alaska, the largest temperate rain forest in the world. The procedure that we employed was described as "ground-truthing the biomass with satellite and aerial photographs." That means that we used clues from satellite and aerial photographs to determine the locations most likely to hold the "temple trees" in the old-growth forests, then investigated and collected data on foot. We identified the species, height, trunk diameter, and age of the largest tree and described the location and ecology of four addition points within a 23-meter radius. Throughout the process of bushwhacking through the forests, data collection, and coding, there were threads of three or four conversations running among the team members. We discussed the link between theory and science, the pain/gain of working with multidisciplinary colleagues, the use of multiple methods to develop and test theory, the strengths, limitations, and acceptable error range of each unique method of data collection (including ground-truthing), and, finally, the genuine struggle to communicate scientific findings to those who were in the midst of making decisions regarding the fate of the trees. Our experience in the Tongass is a model for the wide range of conversations that need to occur if we are to "do justice" for young children who are the subject of investigative interviews.

References

Bearison, D. J. (1990). *They never want to tell you.* Cambridge, MA: Harvard University Press.

Bruck, M., Ceci, S. J., Francoeur, E., & Barr, R. (1995). "I hardly cried when I got my shot!": Influencing children's reports about a visit to their pediatrician. *Child Development,* **66,** 193–208.

Davies, G. (1993). Children's memory for other people. In C. A. Nelson (Ed.), *Memory and affect in development* (Minnesota Symposium on Child Psychology, Vol. **26**). Hillsdale, NJ: Erlbaum.

Fisher, C. B. (1993, Winter). Integrating science and ethics in research with high-risk children and youth. *Social Policy Report: Society for Research in Child Development,* **7,** 1–27.

Lamb, M. E., Hershkowitz, I., Sternberg, K. J., Esplin, P. W., Hovav, M., Manor, T., & Yudilevitch, L. (in press). Effects of investigative utterance types on Israeli children's responses. *International Journal of Behavioral Development.*

Leichtman, M. D., & Ceci, S. J. (1995). The effects of stereotypes and suggestions on preschoolers' reports. *Developmental Psychology,* **31,** 568–578.

Memorandum of good practice. (1992). London: Home Office.

Myers, J. E. B. (Ed.). (1994, June). *Child victim witness investigative pilot project: Research and evaluation final report.* Sacramento: California Attorney General's Office.

National Research Council. (1993). *Understanding child abuse and neglect.* Washington, DC: National Academy Press.

Peterson, C. (1990). The who, when and where of early narratives. *Journal of Child Language,* **17,** 433–455.

Peterson, C. (1996). The preschool child witness: Errors in accounts of traumatic injury. *Canadian Journal of Behavioural Science,* **28,** 36–42.

Peterson, L., Moreno, A., & Harbeck-Weber, C. (1993). "And then it started bleeding": Children's and mothers' perceptions and recollections of daily injury events. *Journal of Clinical Child Psychology,* **22,** 345–354.

Price, D. W. W., & Goodman, G. S. (1990). Visiting the wizard: Children's memory for a recurring event. *Child Development,* **61,** 664–680.

Sternberg, K. J., Lamb, M. E., Hershkowitz, I., Esplin, P. W., Redlich, A., & Sunshine, N. (in press). The relationship between investigative utterance types and the informativeness of child witnesses. *Journal of Applied Developmental Psychology.*

Steward, M. S., O'Connor, J., Acredolo, C., & Steward, D. S. (1996). The trauma and memory of cancer treatment in children. In M. H. Bornstein & J. L. Genevro (Eds.), *Child development and behavioral pediatrics.* Hillsdale, NJ: Erlbaum.

Warren, A. R., Woodall, J. S., Hunt, J. S., & Perry, N. W. (1996). "It sounds good in theory, but . . .": Do investigative interviewers follow guidelines based on memory research? *Child Maltreatment,* **1,** 231–245.

Wood, J. M., McClure, K. A., & Birch, R. A. (1996). Suggestions for improving interviews in child protection agencies. *Child Maltreatment,* **1,** 223–230.

CONTRIBUTORS

Margaret S. Steward (Ph.D. 1965, Yale University) is professor of psychology in the Department of Psychiatry and an associate dean of the School of Medicine at the University of California, Davis. She holds a diplomate in clinical psychology from the American Board of Professional Psychology. Her research, teaching, and clinical interests focus on children and families at risk as a result of prematurity, illness, divorce, and/or abuse. She has been a consultant for the staff of the Sacramento County Multi-Disciplinary Interview Center since its inception and has conducted workshops in the United States and Australia for staff from health, mental health, social welfare, and law enforcement agencies and from the judiciary.

David S. Steward (Ph.D. 1966, Yale University) is research professor at the Pacific School of Religion and the Graduate Theological Union in Berkeley. His research interests include the experiences of children and their families in church, school, and hospital settings and the training of academics and professionals in multidisciplinary settings.

Lisa Farquhar (Ph.D. 1983, University of California, Davis) is associate clinical professor in the Department of Psychiatry at the University of California, Davis, where she provides seminars on child abuse and clinical supervision to graduate students and child psychiatry fellows. In addition, she is a psychotherapist in private practice in Sacramento.

John E. B. Myers (J.D. 1977, University of Utah College of Law) is professor of law at the University of the Pacific, McGeorge School of Law. He served on the California Child Victim Witness Judicial Advisory Committee and chaired the Research and Advisory Panel for the Attorney-General's Office in the State of California. He is the author of books and articles on legal issues in child abuse, including *Child Witness Law and Practice* (1987), *Legal Issues in Child Abuse and Neglect* (1992), and *The Backlash: Child Protection under Fire* (1994).

Michael Reinhart (M.D. 1974, University of California, Los Angeles; M.P.H. 1979, University of California, Berkeley) was assistant professor of pediatrics, director of the Ambulatory Pediatric Clinics, and medical director of the Child Protection Center at the University of California, Davis, Medical Center. He is currently in private pediatric practice in Davis.

Jane Welker (M.S. 1953, University of Chicago) has retired from her role as director of the Early Childhood Laboratory at the University of California, Davis. Currently, she is developing interpretive materials to help children and adults understand our natural world.

Nancy Joye (M.D. 1975, Medical College of Pennsylvania) is associate clinical professor of pediatrics and director of the newborn nursery at the University of California, Davis, Medical Center. One of her major clinical concerns is the identification and protection of infants born into high-risk family settings.

Joseph Driskill (Ph.D. 1996, Graduate Theological Union, Berkeley) is assistant professor in spirituality and pastoral care at the Pacific School of Religion. His research and clinical interests include pastoral counseling and personality development.

Julia Morgan (Ph.D. 1992, Professional School of Psychology, San Francisco) is a psychotherapist in private practice in Sacramento.

Lucy S. McGough (J.D. 1966, Emory University School of Law; LL.M. 1971, Harvard University Law School) is the Vinson and Elkins Professor of Law at the Louisiana State University Law School. She is the author of numerous articles and of *The Child Witness in the American Legal System* (1994). Her research interest is the interface between the disciplines of law and psychology.

Maggie Bruck (Ph.D. 1972, McGill University) is associate professor of psychology and pediatrics at McGill University. Her research with Stephen J. Ceci focuses on the reliability and credibility of young children's testimony.

Stephen J. Ceci (Ph.D. 1976, Exeter University) is the H. L. Carr Professor of Psychology at Cornell University. His research with Maggie Bruck focuses on the reliability and credibility of young children's testimony. They have recently coauthored *Jeopardy in the Courtroom: A Scientific Analysis of Children's Testimony* (1995).

Peter A. Ornstein (Ph.D. 1968, University of Wisconsin) is professor of psychology in the Department of Psychology at the University of North Carolina at Chapel Hill, where he directs the graduate program in developmental psychology. His research has focused on children's memory, especially the development of strategies for deliberate memorization and the long-term retention of salient personal experiences. Increasingly, he has been concerned with the applied implications of research on children's memory, in terms of both understanding children's testimony and the debate surrounding adult claims of recovered as opposed to false memories. He served recently as the cochair of the Working Group on the Investigation of Memories of Childhood Abuse established by the American Psychological Association.

STATEMENT OF EDITORIAL POLICY

The *Monographs* series is intended as an outlet for major reports of developmental research that generate authoritative new findings and use these to foster a fresh and/or better-integrated perspective on some conceptually significant issue or controversy. Submissions from programmatic research projects are particularly welcome; these may consist of individually or group-authored reports of findings from some single large-scale investigation or of a sequence of experiments centering on some particular question. Multiauthored sets of independent studies that center on the same underlying question can also be appropriate; a critical requirement in such instances is that the various authors address common issues and that the contribution arising from the set as a whole be both unique and substantial. In essence, irrespective of how it may be framed, any work that contributes significant data and/or extends developmental thinking will be taken under editorial consideration.

Submissions should contain a minimum of 80 manuscript pages (including tables and references); the upper limit of 150–175 pages is much more flexible (please submit four copies; a copy of every submission and associated correspondence is deposited eventually in the archives of the SRCD). Neither membership in the Society for Research in Child Development nor affiliation with the academic discipline of psychology are relevant; the significance of the work in extending developmental theory and in contributing new empirical information is by far the most crucial consideration. Because the aim of the series is not only to advance knowledge on specialized topics but also to enhance cross-fertilization among disciplines or subfields, it is important that the links between the specific issues under study and larger questions relating to developmental processes emerge as clearly to the general reader as to specialists on the given topic.

Potential authors who may be unsure whether the manuscript they are planning would make an appropriate submission are invited to draft an outline of what they propose and send it to the Editor for assessment. This mechanism, as well as a more detailed description of all editorial policies, evaluation processes, and format requirements, is given in the "Guidelines for the Preparation of *Monographs* Submissions," which can be obtained by writing to the Editor, Rachel K. Clifton, Department of Psychology, University of Massachusetts, Amherst, MA 01003.